Gustavo Gutiérrez and the Liberative Sight of Christ

Gustavo Gutiérrez and the Liberative Sight of Christ

Luke Foster

scm press

© Luke Foster 2024

Published in 2024 by SCM Press

Editorial office
3rd Floor, Invicta House,
110 Golden Lane,
London EC1Y 0TG, UK

www.scmpress.co.uk

SCM Press is an imprint of Hymns Ancient & Modern Ltd
(a registered charity)

Hymns Ancient & Modern

Hymns Ancient & Modern® is a registered trademark of
Hymns Ancient & Modern Ltd
13A Hellesdon Park Road, Norwich,
Norfolk NR6 5DR, UK

All rights reserved. No part of this publication may be reproduced,
stored in a retrieval system, or transmitted,
in any form or by any means, electronic, mechanical,
photocopying or otherwise, without the prior permission of
the publisher, SCM Press.

The author has asserted his right under the Copyright, Designs and
Patents Act 1988 to be identified as the Author of this Work

British Library Cataloguing in Publication data

A catalogue record for this book is available
from the British Library

ISBN 978-0-334-06610-1

Typeset by Regent Typesetting
Printed and bound by
CPI Group (UK) Ltd

Contents

1 Introduction   1

Part One: A World Made Inhumane: Liberation and the History of Salvation

2 Telling the Human Story   21
3 Reading the Human Story   42
4 Christ and the Humanity Before Whom We Speak   58

Part Two: How to Speak of God: Liberation Through Faithful Praxis

5 The Creation of a New Humanity Through Faithful Praxis   81
6 The Faithful Praxis Through which a New Humanity is Forged   98
7 Christ and the Liberation of Humanity Through Faithful Praxis   118

Part Three: Proclaiming God as Father: Liberation and Utopia

8 The Liberation of Utopia   137
9 Liberation and the Humanity that 'Is Not Here'   163
10 Conclusion   182

Bibliography   188
Index   195

I

Introduction

Introduction: *Hasta que la dignidad se haga costumbre*

18 October 2019 is a date that marks a watershed in the recent history of Chile. That Friday afternoon I was in a rush-hour traffic jam travelling through Santiago on my way to speak at a church weekend retreat. A street-vendor knocked on my window and gestured ahead. It was only as the lights turned green and the traffic moved on that I understood what he had been trying to say. First there was the sound of shouting and shots being fired. Then there was the sight of black-clad protesters escaping a curling cloud of tear gas. As we watched the news that weekend, we realized that this was not simply another protest. It was not simply another violent confrontation with the police. In the streets of cities and towns throughout Chile, hundreds and thousands – and in some cases hundreds of thousands – of people were taking part in what has come to be known as the *estallido social*, the social explosion. One of the chants that rang out from those protests was the call to never rest, '*hasta que la dignidad se haga costumbre*' – until dignity becomes the norm. At the retreat that weekend we were reflecting on what it means to be a church in Christ. On the streets that weekend people were protesting about what it is to be a person in poverty.

It is 50 years since Gustavo Gutiérrez published *A Theology of Liberation*, and in his theology he has sought to expose and speak into the tension that I felt so acutely that weekend. Over the half century since Gutiérrez wrote his 'love letter to the church' the social and political context in which his theology is read has been radically transformed.[1] Political orders have been overthrown and new orders have emerged – only for these new orders in their turn to have been shaken and made unstable. For some, new historical and cultural realities have rendered the theology of Gutiérrez irrelevant or inadequate. For others, these changing circumstances have simply served to accentuate the abiding importance of his central concerns. The election of Jorge Mario Bergoglio to the papacy in 2013 marked a new stage in the reception of his theology within the institutional structures of the Roman Catholic Church. The concerns expressed by Pope Francis in *Evangelii Gaudium*, the meeting between the Pope and Gutiérrez in 2013 and the canonization of Oscar Romero in 2018 have, among other events, been read as indicating a renewal of this relation between the Roman Catholic Church and the theology of liberation. Whatever the status of Gutiérrez may be within the hierarchies of the church or academy, the urgency of his voice is not primarily to be heard in the echoes within ecclesiological or academic institutions. It is heard instead in the streets. It is heard as the Church seeks to return from its retreats and enter the streets with the message of Christ.

My purpose in this project is to listen carefully to that voice and, as I make the voice of Gutiérrez heard, contribute to a more faithful understanding and a more careful evaluation of his work. In this way I hope that my project shares something of the approach that Gutiérrez himself sought to learn from Bartolomé de Las Casas: 'One can reach such an understanding, Las Casas stated and advised and, "by commending oneself earnestly to God, by piercing very deeply until one finds the foundations." ... That is what he did.'[2]

Speaking of God as Father in a world that is inhumane: the shape of this study

This study will move forward through a double movement of listening and asking. As I listen to Gutiérrez, I will draw out the importance of both anthropology and Christology to his theological project. In what follows I will identify a Christological anthropology as a central and organizing concern within his theology. I will seek to show that attention to the anthropology of Gutiérrez allows the coherence and continuity of his theological project to come more clearly into view. Rather than approach his theology by means of the option for the poor, the role of praxis, or the concept of the kingdom, my engagement with his anthropology provides a framework within which these other concepts can be more adequately explored. Once this anthropological concern is heard, its Christological form may be discerned. In other words, the theology of Gutiérrez will be heard to proclaim a liberated humanity that is made known in Christ. This attentive listening will also allow for a careful questioning. Having shown the importance and interrelation of anthropology and Christology in Gutiérrez's theology, I will be able to engage in a more rigorous evaluation of his thought.

Introduction

Listening to the theology of Gustavo Gutiérrez

Gustavo Gutiérrez offers his theology as an attempt to answer the question he poses repeatedly throughout his work:

> The question here will not be how to speak of God in a world come of age, but rather how to proclaim God as Father in a world that is inhumane. What can it mean to tell a nonperson that he or she is God's child?[3]

While progressive theology considers the challenge of unbelief, the theology of Gutiérrez addresses itself to the problem of inhumanity.[4] His theology is therefore profoundly anthropological. According to Gutiérrez, to speak of God correctly is to speak of humanity prophetically. The context of such speech is to be the encounter between the concrete human situation and the communion into which God has called his creation. The work of Gutiérrez may therefore be read as an endeavour to articulate a liberative anthropology centred in a vision of Christ. The vision of the Christ encountered in humanity and the humanity that is to be encountered in Christ is generative of his theological project. The sight of Christ encountered amid the poor ushers in a process of transformation – a process that leads to a greater revelation of, and participation in, both Christ and humanity.

The first step of his theological method is the encounter with the Christ revealed in neighbour and the neighbour revealed by Christ, and the direction of a second step follows the contours of this concrete encounter with Christ in the neighbour. In Christ the truth of the poor as children of God is disclosed and in Christ the truth of God as Father of the poor is made known. In Christ the truth of man and the truth of God are together revealed and lived. When read within this framework, what Gutiérrez says of the poet who wrote Job may be found also to be true of him: 'at once more traditional than those who boast of being such, and more innovative than the standards of the mediocre allow them to be'.[5]

Questioning the theology of Gustavo Gutiérrez

By listening carefully to the Christological anthropology of Gutiérrez I hope to offer a more fruitful engagement with his theological project. In response to the statement of the Congregation for the Doctrine of the Faith regarding his theology, Gutiérrez acknowledged that 'these criticisms are important for a deepening and a clearer formulation of these themes'.[6] In what follows I will draw his work further into this process of questioning, critique and clarification.

The central question that emerges from my analysis of Gutiérrez concerns his characterization of the Christ who is foundational to his theological project. For him, Christ is not only the one from whom and of whom theology speaks. In the person of Christ his liberative anthropology holds together. The message of Jesus discloses the truth of God and humanity. In the opening chapter of *A Theology of Liberation*, Gutiérrez contends that 'In revealing God to us, the Gospel message reveals us to ourselves in our situation before the Lord and with other humans.'[7]

The gospel message reveals not only the truth but also how the truth is to be received. Revelation does not take place through a process of abstract or ahistorical speculation, it comes through incarnation. It comes through the incarnation of God among his people and of his people among their neighbours. Gutiérrez warns that coming to know the truth of God in man and the truth of man in God, 'means sinking roots where history is beating at this moment and illuminating history with the Word of the Lord of history'.[8] Christ reveals the truth of which theology is to speak and the way in which this truth is to be received. Christology also establishes the framework within which this truth is to be expressed and understood. The Christological framework that is adopted by Gutiérrez is perhaps most evident in his explanation of how the concept of liberation is to be understood in his work. In *A Theology of Liberation* he characterizes liberation as a 'complex process, which finds its deepest sense and its fullest realization in the saving work of Christ'.[9] Years later, he explains that 'the theological approach here is inspired by the Council of Chalcedon' through which it becomes possible to speak of a 'unity without confusion'.[10] The truth revealed in Christ is central to the message that is proclaimed by Gutiérrez, and the life lived by Christ models how that message is to be discerned. The person of Christ offers a theological and conceptual framework for how that message is to be understood. Over the course of this study I will ask whether his Christology is robust enough to support the weight that his anthropological project calls for it to bear. I will examine and evaluate the way in which Gutiérrez characterizes the person, work and presence of Christ. In this way, I offer a critical engagement with him that is consistent with his own fundamental convictions. By making the fundamental structure of his thought evident I will be able to expose and identify internal inconsistencies that make this structure unstable. Rather than read the theology of Gutiérrez as illustrative of broader theological trends or hold

Introduction

his theology accountable to frameworks that he would not share, I will engage with his theology at the point that he himself places at the heart of his theological project.

The theology of which I speak: an overview of this project

This critical analysis of the Christological anthropology of Gustavo Gutiérrez will unfold in three parts. Each part will consider a distinct facet of his theology and will be structured by the movement from listening to asking that I have already described. I will now turn first to establish the systematic – rather than historical or biographical – approach that will guide my reading of Gutiérrez, before outlining how the argument of this project will unfold across each of these three parts.

Reading the theology of Gutiérrez as a unity

Before summarizing each step of my argument, it is necessary to explain that my engagement with Gutiérrez will be thematic and systematic rather than historical and biographical. As Gutiérrez himself has explained, his theology has undergone significant growth and change over the decades. In his introduction to the revised edition of *A Theology of Liberation*, he compares his theological development to the way in which a husband's love for his wife will deepen and mature as the decades pass. He explains that 'my book is a love letter to God, to the church, and to the people to which I belong. Love remains alive, but it grows deeper and changes its manner of expression.'[11] While I will be attentive to these developments, they will be addressed within my broader structure rather than controlling that broader structure. As I consider each facet of his theology, I will explore both the continuity and the development that are evident in his thought. While the purpose of this project is to give an account of the unity and coherence of Gutiérrez's thought, it will be helpful at this point to provide a brief outline of how his thought has unfolded over the course of his ministry. It is common to observe that his published work may be associated with three broad stages of his life and Gaspar Martinez offers a helpful summary of these stages.[12]

The first stage takes place in the 1950s and 1960s as Gutiérrez studies in Europe and then begins to apply and adapt these theological insights to a Latin American context.[13] This period sees the publication of the texts through which Gutiérrez develops his distinctive theological vision. Key texts in this period include *La pastoral en la Iglesia en América Latina* (1968) and *Hacia una Teología de la Liberación* (1969).[14] In the 1970s his work reaches a second stage in which he articulates his theology of liberation. His most famous work, *A Theology of Liberation*, was published in Spanish in 1971 and in English in 1973. This decade ended with the publication of *The Power of the Poor in History* (1979). During the 1980s and 1990s this theology of liberation underwent a process of reformulation and development. In this stage the language of Marxist social analysis recedes and greater emphasis is placed on the spirituality of the theology of liberation. Texts such as his meditations on a liberative spirituality in *We Drink from our Own Wells* (1983), his commentary *On Job* (1986) and the more systematic text *God of Life* (1989) are characteristic of this period. While Gutiérrez does not abandon the prophetic urgency of his earlier work, the tone is more reflective and less polemical. This is perhaps exemplified by the changes made in the second edition of *A Theology of Liberation* (1986) and the commentaries on his work that he offers in *The Truth Shall Make You Free* (1986) and 'Expanding the View' (1988).

It is helpful to map this outline onto the conferences of the Latin American bishops at Medellín (1968), Puebla (1979) and Santo Domingo (1992). As Martinez points out,

> This division has the advantage of linking Gutiérrez's theological evolution to the two doctrinal milestones of the Catholic Church in Latin America (Medellín and Puebla) and to the later developments at Santo Domingo.[15]

With this framework I would add two further stages which move from Santo Domingo to Aparecida (2007) and then from Aparecida to the present. If the third stage is characterized by retrenchment, then the fourth stage signals a movement towards a greater acceptance of the work of Gutiérrez within the institutional structures of the Roman Catholic Church. Gutiérrez received the final text of the document prepared at Santo Domingo with ambivalence but by the time of their next meeting at Aparecida the Latin American bishops produced a document about which Gutiérrez was far more positive.[16] This renewed confidence is evident in his biography of Bartolomé de Las Casas (1992) and the writings published as *The Density of the Present* (1996). A fifth stage may be associated with the period after Aparecida and the election of Pope Francis. In this period a text such as *On the Side of the Poor* (published in English in 2015), written in collaboration with the Prefect of the Congregation

Introduction

for the Doctrine of the Faith, Cardinal Gerhard Müller, exemplifies a rapprochement with the institutional structures of the Roman Catholic Church. Throughout these stages of ministry, Gutiérrez has been a prolific writer and a sought-after speaker, and his work includes books, articles, homilies and conference addresses. My engagement with Gutiérrez will be thematic and systematic and for that reason I will primarily draw on the texts where he himself expresses his theology in its more developed form. These texts often draw on and adapt what he has published elsewhere and so present themselves as the maturation of a process of theological reflection.

Reading the theology of Gutiérrez: its unity and unities

This project will consider the way in which the work of Gutiérrez as a whole may be read as an attempt to answer the question that I identified at the beginning of this chapter. His work is an attempt to speak of God as Father in a world that is inhumane, and I will show that this question controls the theology of Gutiérrez and leads him to express a Christological anthropology within his theology. The theology of Gutiérrez speaks of the creation of a new and liberated humanity in Christ that is forged by God in three levels or dimensions. There is a liberation from 'oppressive socio-economic structures' on the political level; a 'profound inner freedom in the face of every kind of servitude' on the personal and social level; and a 'liberation from sin which attacks the deepest root of all servitude' at a spiritual level.[17] While these levels may be distinguished, they are united in an ordered relation, with the first and third levels of liberation converging on the second level of personal and social transformation. It is at this second level that the liberation of humanity is made known and the unity of this work is disclosed. As Gutiérrez explores the work of God as it unfolds on this second level, he identifies three concerns that he seeks to address in his attempt to proclaim God as Father in a world that is made inhumane. There is first the historical question posed by 'a world that is inhumane'. Second is the theological question of 'how to speak of God'. Finally, there is the eschatological perspective encountered within the knowledge of God as Father. As I explore Gutiérrez's theology I will attend to these historical, theological and eschatological considerations. Gutiérrez understands each of these areas to involve a dynamic relationship between concepts that are often placed in tension or contradiction. In the liberation of humanity, nature and grace, faith and works, and politics and eschatology are to be distinguished but not separated and I

7

will read the theology of Gutiérrez as a unity of these three unities. In his introduction to the revised edition of *A Theology of Liberation*, Gutiérrez explains the theological grammar within which his theology takes shape. Speaking in this context of the relationship between liberation as gift and as task, Gutiérrez explains that

> these two aspects must be distinguished without being separated, just as, in accordance with the faith of the church as definitively settled at the Council of Chalcedon, we distinguish in Christ a divine condition and a human condition, but we do not separate the two.[18]

In this way Christology is not only an important theme within the theology of Gutiérrez, but it also establishes the framework within which that theology takes shape. As I explore each of these three areas, I will examine the Christology on which their coherence depends.

A world that is inhumane: liberation and the history of salvation

In Part One, I will consider the humanity before whom Gutiérrez speaks and in the first chapter of this part of the project (Chapter 2) I will trace the salvation history recounted by Gutiérrez. Chapter 2 will explore the way in which Gutiérrez relates the work of God to the freedom of humanity in the movement towards liberation and the conception of sin and salvation that takes shape within this narrative. In Chapter 3, I will analyse the hermeneutic by which Gutiérrez reads this history. For Gutiérrez the option for the poor establishes the context in which the work of God in history may be understood. This is not simply an implication of his reading of salvation history, nor is it merely a consequence of his theology. Rather, the option for the poor is the hermeneutic of history and makes possible a faithful theology. Over the course of these two chapters I will aim to establish the connection between anthropology and Christology that emerges within the liberative vision of Gutiérrez. When read within the context of the option for the poor the work of God in history can be recounted as a narrative in which God forms a new humanity in Christ. In Chapter 4 I will examine the Christology central to this narrative, putting to Gutiérrez two questions raised by David Kelsey in his work on theological anthropology.[19] The first question concerns the problems that Kelsey associates with theologies that recount the relationship between God and creation in terms of a single unified narrative. The second question concerns the distinction that Kelsey draws between the description

Introduction

of Jesus' personal identity on the one hand and his ongoing presence on the other. I will explore whether the theology of Gutiérrez is subject to the weaknesses against which Kelsey warns. In short, I will ask whether the theology of Gutiérrez attributes to Christ the concrete particularity on which his anthropology depends.

How to speak of God: liberation through faithful praxis

In Part Two, I turn my attention to the humanity by whom Gutiérrez speaks, considering the way he characterizes the liberative praxis by which a new and liberated humanity is formed. In this praxis faith and works are each the context of the other. Contemplation and action, silence and speech, the prophetic and the mystical are each together the characteristic of the believer's response to Christ in the neighbour. In Chapter 5 I draw on the thought of Paulo Freire to elucidate the framework within which Gutiérrez develops his concept of praxis, and in Chapter 6 outline the steps through which this praxis unfolds. I will consider each step of this movement from sight to judgement to action with reference to a key text by Gutiérrez and respond to a number of important criticisms that have been raised concerning his construction of liberative praxis. I will demonstrate that these criticisms fail to adequately read the relationship between faith and works that emerges in the theology of Gutiérrez. In the final chapter of this part of the project I will address a question that arises out of this analysis. Having described the praxis through which a liberated humanity will be formed, Chapter 7 will examine the relationship between the love of neighbour and the love of God in Gutiérrez's theology. Once again, I will draw on a question posed by David Kelsey and consider the Christological implications of this question. Kelsey argues that 'human love to God and love to fellow creatures must not be conflated'[20] and are 'irreducibly distinct'.[21] I will argue that the theology of Gutiérrez has a tendency towards the conflation against which Kelsey warns and that a consequence of this is that the distinctive work of Christ recedes from view. If Chapter 4 examined the person of Christ in Gutiérrez's anthropology, this chapter turns to consider the work of Christ. While Kelsey's Protestant convictions may be particularly evident in the discussion that takes place in this chapter, I will draw on the questions he raises to explore the extent to which Gutiérrez is consistent with his own convictions and ask whether his Christology succeeds on his own terms.

Gustavo Gutiérrez and the Liberative Sight of Christ

Proclaiming God as Father: liberation and utopia

Finally, in Part Three, I will turn to the way in which Gutiérrez characterizes the liberative Kingdom of God. In this final part of the project, I will outline the relationship between political action and eschatological hope in which a new humanity may be encountered. If Parts One and Two explored the context and methodology of Gutiérrez's anthropological project, this part will consider its content. In Chapter 8, I will analyse the way in which Gutiérrez develops and deploys the concept of utopia. Chapter 9 will examine the account of Christ's presence that emerges in the eschatological vision of Gutiérrez and the role that the resurrection plays within his liberative eschatology. In Chapters 4 and 7 I examined the person and work of Christ. In Chapter 9 I will turn to consider Christ's presence and will argue that the attempt by Gutiérrez to speak of the eschatological reality of a liberated humanity is inhibited by an underdeveloped account of Christ in his personal particularity.

Throughout this project I will be seeking to understand, analyse and examine the theology of Gutiérrez on his own terms. The project will conclude with a summary of my argument and a brief suggestion for how the anthropology of Gutiérrez might be both received and developed in the future.

The voice with which I speak: the perspective of this project

Having summarized the contribution and shape of this project, I will also need to address the perspective from which this dynamic of listening and questioning will take place. All theology is contextual but the theology of Gutiérrez, with its call to be rooted 'where the pulse of history is beating at the moment', makes this question of context especially acute.[22] Before speaking about his theology I need to clarify the context within which my own voice is to be heard. I am an ordained priest in the Church of England but grew up in the Philippines and until recently was based in Chile, where I worked with the Anglican Church of Chile. As a consequence, my engagement with Gutiérrez raises both ecumenical and intercultural questions.

Introduction

Speaking of Gutiérrez with an English accent: the cultural context of this project

The work of listening faithfully across cultures – as with listening faithfully across theological traditions – does not take place in some imagined neutral or objective space. John Parratt observes that 'all theology is ultimately "contextual," that is it arises from specific historical context and it addresses that context'.[23] This context is not to be escaped. It has to be identified, acknowledged and examined. Graham Ward makes a helpful comparison with the process of learning a language. The acknowledgement of distance and difference need not inhibit cross-cultural understanding; it is the condition and characteristic of such understanding:

> The other ... will always remain other. I can learn to speak Punjabi, Yiddish or Polish fluently, but my mother language remains my mother language; I cannot (and nor should I attempt to) transcend the context I inhabit, and have been called to inhabit.[24]

My ministry with the Anglican Church in Chile was conducted in Spanish. However much time I dedicated to learning the language it was impossible to hide the culture from which I came and the distinctive accent with which I spoke. My approach here accepts this reality. As I speak of the theology of Gutiérrez, I will do so with an English accent.

My engagement with Gutiérrez will not take place in a supposed objective and culturally neutral space. Instead, the purpose of this project is to engage with the theology of Gutiérrez in a space that Jung Young Lee characterizes as the margins.[25] The language of marginality is often used to describe situations of exclusion and oppression but, while not unrelated to this reality, the concept as deployed by Lee refers to a much broader dynamic of distance from a centre in which identity is constructed through exclusion rather than in relation.[26] I am not attributing to myself the marginality of the poor, excluded and oppressed. Instead, I am recognizing that reading Gutiérrez draws me into a new cultural and ecclesial context. Rather than presuming that I can abandon my context or impose my context on Gutiérrez, the language of marginality as used by Lee recognizes that 'to be in-between two worlds means to be fully in neither'.[27] Lee calls for all theological enquiry to share in the marginality that characterizes the revelation of God in Christ. In what he holds to be 'an essential point of the Incarnation' Lee describes Jesus as 'alienated from and placed in-between two worlds without belonging to either. He entered a neither/nor category.'[28]

Gustavo Gutiérrez and the Liberative Sight of Christ

According to Lee, Jesus 'lived in-beyond and was in-between and in-both simultaneously'.[29] I do not write this project from a position of supposed neutrality or objectivity. I do not seek to establish a centre ground. Instead, this project will place itself at the margins of two cultural worlds. Once again, I am using the image of the margin in its broadest sense to describe a dynamic that brings together two worlds. As I write of *Gutiérrez* I move to the margin of my context. That it is *I* who write of Gutiérrez means that he is drawn to the margins of his.

The nature of this engagement with Gutiérrez is analogous with what has been described as mestizaje theology.[30] To be clear, I am not seeking to appropriate this theological identity or place my project specifically within this cultural context.[31] However, the character of mestizaje theology provides a helpful example of the intercultural dynamic at play within this project. It speaks of an 'ambiguous "in-between" identity' that provides 'the basis for a new, more universal identity, a new source of belonging, and a call to service'.[32] It is a theology that takes shape at the margins and in 'the border lands'.[33] Harvey Sindima explains that 'Mestizo affirms both the identities received while offering something new to both. Being an insider-outsider and outsider-insider to two worlds at the same time, we have the unique privilege of seeing and appreciating both worlds.'[34] The language of mestizaje by its nature speaks of a complex and multifaceted reality. Gutiérrez suggests that the concept can be used to convey a broader intercultural dynamic that is present in the contemporary world. He observes that 'mestizaje today, it is a planetary reality'.[35] It is a concept that offers an analogy for other intercultural dynamics.

I write this project as someone who has lived over half their life outside their 'passport' country. I was raised as a 'third culture kid' and while in Chile raised my own children in this 'third culture'.[36] This project arises out of, and is characterized by, the 'ambiguous "in-between" identity' described by Elizondo and Sindima. Once again, I do not presume to identify this project as a work of mestizo theology. It may perhaps be described as a work of 'third culture theology'. It is important to emphasize that this 'third culture' is not a flat or undifferentiated space, and my location within it is marked by the fact that I am from a background associated with social privilege. My experience – and the experience of my children – is very different to the experience of, for example, a Venezuelan or Haitian family who have come to Chile in search of work. The distinctive perspective of this 'third culture' and the differences within this space itself make it all the more important to cultivate what may be described as a self-aware attention to the other. As I seek to inhabit and understand Chilean culture, I seek to live and serve in

Introduction

a way that 'affirms both the identities received while offering something new to both'. I seek to be attentive to where I am and self-aware of where I am from. In the same way I seek to understand and inhabit the culture within which Gutiérrez writes, all the while being conscious of the culture within which I write. As both cultures are received something new may be born. The 'third culture' that emerges through this intercultural exchange corresponds to the 'three-way conversation' that is called for by Benno van den Toren.[37] There is a danger that intercultural encounters take place within the frameworks and assumptions of theologians from the West. The consequence is that 'the perspective that their dialogue partners consider to be decisive for their self-understanding is excluded as a proper theme of research and dialogue'.[38] Instead, it is important to take seriously the religious commitments within which the theology of a dialogue partner takes shape. For this reason, Benno van den Toren argues that

> Intercultural theological dialogue is therefore in principle a trialogue, a three-way conversation between representatives of the global church in which the third or rather the first voice is the voice of God who Himself in the scriptures and through the Holy Spirit addresses His church.[39]

This book seeks to draw the theology of Gutiérrez into this kind of 'three-way conversation'. It takes seriously the way in which Gutiérrez places himself within the dynamic and historic orthodoxy of the Christian church. As I examine and question the Christology within which the anthropology of Gutiérrez takes place, I am simply following his lead in recognizing that 'the Bible reads us'.[40] Gutiérrez places his theology before the God whose voice is heard in the Bible and the church. As a consequence, my engagement with the theology of Gutiérrez will involve a participation in a 'three-way conversation'. Careful attention to the theology of Gutiérrez will also involve a careful attention to 'the voice of God who Himself in the scriptures and through the Holy Spirit addresses His church'.

David Kelsey and the Protestant perspective of this project

I will seek to foreground the cultural and ecclesial context of my voice by drawing Gutiérrez into conversation with the theological anthropology developed by David Kelsey. When considering the Christological anthropology of Gutiérrez, there are other theologians who are closer to his cultural and ecclesial context and I will be drawing on their insights throughout this project. However, rather than adopt another voice or appropriate another perspective, I am choosing to acknowledge my distance from the context of Gutiérrez. My aim is for this distance to provide space for a distinctive perspective through which new insights may emerge. One of the ways in which I will respect this distance is to draw on Kelsey's anthropology. I have chosen to bring Kelsey into conversation with Gutiérrez for two reasons. The first reason relates to the intercultural and ecclesial dynamic that I have already mentioned. I will use David Kelsey to give expression to some of the questions that the work of Gutiérrez will provoke within my theological context. I am writing from a Protestant perspective and my engagement will – to take an image that I have already used – be marked by a distinctively Protestant 'accent'. In this way I will not only be raising questions that Protestants might need to consider in their reception and development of Gutiérrez's theology. I also hope to shed light on those areas in his theology where he appears to be inconsistent with his own convictions and in tension with his stated purposes. As I pose to Gutiérrez the questions developed by Kelsey, I do not mean to impose Kelsey's answers and alternatives on Gutiérrez. Instead, by foregrounding the space between our cultural and ecclesial contexts I hope to cultivate the self-aware attention to his work that will enable me to more clearly hear and more carefully evaluate his work. For this reason, although I will draw on themes developed by David Kelsey and explore questions raised in his work, I will not be attempting to offer an overall exposition or evaluation of his theological anthropology. Such an engagement with Kelsey is beyond the scope of this project and would draw attention away from my focus on the Christological anthropology of Gutiérrez. A second reason for drawing on Kelsey is that his recent work on anthropology makes him a natural conversation partner for this project. The scope of his work and its impact on the field establish Kelsey as an important voice in any contemporary discussion of anthropology.[41] Furthermore, Kelsey presents Christ as the one in whom the 'triple helix' of humanity's eccentric existence is held together.[42] Kelsey's Christological approach establishes a valuable point of contact with the Christological framework within which the anthropology of Gutiérrez takes shape. In this way I hope to develop a systematic engagement with Gutiérrez that is attentive to the fundamental commitments that give coherence to his thought. An atomistic or superficial reception of Gutiérrez may, for example, hear his call to address a world made inhumane without recognizing the convictions and concerns that characterize his proclamation of God as Father. Such a reception would presume to hear his anthropo-

Introduction

logical concerns apart from the Christological framework through which they take shape. A protestant reception of Gutiérrez must be attentive to the particular contours of his Christology and consider how it compares to the Christological constructions of the listening community before the contribution of Gutiérrez's anthropology can be authentically received. It is not my purpose in this project to identify precisely what gifts will be received and which wounds will be healed.[43] It is also beyond the scope of this project to explore the questions that Gutiérrez might ask of Kelsey or the ways in which Gutiérrez might critique the methodology and structure of his anthropology. Instead, in my process of listening and asking I hope to cultivate a dynamic of self-aware attention to the other that will in turn facilitate a process of authentic learning and receiving.

Conclusion: opening a window onto the theology of Gutiérrez

On 18 October 2019 a street-vendor approached my car. I didn't understand what he was saying. Nor did I try. Instead, I checked that my door was locked and my window was up. The moments before I heard and saw the beginnings of the *estallido social* I was playing my small part in its many and messy causes. I was another person who had closed themselves off. Another person who did not let themselves hear the warning of what was to come. The theology of Gutiérrez is a call to see the humanity of those who are outside. To hear their voice and so to understand our world.

The cry that has been heard in Chile since the *estallido social* was a political and economic protest. As a political and economic protest it poses an anthropological question. As an anthropological question it provokes a theological challenge. It is a question that must be heard and a challenge that must be felt until humanity is seen in all its dignity and reality. Or to put it in the words that have been heard in the streets of Chile since 18 October 2019: *hasta que la dignidad se haga costumbre.*

Notes

1 Gustavo Gutiérrez, *A Theology of Liberation: History, Politics, and Salvation*, trans. Caridad Inda and John Eagleson (London: SCM Press, 2010), p. 44.

2 Gustavo Gutiérrez, *Las Casas: In Search of the Poor of Jesus Christ* (Eugene, OR: Wipf & Stock, 2003), p. 15.

3 Gustavo Gutiérrez, *The Power of the Poor in History*, trans. Robert R. Barr (Maryknoll, NY: Orbis Books, 1983), p. 57. Gutiérrez returns to this concept in the final chapter. This concern is evident at an early stage in his theology. See for example Gustavo Gutiérrez, 'Faith as freedom: solidarity with the alienated and confidence in the future', *Horizons* 2, no. 1 (1975), p. 43.

4 The distinction between the challenge of the 'non-believer' and the challenge of the 'non-person' is central to the contrast Gutiérrez draws between liberation theology and progressivist theology in his paper 'Two theological perspectives: liberation theology and progressivist theology' in *The Emergent Gospel: Theology from the underside of history: papers from the Ecumenical Dialogue of Third World Theologians, Dar Es Salaam, August 5–12, 1976*, ed. Sergio Torres González (Maryknoll, NY: Orbis Books, 1978), pp. 227–55.

5 Gustavo Gutiérrez, *On Job: God-talk and the Suffering of the Innocent*, trans. Matthew J. O'Connell (Maryknoll, NY: Orbis Books, 1987), p. 93.

6 Gustavo Gutiérrez, 'Criticism will deepen, clarify liberation theology' in *Liberation Theology: A documentary history*, ed. Alfred T. Hennelly (Maryknoll, NY: Orbis Books, 1990), p. 423.

7 Gutiérrez, *A Theology of Liberation*, p. 51.

8 Gutiérrez, *A Theology of Liberation*, p. 59.

9 Gutiérrez, *A Theology of Liberation*, p. 76.

10 Gustavo Gutiérrez, *The Truth Shall Make You Free: Confrontations*, trans. Matthew J. O'Connell (Maryknoll, NY: Orbis Books, 1990), p. 122.

11 *A Theology of Liberation*, p. 44. This introduction was also published separately as Gustavo Gutiérrez, 'Expanding the view' in *Expanding the View: Gustavo Gutiérrez and the Future of Liberation Theology*, ed. Marc H. Ellis and Otto Maduro, trans. Matthew J. O'Connell (Eugene, OR: Wipf & Stock, 1990), pp. 3–36.

12 Gaspar Martinez, *Confronting the Mystery of God: Political liberation and public theologies* (New York: Continuum, 2002), p. 120.

13 For an exploration of how this period gave shape to what would become the theology of liberation, see, for example, Roberto Oliveros Maqueo, *Liberacion y Teologia: Génesis y Crecimiento de Una Reflexion (1966–1976)* (Lima: Centro de Estudios y Publicaciones, 1977); Christian Smith, *The Emergence of Liberation Theology: Radical religion and social movement theory* (Chicago, IL: University of Chicago Press, 1991); and Diana Sorensen, *A Turbulent Decade Remembered: Scenes from the Latin American sixties*, Cultural Memory in the Present (Stanford, CA: Stanford University Press, 2007).

14 Unless otherwise indicated, in this and the next paragraph the year given in brackets indicates the first publication of the text in Spanish.

15 Martinez, *Confronting the Mystery of God*, p. 120.

16 See the discussion of the document produced by the bishops at Aparecida in Gustavo Gutiérrez, 'The option for the poor arises from faith in Christ', *Theological Studies* 70, no. 2 (2009), pp. 317–26.

17 Gutiérrez, *A Theology of Liberation*, p. 34.

18 Gutiérrez, *A Theology of Liberation*, p. 35.

19 David H. Kelsey, *Eccentric Existence: A theological anthropology*, 1st edn, 2 vols (Louisville, KY: Westminster John Knox Press, 2009). I will explain in more detail below my reasons for drawing Kelsey into conversation with Gutiérrez in this way.

Introduction

20 Kelsey, *Eccentric Existence*, p. 712.
21 Kelsey, *Eccentric Existence*, p. 826.
22 Gutiérrez, *A Theology of Liberation*, p. 59.
23 John Parratt, 'Introduction' in *An Introduction to Third World Theologies*, ed. John Parratt (Cambridge: Cambridge University Press, 2004), p. 2.
24 Graham Ward, 'Intercultural theology and political discipleship' in *Intercultural Theology: Approaches and themes*, ed. Mark J. Cartledge and David Cheetham (London: SCM Press, 2011), p. 42.
25 Jung Young Lee, *Marginality: The key to multicultural theology* (Minneapolis, MN: Fortress Press, 1995).
26 Lee, *Marginality*, p. 171.
27 Lee, *Marginality*, p. 45.
28 Lee, *Marginality*, p. 82.
29 Lee, *Marginality*, p. 89.
30 Arturo J Bañuelas, ed., *Mestizo Christianity: Theology from the Latino Perspective* (Eugene, OR: Wipf & Stock, 2004).
31 Elizondo describes the tragic and specific history of violence from which this identity was born – and in which this identity continues to be forged. Virgil P. Elizondo, 'Mestizaje as locus of theological reflection' in *Mestizo Christianity: Theology from the Latino perspective*, ed. Arturo J Bañuelas (Eugene, OR: Wipf & Stock, 2004), pp. 5–27.
32 Virgilio Elizondo, 'Jesus the Galilean Jew in Mestizo theology', *Theological Studies* 70, no. 2 (May 2009), p. 279. A broader use of this concept is exemplified in the way in which it is used by Muñoz to provide a framework for describing a distinctively Anglican theological identity. Daniel Muñoz, 'Anglican identity as Mestizaje ecclesiology', *Journal of Anglican Studies* 16, no. 2 (2018), pp. 83–102.
33 Harvey J. Sindima, *The Gospel According to the Marginalized*, Martin Luther King, Jr Memorial Studies in Religion, Culture, and Social Development, vol. 6 (New York: Peter Lang, 2008), p. 196.
34 Sindima, *The Gospel According to the Marginalized*, p. 195.
35 Simon C. Kim, 'Appendix B: An interview with Gustavo Gutiérrez December 8, 2009' in *An Immigration of Theology: Theology of Context as the Theological Method of Virgilio Elizondo and Gustavo Gutiérrez*, p. 258.
36 This term was coined by Useem and Useem to describe children who live for extended periods of time in foreign countries. They are not immigrants nor are they visitors. They do not belong to either the home or the host culture. Their identity is forged within a 'third culture'. John Useem and Ruth Useem, 'The interfaces of a binational third culture: a study of the American community in India', *Journal of Social Issues* 23, no. 1 (January 1967), pp. 130–43. For a more recent articulation of the concept, see David C. Pollock and Ruth E. Van Reken, *Third Culture Kids: Growing up among worlds*, rev. edn (Boston, MA: Nicholas Brealey, 2009).
37 Benno van den Toren, 'Intercultural theology as a three-way conversation: beyond the western dominance of intercultural theology', *Exchange* 44, no. 2 (8 June 2015), p. 133.
38 Van den Toren, 'Intercultural theology as a three-way conversation', p. 138.
39 Van den Toren, 'Intercultural theology as a three-way conversation', p. 142.
40 Gustavo Gutiérrez, *We Drink From Our Own Wells: The Spiritual Journey of*

a People (Maryknoll, NY: Orbis Books, 2003), p. 34; see also Gutiérrez, *The Truth Shall Make You Free*, p. 47.

41 See, for example, the collection of essays published in G. Outka, *The Theological Anthropology of David Kelsey: Responses to Eccentric Existence* (Grand Rapids, MI: William B. Eerdmans, 2016).

42 Kelsey, *Eccentric Existence*, p. 11.

43 For the 'allegory of the wounded body needing healing', see Ladislas Örsy, 'Authentic learning and receiving – a search for criteria' in *Receptive Ecumenism and the Call to Catholic Learning: Exploring a way for contemporary ecumenism*, ed. Paul D. Murray and Luca Badini Confalonieri (Oxford: Oxford University Press, 2008), p. 41.

PART ONE

A World Made Inhumane: Liberation and the History of Salvation

2

Telling the Human Story

In order to proclaim God as Father in a world that has been made inhumane, Gutiérrez recounts a narrative of human history whose end is an experience of fellowship with God. The story of humanity as told by Gutiérrez moves from God's work in creation towards an eschatological consummation in which the human person comes to know and be known in the communion of 'the Pauline face to face'.[1] Thus his anthropology takes shape within a unified narrative of history in which humanity reaches its fruition in a vision of God in Christ that is to be encountered within a concrete experience of community.

In this chapter I will first describe the unity that Gutiérrez discerns in the narrative of history and will then outline the narrative that takes shape through this unity. The next chapter will explore the hermeneutic through which both this unity and this narrative are discerned by Gutiérrez in history. Together these two chapters will trace out the framework within which his theological anthropology takes shape.

The unity of history

As Gutiérrez recounts the history of humanity, he brings together God's gracious work and humanity's free response into a single story of salvation. This unified history reaches its climax in Christ as he is made known through the neighbour. As Gutiérrez tells the story of humanity, 'the connection between grace and nature, between God's call and the free response of human beings, is located within a single Christo-finalized history'.[2] In this encounter with Christ in the neighbour 'the grace of the vision of God' is given and leads humanity to its fulfilment in communion with God and neighbour.[3] Expressed in other words, the encounter with Christ in the neighbour is also an encounter with the truth of the neighbour's identity as a child loved by God. As Christ is revealed through the neighbour and the neighbour through Christ, 'both movements need each other dialectically and move towards a synthesis' within which communion with God and with neighbour each lead the other to greater intimacy and truth.[4] Unfolding through history and forged within community, the humanity proclaimed by Gutiérrez is shaped by the loving encounter with Christ that is offered by the neighbour – a love by which the neighbour is seen and known in the truth of their humanity.[5]

The single vocation to communion

For Gutiérrez the distinctive voices of nature and grace come together in a harmonious call to a single human vocation of communion with God. Arguing that human fulfilment can be found only in the communion given in the vision of God, he concludes that:

> The natural and the supernatural orders are therefore intimately unified. In the concrete situation there is but one vocation: communion with God through grace. In reality there is not pure nature ... there is no one who is not invited to communion with the Lord, no one who is not affected by grace ... we know humanity only as actually called to meet God.[6]

What Gutiérrez describes as 'the single vocation to the grace of communion with God'[7] is itself realized within the diverse and concrete contexts of community.[8] The integration of the vocation to which humanity is called – and in which humanity finds its liberty and identity – corresponds to the integrated history within which this vocation is to be pursued. Gutiérrez observes this pattern in his reading of twentieth-century discussions of nature and grace 'in the gradual forsaking of such expressions as *supernatural end*, *supernatural vocation*, and *supernatural order* and in the ever-increasing use of the term *integral*'.[9] The unified vocation of humanity unfolds within the unified narrative of history. Cautioning that 'the process is single not monolithic', Gutiérrez argues that his account of history is characterized by 'neither separation nor confusion, neither verticalism nor horizontalism', but rather is structured by the 'Chalcedonian principle' that offers a relation of 'unity without confusion, distinction without separation' in its articulation of 'total liberation in Christ'.[10]

While Gutiérrez characterizes his work as a development of the conclusions drawn by 'recent discussion on the relationship of grace to nature', he is at pains to resist a reductive association of his work with one or other supposed voice within this discussion.[11] At the presentation of his work to the Catholic Institute of Lyons for consideration as a doctoral thesis, Gutiérrez describes his encounter with the thought of such theologians as de Lubac, Blondel and Rahner during his earlier studies at the faculty.[12] During his studies he concluded that 'the question needed to be approached not in terms of abstract notions of nature and supernature but from the historical, Augustinian viewpoint'.[13] According to Gutiérrez, such a viewpoint allows for a relation without elision of the natural and supernatural in the call of humanity towards communion with God and neighbour. He describes how,

> In my first years of studies at this faculty, when we were studying the treatise on grace, I was greatly struck by the magnificent idea of the unmerited character of God's love and free initiative. This Pauline and Augustinian insight left its mark on my theological studies.[14]

This grace is to be understood not only 'as a fundamental datum of our Christian life in relation to God, but also as a human quality' such that 'the encounter with God is also an encounter with ourselves'.[15] Rather than structuring nature and grace as two abstract planes that may be coordinated by subordination or elevation, Gutiérrez claims to pursue 'a retrieval of the traditional approach ... which says that human history is permeated at every point by the opposition between grace and sin'.[16] The relation of nature to grace is only to be understood when viewed from the perspective of the call to communion with God and neighbour that is pursued within history. Gutiérrez concludes that 'in the final analysis, history is one – that is, every human life is ultimately a yes or no to God, to God's offer of grace' that is mediated by the concrete conditions and relations of life in community.[17]

The vocation given in creation

The single vocation to communion with God and neighbour that relates nature to grace in a single narrative of human history is given to humanity with creation. In his reading of the stories of creation and redemption as they are recounted and interwoven by the Pentateuch, Gutiérrez observes that 'creation appears as the first salvific act' and concludes that 'the work of creation is regarded and understood only in this context'.[18] Creation thereby speaks of both a transcendence and immanence that finds its unity in the establishment of humanity within a liberated community. Creation sets before humanity the liberation for which it is purposed and redemption casts humanity upon the creative gratuity of God that makes such liberation possible. As Israel hears in their sacred narratives that 'creation is the work of the redeemer',[19] they are called to read in the created world around them 'a revelation of the gratuitousness of God's love' that is to be the pattern of the life to which they have been saved.[20] The revelation in creation of gracious love calls the people of God to a participation in the creation of the community in which this love is to be made known. Creation reveals to humanity the gratuitous love of the redeemer. Liberation is made possible by the gratuitous love of the creator. Gratuity and exigency do not exclude each other; rather, they each provide the purpose and possibility of the other. As a consequence, Gutiérrez concludes that, 'there is nothing more demanding, nothing more productive of commitment in daily life, than the gratuitousness that has its source in the love of God'.[21] Just as 'Yahweh's historical actions on behalf of the people are considered creative',[22] so too, 'by working, transforming the world, breaking out of servitude, building a just society, and assuming its destiny in history, humanity forges itself'.[23] The word of God in creation calls forth its echo in history as communities are formed that express and incarnate the gratuitous love of the creator.

The vocation drawn forth by eschatology

The creative gratuity from which liberation in history flows finds its counterpart in the eschatological gratuity to which it is drawn. Gutiérrez describes the vocation to communion with God as the eschatological hope and argues that the 'attraction of "what is to come" is the driving force of history'.[24] As a consequence, this eschatological hope 'not only is not foreign to the transformation of the world; it leads necessarily to the building up of the fellowship and communion in history'.[25] Through its eschatological hope the church proclaims that the 'day of Yahweh will, in the final analysis, be a state of communion with God and fellowship among human beings'.[26] The inseparable – though distinguishable – unity of this communion with God and neighbour is the vocation and future hope that gives history unity and meaning. Gutiérrez is careful to clarify that the 'final meaning' that this vocation gives to history does not imply 'that the kingdom is located at the chronological end of the process'.[27] Rather, he describes this communion as a hope 'that is, if I may coin a word, "kairologically" at hand and in the process of being brought to completion' and so to be discerned in the 'historical density' of the present concrete experience.[28] The future is not to be considered in abstraction from the present; rather, it is disclosed and encountered in the present. Gutiérrez cautions that theology 'means sinking roots where the pulse of history is beating at this moment and illuminating history with the Word of the Lord of history, who irreversibly committed himself to the present moment of humankind to carry it to its fulfilment'.[29] An openness to neighbour is at the same time an openness to the future that entrusts itself to the gratuitous purposes and promises of God. Openness to the future is lived in a commitment to the present in which the gratuitous love for God is imaged forth. As such, faithful love discloses eschatological hope in the midst of history.

Gutiérrez seeks to place the eschatological promise within a framework that neither negates history nor deprecates humanity. Instead, it is to be the purpose and possibility of both. On the one hand, the word of God by which communion is promised to humanity does not lead to an abandonment of history but rather is that which gives history its meaning. The eschatological promise 'is inexhaustible and dominates history because it is the self-communication of God' which leads humanity in history 'through incipient realizations towards its fulness'.[30] Gutiérrez argues that an 'opening of eschatology to the future is inseparably joined with its historical contemporaneity and urgency'.[31] Eschatological hope 'liberates history because of its openness to the God who is to come'.[32] Just as creation establishes the gratuitous love of God as the foundation of all, eschatology reveals the gratuitous love of God as the purpose of all. History is thus liberated from the impersonal and mechanistic processes that point only towards an end in oppression and death. Instead, history must be read through a hermeneutic of hope in which a faith in the God of life leads each neighbour to turn to the other in love. Not only does history find its reality in the freedom offered by eschatology; humanity may encounter in the present the freedom promised by the future.[33] The call of eschatology is thus heard in history and speaks of a movement towards being, in words that Gutiérrez draws from *Populorum progressio*, 'more human ... finally and above all'.[34] I will engage in a more detailed evaluation of this eschatological framework in the final chapters of this project. At this stage, however, I simply seek to clarify the role that this eschatology plays within the story of humanity as it is told by Gutiérrez. The commitment to the liberation of the neighbour images within history the intervention of God to save. A hope in the future grounded in a faith in the promises of God frees humanity to live in a gracious love.

Gustavo Gutiérrez and the Liberative Sight of Christ

The vocation that unfolds in history

Given in creation and drawn forth by eschatology, the vocation to communion with God and within humanity unfolds through history, and for Gutiérrez this history can only be understood when read as a narrative of liberation. Reflecting on Ephesians 1.4 he observes both the purpose established by God for humanity and the implication this has for the reading of history:

> The choice or election was to make us adoptive sons and daughters, and, contrary to the picture we sometimes draw for ourselves, it took place before creation. The 'before' does not indicate chronological precedence but a precedence of meaning and finality; we live in 'a "Christo-finalized" history'.[35]

For Gutiérrez the 'priority' and 'ultimacy' outlined in such passages are not coordinates of time but rather of meaning. History is characterized by its origin and end in Christ – that is, by its conception in and growth towards the vocation to communion with God and neighbour. To speak of history as Christo-*finalized* is to speak of the orientation that gives history its unity and meaning. To speak of history as *Christo*-finalized is to speak of the character of this unity and meaning. According to Gutiérrez the unity and meaning of history are given in the communion realized in Christ – but this unity and meaning are to be understood according to the 'Chalcedonian principle' revealed in Christ.[36] As such, Gutiérrez seeks to tell the story of human history in such a way as to articulate, on the one hand, the relation of both divine immanence and transcendence to history and, on the other hand, the reality of human freedom and the intimacy of divine presence within history.

Placing history within the context of the gracious love from which and to which it flows, the work of God to liberate within history may be encountered as expressive of both his holy otherness from, and just commitment to, the historical process. There need be no conflict between either of these realities because 'according to the Bible, God's interventions in the life of God's people do not imply any kind of immanentism or any dissolution of God into history; rather they emphasize that God is the absolute and transcendent source of being'.[37] The holiness that secures the free relation of God to history is the holy freedom that finds expression in the liberative work of God in history. It is because God is holy that he can and does act in grace to express his love within human history. For Gutiérrez,

... the scriptures teach us that the God of the Bible irrupts into history, but at the same time they show us that God is not as it were watered down by the historical process ... the God of the covenant is 'Wholly Other,' the Holy One. These two distinct aspects of God each imply the other.[38]

The historical process neither constitutes nor constrains the divine. Rather, it is a history that receives its meaning and orientation from God; it is within history that the free and thereby gracious God makes himself known. The story of history told by Gutiérrez receives its unity from the vocation to communion that is offered by God in his freedom and grace and that is achieved by God as that same freedom and grace find expression in human history.

The account of human history offered by Gutiérrez does not only seek to express the relation-in-distinction of divine immanence and transcendence. It also seeks to secure the twin realities of human freedom within history and divine presence to humanity. As the vocation to communion unfolds within history, Gutiérrez seeks to tell the story in a way that preserves the integrity of both of the characters within its narrative. God is known in both his freedom from and his commitment to this history. In a similar way, humanity is characterized through both a radical relation to the God of history and a real responsibility within the processes of history. While 'salvation in Christ gives human history as a whole its ultimate meaning', Gutiérrez is cautious to emphasize that 'this salvation is already present in history; God's saving action is working upon history from within'.[39] Indeed, the plans and purposes that God reveals for human history are to be seen as the possibility for the freedom and autonomy of that history.

In his reflections on the book of Job, Gutiérrez describes the 'communion of two freedoms' that takes shape through an encounter with the liberative work of God. In the power of God to tame Behemoth there is the recognition that 'there are chaotic forces within creation, but the cosmos is not a chaos'.[40] Neither mechanistic systems of retribution and reward nor chaotic conflicts of power and oppression are the ultimate reality of creation. Instead, in Job's '"face-to-face" encounter with God' he is able to savour the reality that 'faith, hope, and love abide, "but the greatest of these is love"'.[41] The unity of history is discovered in this encounter with God – and with it the possibility and purpose of human freedom. Not only is this freedom grounded in the power of God over his creation, it is given through the humility of God before his creation. There is in the final chapters of Job a revelation of the '"weak" God who is heedful of human freedom and its historical rhythm' and so will 'stop at the threshold of their freedom and ask for their collaboration in the building of the world and in its just governance'.[42]

However, even this 'weakness' is itself an expression – rather than an attenuation – of God's freedom. By offering to Job a revelation of his creative power God reveals not only his power to keep creation from bondage to chaos but also his power to open creation up to free and responsible action. The comfort that Job encounters having 'seen' God is deeper than the answers that he had sought and been offered among those who had only 'heard' of God. The power of God is not to be found in a rigid and impersonal moral order; it is instead to be experienced in the responsibility and creativity of human freedom. The narrative of Job enacts an interrelation of divine and human freedoms that is secured through the divine commitment and human vocation to communion.

As a consequence, when Gutiérrez speaks of the 'unity of God and man' he speaks of a relation whose intimacy is secured through distinction.[43] The story of history is therefore told as a movement through and for human freedom. When made conscious of the gratuitous love that is the foundation and purpose of history, humanity is able to participate in and image forth that creative grace in the concrete contexts of community and history. A faith in God as creator allows for a consciousness of the true freedom and real responsibility of humanity as creature: 'Biblical faith does indeed affirm the existence of creation as distinct from the Creator; it is the proper sphere of humankind, and God has proclaimed humankind lord of this creation.'[44] Within such a sphere a person is to become 'ever more conscious of being an active subject of history'.[45] In the consciousness of this identity, a person 'emerges as a free and a responsible being, a person in relationship with other persons, as someone who takes on a historical task'.[46] The human creature is to image forth the creative work of God as they take responsibility for the creative work of liberation. For this reason, Gutiérrez discerns within the movement of history a dynamic that 'coincides with the Christian vision of human nature' as we are increasingly called to 'perceive ourselves as a creative subject' and so to participate in 'the possibility of being more fully human'.[47] For Gutiérrez, to speak of a single vocation unfolding through a unified historical narrative is not to dissolve human freedom and integrity before an impersonal divine plan. Rather, the movement that he discerns unfolding through history is a movement towards an ever-clearer consciousness of an ever-greater responsibility that is expressed in an ever-increasing freedom and creativity. Where Gutiérrez sees the unfolding of the historical narrative he sees, at the same time, the emergence of humankind as an active and creative agent. He seeks to recount a historical narrative that, far from subordinating humanity to a prior plan, is purposed to make possible for humanity an ever-increasing freedom, responsibility and agency.

While it has been suggested that in his earlier work Gutiérrez may 'at times appear to interpret human action in Promethean, or even Pelagian terms', later writings express the nuance of his narration of human history.[48] In his narration of history as the unfolding of the human vocation to communion given by God, Gutiérrez cautions his readers to hear 'two correctives' that the prophets offer to our readings of this story.[49] First, there is the conviction 'that no place and no historical event can contain God'.[50] While present to and with history, God remains always uncontained and unconstrained by it. The freedom and generosity of his love will always exceed the social, structural and temporal encounters in which it is revealed. As such there is always a further word of judgement and a further word of hope to be heard within any given historical situation or experience. Any narration of human history must therefore recognize its limits and its contingency before the limitless and uncontainable God. Furthermore, the second corrective proclaimed by the prophets warns that the work of God in history will often be hidden and humble:

> The Lord certainly dwells within history, but, as the prophet makes clear, God's presence is often hidden; God is present in what is insignificant and anonymous. ... God is present in history with its tensions, successes, and conflicts, but finding God requires a search.[51]

The narrative of human history and the unfolding movement of humanity towards its vocation involves failure and frailty, paradox and pain. Anticipating the critique that might be offered against such an integrated historical narrative, Gutiérrez emphasizes the importance – and the character – of the unity revealed in Christ:

> It is right to recognize that the postmodern critique helps us to not fall into rigid and starched schemes as we interpret the course of history ... However, having said this, it is necessary to remember that in a Christian perspective, history has its centre in the coming of the Son, in the Incarnation, without this meaning that human history ineluctably advances following paths traced and dominated by a strong guiding thought.[52]

This is not a reductive account of an inevitable and ultimately impersonal 'promethean' progress. It is instead a story in which humanity in all the complexity of its concrete reality is led into fellowship together as members of the family of God. The tone in which this story is told is not that of either triumphalism or authoritarianism. Instead, this story is heard in the voice of Job confessing faith amid the dust and ashes; of John calling for justice from the wilderness; and of Jesus crying out for forgiveness on the cross.

The vocation revealed in the incarnation

For Gutiérrez the incarnation reveals and actualizes the communion to which humanity is called and in which it is to be formed. Tracing the revelation of this vocation through the scriptures, Gutiérrez observes that 'the active presence of God in the midst of the people is a part of the oldest and most enduring Biblical promises',[53] which is ultimately 'fulfilled with the Incarnation of the Son of God'.[54] The promise of God that unfolds through history is the gift of his self-communication and 'with the Incarnation of the Son and the sending of the Spirit of Promise this self-communication has entered into a decisive stage'.[55] At the incarnation this promised presence achieves and expresses a universal and integrated scope of human communion with God.[56] The fulfilment of this promise in Christ reveals the purpose of God for humanity, in which 'all persons are in Christ efficaciously called to communion with God' through the 'universal lordship of Christ in whom all things exist and have been saved'.[57] The vocation that is given in creation and is the content of the eschatological promise is revealed and realized in the coming of Christ: 'Since the Incarnation, humanity, every human being, history, is the living temple of God. The "pro-fane" which is located outside the temple no longer exists.'[58] As Christ brings God and humanity together in his person, and as Christ in his proclamation reveals the way to love of God and neighbour, he makes known and present the communion to which humanity has been called and in which humanity is formed.

Not only does the incarnation disclose the vocation to which humanity is called, it also 'embodies' the structure of the history through which this vocation unfolds. This communion with God takes place within concrete and historical encounters with the neighbour. According to Gutiérrez 'the "union with the Lord" which all spirituality proclaims' is only encountered in the dual movement to God and neighbour whose 'synthesis is found in Christ', in whom 'humankind gives God a human countenance and God gives it a divine countenance'.[59] As a consequence, Christ reveals not only the fellowship of the communion to which humanity is called but also the unity of the history within which this communion is to be achieved. Just as the unity of God and Man is encountered in Christ, so too in Christ is heard a call to love both God and Man. The love that seeks fellowship with the neighbour is a love found in fellowship with God. Gutiérrez emphasizes that 'Christ, who is both God and human, is the basis of a unity that does not do away with distinctions but does prevent confusions and separations.'[60] The 'Chalcedonian principle' that is demanded by the fact of the incarnation is to structure how the story of human history is told.[61] It is to be recounted as a story in which both God and humanity participate as free and creative actors as together they move towards a universal and integral communion.

Conclusion

Gutiérrez narrates the story of human history as a unity within which the liberative work of God unfolds to form mankind in its fullness. A single vocation to communion with God is the gift offered in creation, the promise held forth by eschatology, and the salvation revealed and realized at the incarnation. As a consequence of this single vocation, history receives its meaning and unity. A meaning and unity whose integrity is structured by the communion in which it is forged – the communion of God and humanity acting together in freedom, grace and love.

The history of salvation

Having identified the importance of this unity, I will now follow the unfolding of this vocation in the history narrated by Gutiérrez. In this section I will first trace the movement from sin to salvation in the redemptive narrative recounted by Gutiérrez and then explore the three levels of liberation in which the action of this narrative is to take place.

Sin and inhumanity: the bondage of broken communion

The history of salvation narrated by Gutiérrez moves from the vocation to communion that is given in creation to its violation in the refusal and rejection of love that characterizes sin. This is not to suggest that he outlines a chronological movement from a state of perfection through a historical fall into a state of sin. There is, however, a conceptual movement that corresponds to these narrative moments. According to Gutiérrez, sin in all its forms is to be understood as – and has its origins in – a fall from love. This 'fall' from the vocation to which humanity is called takes place in the choice for the idolatrous god of death and in the rejection of the loving God of life.

Gutiérrez defines sin as a 'rejection of love'[62] and the 'breach of friendship between God and others'[63] which gives rise to injustice, conflict and oppression.[64] This account of sin does not narrate a tension between grace and nature nor a dissolution from the former to the latter. Rather, the movement of this 'fall' is from community to conflict, from harmony to hatred. In the rejection of love and the rupture of relationships there is a denial of both nature and grace. That is, there is a denial of life. Sin is the falling from the communion of love in which human life is forged. It is the bondage of death rather than the liberty of life. For this reason Matthew 25 becomes a programmatic text for the analysis and explanation of sin within the theology of Gutiérrez.[65] As Jeffrey Siker observes, 'the exodus story is not ... the crucial story or theme underlying Gutiérrez's liberation theology'.[66] Rather, it is important to recognize that 'from the New Testament, indeed from all of scripture, the single most important passage for Gutiérrez is clearly Matt. 25.31–46'.[67] This narrative characterizes sin as the rejection of life in the refusal to love the neighbour – and, in the neighbour, Christ.[68] The inhumanity of sin is not understood as the loss of a gift of grace or a degeneration from an ontological state. It is, rather, understood as the breach of the communion to which humanity is called and in which humanity is to be formed. It is the choice of death over life in the rejection and turning away from Christ in the neighbour.

Arguing that 'human existence in the last instance is nothing but a yes or a no to the Lord',[69] Gutiérrez characterizes each moment as a confrontation with the question, 'Whom in practice do you serve? The God of life or an idol of death?'[70] Sin consists in concrete decisions and social structures that express this 'no' to the Lord and servitude to the idol of death. Realized in this rejection of love, sin is a term that describes a historical and relational dynamic. According to Gutiérrez, sin 'cannot be encountered in itself, but only in concrete instances, in particular alienations'.[71] Observing that 'Gutiérrez stresses that sin only becomes actual in deeds', Thomas Lewis highlights the importance of this relational and social quality of sin.[72] Rather than describing an impersonal force or abstract condition, sin is expressive of a concrete decision that realizes a relation: a service of God or an idol, the turn outward to neighbour or inward to self, the commitment to creation or to the 'fetishes' of human hands.[73] For this reason sin – both in its personal and public expressions – must be considered as a social reality that courses through human history. The confrontation with sin and the condemnation of the idols of death do not take place on some separate 'spiritual' plane of subjective interiority. Rather, even the subjective and private decisions of the individual are themselves caught up in this narrative of human history. The conflict between the God of life and the idols of death is played out in concrete contexts where communion may be either breached or built. Within individual decisions and corporate social structures may be heard the 'yes' or 'no' to the call to communion in Christ.

Given the relational quality of this 'fall' from the vocation to which humanity is called, sin is necessarily a historical reality that is encountered within concrete decisions and structures that express a denial of life and a bondage to the idols of death. Realized within these concrete contexts of human history, sin must be understood as partaking in the distinct but inseparable dimensions that structure these contexts. Sin is therefore not only 'a personal, free act' but also, 'like every human act, necessarily has a social dimension'.[74] While not forgetting that 'sin is always the result of a personal, free act', the language of sin is also 'applicable to structures'.[75] Once sin is understood as such a 'social, historical fact ... the collective dimensions of sin are rediscovered'.[76] The personal, social and political facets of human life are each marked by the sin that resists and ruptures the communion in which this life is truly to be found.

Salvation and humanity: liberation forged in fellowship

Whereas sin expresses a rejection of the human vocation to communion, salvation is the movement towards its fulfilment. According to Gutiérrez, the narrative of salvation leads humanity to the end purposed in creation. He urges that, 'it is important to keep in mind that beyond – or rather, through – the struggle against misery, injustice and exploitation, the goal is *the creation of a new humanity*'.[77] Salvation involves neither an escape from history nor a simple change within history. It does not simply involve the deliverance from a certain circumstance or the elevation to a particular condition. It does not simply concern a change in the historical context or in the human person. Rather, salvation consists in the forging of humanity itself. Gutiérrez speaks of the process of history and 'temporal progress as a continuation of the work of creation' in its movement towards the fulfilment of the communion purposed to humanity.[78] Rather than speaking of an elevation of the human condition or a transformation of human circumstances, salvation expresses the forging and fulfilment of the truth of humanity. In his discussion of *Populorum progressio* Gutiérrez notes the concern to 'rise gradually to a more human state of things' that derives from 'a fuller idea of what it is to be human, the reaffirmation of the single vocation to the grace of communion with God'.[79] Salvation is neither a reductive alleviation in circumstances nor an abstracted elevation of condition. It is, instead, the creation of a humanity fulfilled in the communion for which it is purposed.

The salvific purpose of communion itself unfolds through a process of communion. Just as the end for which humanity is purposed is the love of God and neighbour, so the means by which this end is attained involves a sharing in the life of God and a service of the life of the neighbour. Salvation is characterized through an integrated working of God and humanity and Gutiérrez is emphatic that it comes and is received as a gift: 'Communion with the Lord and with all humans is more than anything else a gift ... There is a real love only when there is free giving – without conditions or coercion. Only gratuitous love goes to our roots and elicits true love.'[80] The forging of humanity in its personal, social and political integrity is made possible by the creative and redemptive giving of God. Human community is possible in divine self-communication. This gratuitous love and self-communication find their climactic expression in the coming of Jesus Christ. Gutiérrez concludes his reflections on the book of Job by joining the biblical author in directing the reader 'towards that gratuitousness of the Father's love that will be the heart of the proclamation and witness of Jesus Christ. He seeks a way; he offers himself as "the way" (John 14:6).'[81]

The love proclaimed by and known in Jesus is constitutive of the new humanity forged in community. The Son who is 'face to face with the Father'[82] shares this communion with those who will 'receive the gift of becoming children of God'.[83] This gift is the powerful and efficacious call in Christ to communion with God – a call proclaimed and fulfilled through Christ. In Christ the vocation to which humanity is called is both definitively revealed and irreversibly enacted. The new humanity created through the history of salvation is freely announced and achieved as God gives himself to – and in – humanity through the incarnation of his Son, Jesus Christ.

Flowing from the gratuitous love of God, the history of salvation unfolds through the liberative work of humankind. As the Son comes to humanity from the Father, so humanity is called to image this movement in love towards the neighbour. Like the 'reflected light' of John the Baptist by which he was able to 'help others and illumine the way that leads to the Lord', the life freely given by God must be made to shine through concrete decisions and actions.[84] As they image forth the creative gratuity of God, people are called to participate in the forging of a new humanity and to become 'artisans of this process'.[85] Observing that 'the grace of God is a gift, it is also a task', Gutiérrez draws on the example of Paul's exhortation to Philemon to demonstrate how the grace of God 'opens the door to the possibility of limitless work on Philemon's part in the service of his brother, who, in this case, is a man who is not acknowledged to be a human being with all human rights'.[86] The gospel calls for Christians to image forth the creative gratuity of God as they forge the new humanity revealed in Christ. In the freedom of this 'limitless work', Gutiérrez argues that Christians 'must in one or other fashion daily "invent" their life of love and commitment'.[87] As a consequence he concludes that 'by working, transforming the world, breaking out of servitude, building a just society, and assuming its destiny in history, humankind forges itself'.[88] In daily decisions of love and commitment a new humanity is forged that continues and brings to completion the creative and salvific work of God. The communion given to humanity as its destiny is also a task given to humanity as a responsibility.

The purpose of salvation is the creation of humanity and the process of salvation unfolds through the interplay of divine gratuity and human responsibility.[89] In other words, the story of salvation as told by Gutiérrez is a narrative by which humanity is formed through and for communion with God and neighbour.

The three facets of liberation to communion

As a social and historical reality, the salvation of humanity is a differentiated integrity that concerns the personal, social and political realities that constitute human identity and community. Reflecting on the structure of salvation that he delineated in *A Theology of Liberation*, Gutiérrez emphasizes that 'The idea that "there are three levels of meaning in a single, complex process, which finds its deepest and its fullest realization in the saving work of Christ" (*Liberation* p. 25) is fundamental to my perspective.'[90] The three levels that Gutiérrez distinguishes may be described as the political and structural, the personal and social and the subjective and spiritual.[91] It is necessary to attend to the three levels that constitute the complexity of this salvation before recognizing the unity to which they are drawn in Christ.

The first level identified by Gutiérrez is that found within the 'the political sphere'.⁹² To speak of the political in this sense is not to be restricted to institutional structures and affiliations.⁹³ It addresses itself instead to the reality of a humanity that seeks to 'be the artisan of its own destiny' by taking responsibility for the ways in which relationships are structured within community, with the result that 'nothing lies outside the political sphere'.⁹⁴ Gutiérrez explains that 'social and political liberation aims at eliminating the proximate causes of poverty and injustice' without seeking to restrict the work of salvation and liberation to this dimension.⁹⁵ Indeed, this aim demands a consideration of the second dimension of liberation. If the first dimension concerns the political structures that provide the context for human relations, the second dimension describes the personal and social dynamics that form – and are formed by – these broader structures.

When viewed from this second perspective, liberation places its emphasis on human freedom and agency within history and demands that the 'interior freedom of the human being' be taken seriously.⁹⁶ This personal freedom is not only the 'the goal of liberation but the necessary condition for any authentic political liberation'.⁹⁷ The attention to the personal is not to lead to an atomized individualism. Rather, valorization of the personal sphere reveals the universal extent of the liberation that is envisaged. It indicates that it is not sufficient for there to be a generalized or abstract freedom at the structural level – this liberation is to be the reality of all people at the deepest and most personal level. It proclaims the reality that liberation concerns persons – and, further, that liberation is to concern *all* persons. Gutiérrez cautions that a commitment to the first level of liberation without concern for the second can lead to injustice and oppression:

> If there is no daily friendship with the poor and appreciation of the diversity of their desires and needs as human beings, we can – it seems cruel to say it, but experience teaches us – transform the search for justice into a pretext, and even a justification, to mistreat the poor, pretending to know better than they what they want and need.⁹⁸

The pursuit of liberation must never degenerate into an idol before which the concrete reality of individual persons is sacrificed. It is instead a vocation that must '*da su plena densidad al presente*' ('accord to the present the fullness of its density').⁹⁹ Such a perspective allows liberation to be discovered within the lived and concrete reality of all people.

The final dimension of liberation concerns the deliverance from sin. As Gutiérrez explains:

Christ the Saviour liberates from sin, which is the ultimate root of all disruption of friendship and of all injustice and oppression. Christ makes humankind truly free, that is to say, he enables us to live in communion with him; and that is the basis for all human fellowship.[100]

This third perspective on liberation reveals the dynamic that energizes and establishes the others. While it concerns what might be described as the 'spiritual' dimensions of human life, it also directs attention to the way in which these spiritual dynamics themselves unfold within the social and political spheres.

These three dimensions together offer a unified and integrated account of the liberation achieved in the work of salvation.[101] Gutiérrez seeks to outline an 'integral liberation' whose salvation 'extends to all dimensions of the human'.[102] These structural, social and spiritual aspects each inform the other but there is a clear order between them. The first level is guided by the second, and the third is that which energizes the first and second. However, it is in the second level of interpersonal relation unfolding through history that the first and third are to meet. As such, this second level is a focal point of the liberative work of God in history because it offers the perspective by which the new and liberated humanity may be seen: 'In this perspective the unfolding of all the dimensions of humanness is demanded – persons who make themselves throughout their life and throughout history. The gradual conquest of true freedom leads to the creation of a new humankind.'[103] Gutiérrez cautions that while the structural change at the first level of liberation offers a necessary condition for this humanity, it is not in itself a sufficient condition. For structural and political change to take place on this first level it is necessary that it take shape through the liberated relations of the new humanity that is encountered at the second level.[104] In a similar way, the spiritual change rooted in the third level is only realized in the fruit that it bears in the lived relations that are expressed on the second level. As such, political action on the one hand and gospel proclamation on the other find their focus in the creation of a new humanity forged within community. As Gutiérrez argues, 'Faith and political action will not enter into a correct and fruitful relationship except through the effort to create a new type of person in a different society.'[105] The salvation proclaimed by Gutiérrez is a complex unity centred in the creation of a new humanity.

The humanity to which this process moves is finally and fully revealed in Christ and so it is in Christ and his church that the unity and totality of salvation may be discerned. Gutiérrez clarifies the unity of liberation

Gustavo Gutiérrez and the Liberative Sight of Christ

achieved by Christ in the commentary he offers on *A Theology of Liberation* in a later text. His commentary is worth citing at length:

> The complex unity comes, in the final analysis, from 'Christ the saviour,' who 'liberates from sin, which is in the ultimate root of all disruption of friendship and of all injustice and oppression [first level]. Christ makes humankind truly free [second level] – that is to say, he enables us to live in communion with him; and this is the basis for all human fellowship [third level]' (*Liberation*, p. 25).[106]

In Christ the complex unity of the work of salvation may be achieved. In Christ is revealed and realized the humanity in community to which the narrative of history moves. Gutiérrez narrates the story of human history as the movement from the breach of communion and the bondage of inhumanity to the restoration of community and the liberation of humanity. This movement finds its unity, possibility and purpose in the person of Jesus Christ.

Conclusion

Gutiérrez recounts the history of humanity as a single story whose unity is revealed and realized in Christ. As the narrative of salvation history moves towards the creation of a new humanity it is important to recognize the sight of Christ that Gutiérrez offers as the means by which this new humanity is forged. The Christ encountered in the neighbour and the neighbour encountered in Christ together become the climactic moment of the narrative recounted by Gutiérrez. It is to a consideration of this sight that I now turn.

Notes

1 Gustavo Gutiérrez, *The Truth Shall Make You Free: Confrontations*, trans. Matthew J. O'Connell (Maryknoll, NY: Orbis Books, 1990), p. 117. So also Gustavo Gutiérrez, *On Job: God-talk and the suffering of the innocent*, trans. Matthew J. O'Connell (Maryknoll, NY: Orbis Books, 1987), p. 85.

2 Gutiérrez, *The Truth Shall Make You Free*, p. 126.

3 Gustavo Gutiérrez, *A Theology of Liberation: History, politics and salvation*, trans. Caridad Inda and John Eagleson (London: SCM Press, 2010), p. 98.

4 Gutiérrez, *A Theology of Liberation*, p. 196.

5 Gustavo Gutiérrez, *The Power of the Poor in History*, trans. Robert R. Barr (Maryknoll, NY: Orbis Books, 1983), p. 193.

6 Gutiérrez, *A Theology of Liberation*, p. 98.
7 Gutiérrez, *A Theology of Liberation*, p. 170.
8 Gustavo Gutiérrez, '¿Dónde Dormirán Las Pobres?' in Gustavo Gutiérrez, Javier Ihuiñiz et al., *El Rostro de Dios En La Historia*, CEP 175 (Lima: Pontificia Universidad Católica del Perú, Departamento de Teología, 1996), p. 20.
9 Gutiérrez, *A Theology of Liberation*, p. 99.
10 Gutiérrez, *The Truth Shall Make You Free*, p. 14.
11 Gutiérrez, *The Truth Shall Make You Free*, p. 124.
12 Gutiérrez, *The Truth Shall Make You Free*, p. 22.
13 Gutiérrez, *The Truth Shall Make You Free*, p. 22.
14 Gutiérrez, *The Truth Shall Make You Free*, p. 34.
15 Gutiérrez, *The Truth Shall Make You Free*, p. 51.
16 Gutiérrez, *The Truth Shall Make You Free*, p. 124.
17 Gutiérrez, *The Truth Shall Make You Free*, p. 22.
18 Gustavo Gutiérrez, *The God of Life*, trans. Matthew J. O'Connell (Maryknoll, NY: Orbis Books, 1991), p. 152.
19 Gutiérrez, *The God of Life*, p. 153.
20 Gutiérrez, *The God of Life*, p. 77.
21 Gutiérrez, *The Truth Shall Make You Free*, p. 51.
22 Gutiérrez, *The God of Life*, p. 153.
23 Gutiérrez, *The God of Life*, p. 157.
24 Gutiérrez, *A Theology of Liberation*, p. 163.
25 Gutiérrez, *A Theology of Liberation*, p. 54.
26 Gutiérrez, *The God of Life*, p. 98.
27 Gutiérrez, *The God of Life*, p. 101.
28 Gutiérrez, *The God of Life*, p. 102.
29 Gutiérrez, *A Theology of Liberation*, p. 59.
30 Gutiérrez, *A Theology of Liberation*, p. 160.
31 Gutiérrez, *A Theology of Liberation*, p. 200.
32 Gutiérrez, *A Theology of Liberation*, p. 204.
33 'In other words what is at stake above all is a dynamic and historical conception of the human person, oriented decisively and creatively toward the future, acting in the present for the sake of tomorrow' (Gutiérrez, *A Theology of Liberation*, p. 71).
34 Paul VI, *Populorum Progressio* (Vatican City: Libreria Editrice Vaticana, 1967), 21, https://www.vatican.va/content/paul-vi/en/encyclicals/documents/hf_p-vi_enc_26031967_populorum.html, quoted in Gutiérrez, *A Theology of Liberation*, p. 170. The translation of *A Theology of Liberation* at this point follows Gutiérrez's citation of the Spanish version of *Populorum Progressio*.
35 Gutiérrez, *The Truth Shall Make You Free*, p. 125.
36 Gutiérrez outlines the importance of this conceptual structure to his theological project in *The Truth Shall Make You Free*, pp. 121–4.
37 Gutiérrez, *The Truth Shall Make You Free*, p. 2.
38 Gutiérrez, *The God of Life*, p. 27.
39 Gutiérrez, *The God of Life*, p. 117.
40 Gutiérrez, *On Job*, p. 80.
41 Gutiérrez, *On Job*, p. 85.
42 Gutiérrez, *On Job*, p. 79.

43 Gutiérrez, *A Theology of Liberation*, p. 52.
44 Gutiérrez, *A Theology of Liberation*, p. 95.
45 Gutiérrez, *A Theology of Liberation*, p. 79.
46 Gutiérrez, *A Theology of Liberation*, p. 81.
47 Gutiérrez, *A Theology of Liberation*, p. 95.
48 Brackley, *Divine Revolution*, p. 87. Brackley argues that whereas the precise contours of the relation between, for example, divine grace and human action may have been under-developed during the first stages of his theological project, 'Gutiérrez later addressed these issues with extraordinary depth and eloquence' (Dean Brackley, *Divine Revolution: Salvation and liberation in Catholic thought*, Eugene, OR: Wipf & Stock, 2004, p. 90).
49 Gutiérrez, *The God of Life*, p. 78.
50 Gutiérrez, *The God of Life*, p. 79.
51 Gutiérrez, *The God of Life*, p. 80.
52 'Es justo reconocer que la crítica posmoderna nos ayuda a no caer en esquemas rígidos y almidonados para interpretar el curso de la historia ... No obstante, dicho esto, es necesario recordar que en una perspectiva cristiana la historia tiene su centro en la venida del Hijo, en la Encarnación, sin que esto quiera decir que la historia humana avanza ineluctablemente siguiendo cauces trazados y dominados por un férreo pensamiento rector' (Gutiérrez, '¿Dónde Dormirán Los Pobres?', p. 43; my translation).
53 Gutiérrez, *A Theology of Liberation*, p. 179.
54 Gutiérrez, *A Theology of Liberation*, p. 181.
55 Gutiérrez, *A Theology of Liberation*, p. 160.
56 Gutiérrez, *A Theology of Liberation*, p. 182.
57 Gutiérrez, *A Theology of Liberation*, p. 99.
58 Gutiérrez, *A Theology of Liberation*, p. 183.
59 Gutiérrez, *A Theology of Liberation*, p. 196.
60 Gutiérrez, *The Truth Shall Make You Free*, p. 125.
61 Gutiérrez, *The Truth Shall Make You Free*, pp. 121–4.
62 'We insist that in the final analysis the root of social injustice is the rejection of love – that is, sin' (Gutiérrez, *The Truth Shall Make You Free*, p. 31).
63 'Sin – a breach of friendship between God and others – is, according to the Bible, the ultimate cause of poverty, injustice and the oppression in which persons live' (Gutiérrez, *A Theology of Liberation*, p. 74).
64 Gutiérrez, '¿Dónde Dormirán Los Pobres?', p. 47.
65 Jeffrey S. Siker, 'Uses of the Bible in the theology of Gustavo Gutiérrez: liberating scriptures of the poor', *Biblical Interpretation* 4, no. 1 (1 January 1996), p. 44.
66 Siker, 'Uses of the Bible', p. 44.
67 Siker, 'Uses of the Bible', p. 45.
68 Gutiérrez expounds 'the essence of the gospel message' that he considers to be summarized by Matthew 25.31–46 in *A Theology of Liberation*, pp. 186–7.
69 Gutiérrez, *A Theology of Liberation*, p. 149.
70 Gutiérrez, *The God of Life*, p. 49.
71 Gutiérrez, *A Theology of Liberation*, p. 174.
72 Thomas A. Lewis, 'Actions as the ties that bind: love, praxis, and community

in the thought of Gustavo Gutiérrez', *Journal of Religious Ethics* 33, no. 3 (September 2005), p. 551.

73 Gutiérrez outlines the characteristics of idolatry in *The God of Life*, pp. 49–53.

74 Gutiérrez, *A Theology of Liberation*, p. 348 n. 101.

75 Gutiérrez, *The God of Life*, p. 137.

76 Gutiérrez, *A Theology of Liberation*, p. 174.

77 Gutiérrez, *A Theology of Liberation*, p. 145. Emphasis original.

78 Gutiérrez, *A Theology of Liberation*, p. 171.

79 Gutiérrez, *A Theology of Liberation*, p. 170.

80 Gutiérrez, *A Theology of Liberation*, p. 195.

81 Gutiérrez, *On Job*, p. 97.

82 Gutiérrez, *The God of Life*, p. 84.

83 Gutiérrez, *The God of Life*, p. 83.

84 Gutiérrez, *The God of Life*, p. 82.

85 Gutiérrez, *A Theology of Liberation*, p. 137.

86 Gutiérrez, *The Truth Shall Make You Free*, p. 140.

87 Gutiérrez, *The Truth Shall Make You Free*, p. 141.

88 Gutiérrez, *A Theology of Liberation*, p. 157.

89 Gustavo Gutiérrez, 'Expanding the view' in *Expanding the View: Gustavo Gutiérrez and the Future of Liberation Theology*, ed. Marc H. Ellis and Otto Maduro, trans. Matthew J. O'Connell (Eugene, OR: Wipf and Stock, 1990), p. 26.

90 Gutiérrez, *The Truth Shall Make You Free*, p. 121.

91 Gutiérrez, *A Theology of Liberation*, p. 175.

92 Gutiérrez, *The Truth Shall Make You Free*, p. 129.

93 Gutiérrez, *The Truth Shall Make You Free*, p. 130.

94 Gutiérrez, *A Theology of Liberation*, p. 81.

95 Gutiérrez, *The Truth Shall Make You Free*, p. 130.

96 Gutiérrez, *The Truth Shall Make You Free*, p. 134.

97 Gutiérrez, *The Truth Shall Make You Free*, p. 135.

98 'Si no hay amistad cotidiana con el pobre y valoración de la diversidad de sus deseos y necesidades en tanto ser humano podemos – parece cruel decirlo, pero la experiencia lo enseña – transformar la búsqueda de la justicia en un pretexto, y hasta en una justificación, para maltratar a los pobres, pretendiendo conocer mejor que ellos lo que quieren y necesitan' (Gutiérrez, '¿Dónde Dormirán Los Pobres?', p. 51; my translation.

99 Gutiérrez, '¿Dónde Dormirán Los Pobres?', p. 43. My translation.

100 Gutiérrez, *A Theology of Liberation*, p. 76.

101 Gutiérrez describes 'three levels of meaning of a single, complex process which finds its deepest sense and its fullest realization in Christ'. Gutiérrez, *A Theology of Liberation*, p. 76.

102 Gutiérrez, *The Truth Shall Make You Free*, p. 141.

103 Gutiérrez, *A Theology of Liberation*, p. 75.

104 Gutiérrez, *The God of Life*, p. 133.

105 Gutiérrez, *A Theology of Liberation*, p. 221.

106 Gutiérrez, *The Truth Shall Make You Free*, p. 122. Commentary in square brackets original.

3

Reading the Human Story

According to Gutiérrez this movement of humanity towards communion with God and neighbour through an encounter with Christ in community is discerned when history is read from the perspective of a preferential option for the poor.

In the theology of Gutiérrez the preferential option for the poor is 'a deep, ongoing solidarity, a voluntary daily involvement with the world of the poor' that establishes the context for theological reflection.[1] Arguing that the priority of this preference 'has its roots in biblical revelation and the history of the church', Gutiérrez traces this preference from the story of Cain and Abel at the start of the Bible through the teaching of Jesus and the preaching of the Apostles at its climax.[2] The preferential option for the poor that he draws from the biblical revelation is not simply a part of the message of Scripture, but rather offers the perspective by which the message of the gospel may itself be heard. According to Gutiérrez, this has been the perspective to which the church has been called throughout her history – a call that has been heard with particular clarity in Latin America since the Second Vatican Council. He recalls the declaration of John XIII in the month before the Council that 'the church is and wishes to be, the church of all, and especially the church of the poor',[3] and after the Council the bishops of Latin America sought to apply the theology expressed in such documents as *Lumen Gentium* with an exhortation to a 'preference to the poorest and neediest, and to those who are segregated for any reason'.[4] Gutiérrez observes[5] that 'in Medellín, the three words (option, preference, poor) are all present, but it was only in the years immediately following Medellín that we brought these words into a complete phrase' whose formulation received a 'powerful endorsement' at the Puebla Conference of 1979.[6]

Taught by Scripture and proclaimed in the church, the preferential option for the poor is a commitment by the disciple of Christ to the neighbour in Christ – a commitment that is called for both by divine revelation and the context in which divine revelation is to be received. Before I trace out the contours of this concept, I will need to clarify the role that the preferential option for the poor plays in the thought of Gutiérrez. I will show that the preferential option for the poor is not simply the application of a theology. Instead, Gutiérrez contends that it is the context in which a truly Christian theology must emerge. Having recognized this role, it will be possible to trace out its shape. In the second part of this chapter, I will explore the way in which Gutiérrez characterizes the preferential option for the poor. While arguing for the biblical and ecclesial warrant for the concept, he acknowledges that it is susceptible to misunderstanding. In order to understand the spiritual reality that he seeks to invoke in the call to a preferential option for the poor I will explore each of the three elements of the phrase. I will consider first the phenomenon of the poor, then the dynamic of preference, and finally the concept of the option. Each facet of the phrase discloses the relation between concerns that are often considered to be in conflict or contradiction.

The preferential option for the poor: a hermeneutic of history

For Gutiérrez the preferential option for the poor is not simply the consequence of a particular theology; rather, it is the necessary context for a truly Christian theology. While language that speaks of a preferential option for the poor can be heard within many different parts of the church, this shared language belies significant theological differences. On the one hand, this language may be deployed within a broader ethical framework. Whatever the concerns or priorities that give shape to this ethical framework, the preferential option for the poor is considered to be a particular and perhaps especially relevant expression of Christian charity and love.[7] On the other hand, the option is considered to provide the context within which theological and ethical reflection must take place. If one approach speaks of the option within a pre-existing ethical framework, the other approach establishes the option as a theological and ethical framework. This treatment of the option considers it to be not simply the moral implications of theology but rather 'in some sense pre-moral: it affects epistemological matters as well as the ethical reflections based thereupon'.[8] The preferential option for the poor involves a reading of history and conversion to the neighbour that give acts of charity their possibility and meaning. For this reason, Rebecca Chopp is correct to conclude that:

> The option for the poor, in the nature of theological reflection, is therefore not first of all an ethical claim, though of course this theological insight has ethical implications. Rather, the option for the poor is

Gustavo Gutiérrez and the Liberative Sight of Christ

Gutiérrez's hermeneutical strategy, a wager that we shall understand differently as we risk encountering God in the poor.[9]

The option for the poor offers the 'hermeneutical strategy' through which history can be read, its narrative discerned, and its ethical call heard. Observing that 'the essence of Christian faith is to believe in Christ', Gutiérrez argues that 'to have faith in Christ is to see the history in which we are living as the progressive revelation of the human face of God'.[10] The commitment of God to humanity that is realized at the incarnation and that continues to be revealed in history is the definitive fact of the Christian faith. Gutiérrez argues that the preferential option for the poor is an expression of faith in the God who reveals himself at the incarnation and throughout human history. It is in the preferential option for the poor that the unity of history is heard and the 'human face of God' is to be discerned so that the communion to which humanity is called may at last be achieved.

The option: confirmed by God in Jesus

According to Gutiérrez, therefore, the preferential option for the poor is an expression of the faith that is demanded by the incarnation. Faith in Christ involves a faith in the Christ who lived in particular historical and social circumstances. Faith in Christ is an echo in the human heart of the commitment of God in Christ to the poor, marginalized and oppressed. Gutiérrez observes that the biblical theme of God's presence to humanity in history 'reaches its fullest form in the Incarnation in Jesus the Galilean, the poor man of Nazareth'.[11] The Jesus confessed by faith is a person who lived 'in a particular place and at a particular time'[12] and whose meaning is found within these 'historical coordinates' of his life'.[13] The commitment by God to humanity is not a commitment to an idea or abstraction; rather, it is the commitment revealed in Jesus, a man born amid poverty, oppression and exclusion. Faith proclaims that 'God became flesh and is present in history but because God identifies with the poor of the world, God's face and action are hidden in them.'[14] At the incarnation faith encounters the presence of God with humanity in history. However, this is not an abstract presence in a generalized humanity within a spiritualized history. Rather, it is the specific and concrete history of Jesus that reveals how God is present in the specific and concrete realities of the history of humanity as a whole. Given that God has revealed himself specifically in Jesus in the gospel, God reveals himself especially among the poor in history.

Reading the Human Story

The option: revealed in the poor

The faith that sees in the gospel the face of God revealed in Jesus will see this face revealed in history amid the poor and excluded. The history of God's work of creation and liberation can be discerned among the darkness and death that seem to shroud human history. This work may be discerned when that history is read from the perspective of the preference for the poor that is established by God at the incarnation. Reflecting on a poem by César Vallejo, Gutiérrez considers the hope offered by a seller of lottery tickets. Amid the fickleness of fortune and the experience of lost hope it is in 'this tattered fellow' that 'we might run into fortune' and encounter 'this God who so mysteriously is linked to the marginalized of history and who is hidden'.[15] As Gutiérrez observes at another point when reflecting on the same poem: 'But every person is a lottery vender who hawks tickets for "the big one": our encounter with that God who is deep down in the heart of each person.'[16] The faith that can see the glory of God in the face of Christ can discern the presence of Christ in the face of the neighbour. Despite the seemingly impersonal process of history that is invoked by the image of the lottery ticket, and within the realities of poverty and exclusion that are expressed in the figure of the seller, faith discerns the presence and work of God.

The dynamic that is expressed in the poem by Vallejo is explored within the drama of the book of Job. The tension of the drama arises out of the inability of Job to discern and understand the presence and work of God in the midst of his suffering and pain. Job's experience confronts him with the possibility that either injustice or at the very least the forces of chaos are the basic characteristic of human existence.[17] History for Job appears to be a narrative of death and disorder rather than a story that leads to liberation and life. The drama of Job begins with an understanding of God given through the 'hearsay' of his friends or cultural traditions.[18] It reaches its climax in an encounter with God in his self-revelation. In this encounter Job is shown that 'God does indeed have plans and the world is not a chaos as Job had pictured it', and amid the seeming chaos and injustice of his experience he is led to discern 'a plan of gratuitous love'.[19] While Job has been bound by his own – and his friends' – reading of history, the speeches of God allow him to 'leap the fence of this sclerotic theology that is so close to idolatry' and to 'run free in the fields of God's love' as he discovers that 'the world outside the fence is a world of gratuitousness'.[20] Where Job sees in his own life only chaos and injustice – where the passer-by sees in the lottery seller only wretchedness and hopeless dreams – faith may hear the call of God to know his love.

By first making known the gratuity of his love, God allows Job to penetrate more deeply into the reality of his justice. History does not receive its order and meaning from a rigid and impersonal system. The truth of history is found in God's gracious love. Before the story of history can be read and its meaning understood, there must be an encounter with a limitless and uncontainable love that 'Yahweh has established as the fulcrum of the world'.[21] Read within the context of this love the work of God in history may be discerned: 'God's freedom comes to light in the revelation that divine gratuitous love has been made the foundation of the world and that only in the light of this fact can the meaning of divine justice be grasped.'[22] An encounter with the gratuitous love of God allows for the meaning and order of history to be disclosed. This freedom and gratuity find climactic expression through the identification of God with the poor, suffering and excluded. What is declared to Job at the end of the book is revealed to the reader throughout its drama: that the God who calls for trust from Job is the God who first trusts in Job.[23] God identifies himself with Job and binds himself to him in his suffering. At the end of the book the speeches of God reveal to Job the grace and justice of God. Throughout the book, the figure of Job expresses to the reader the grace and justice of the God who identifies himself with the one who endures injustice, pain and loss.

As God comes to Job, he does not deny the pain of his suffering or seek to deprecate his protest against injustice and death. Rather, in the figures of Behemoth and Leviathan God evokes the reality of his experience in all its ferocious inhumanity. However, as God describes these 'symbols of the wicked', Job is reminded that 'like everything that exists, the enormous forces of chaos and disorder are subject to divine power'.[24] The creative gratuitousness that is expressed in the first speech (Job 38.1—39.30) and the just power that is displayed in the second (Job 40.6—41.34) must be heard in the context of the previous chapters of suffering. While the gratuitous love of God and the just purposes of God are declared by God in his speeches at the end of the book, these realities are dramatized in the fact of his presence with his servant throughout the book as a whole. It is through Job that the vision of God is given. It is to and through the one who suffers that the truth of God is revealed. As such, Job, a suffering servant of God, anticipates the coming of Jesus who 'teaches us that talk of God must be mediated by the experience of the cross'.[25] In his creative freedom God binds himself 'to those whom the powerful and the self-righteous of society treat unjustly and make outcasts'.[26] It is in the power of his justice that in the midst of death God can work resurrection and new life.[27] As the readers encounter in Job the reality of suffering and confusion, they are able to hear through Job the revelation of divine justice and love. To read the history of God's presence to humanity and to speak of the purpose of God for humanity it is necessary to see in Job, in Jesus, in the oppressed and in the poor, the wisdom and strength of God. As Gutiérrez observes:

> Communion in suffering and in hope, in the abandonment of loneliness and in trusting self-surrender in death as in life: this is the message of the cross, which is 'folly to those who are perishing, but to us who are being saved it is the power of God' (1 Cor. 1.18).[28]

In the cross, death and injustice claim the victory. In the cry of Christ on the cross, faith is given the final word. In the suffering of Job the brutality of Behemoth is exposed. In the presence of God to Job, the bondage of Behemoth and the victory of love are proclaimed.

As read by Gutiérrez, the text of Job is not a parable that provides a resolution at its conclusion. Rather, it is a drama whose truth is disclosed as the reader is drawn into its action. The suffering of Job mediates to the reader a voice of solidarity and compassion. The silence that enfolds God throughout the majority of the book is itself a revelation of his presence with and commitment to a suffering humanity. As the protest and complaint of Job unfold throughout the book, God gives preference to this expression. While the experience of Job leads him to fear that 'human beings are insignificant', the space given to his voice expresses in dramatic form what God proclaims in poetic form at the end of the book: that 'they are great enough for God, the almighty, to stop at the threshold of their freedom'.[29] As the drama of the book unfolds, God gives preference to the experience of Job and, when God does speak, the truths proclaimed in the final chapters of the book serve to accentuate the revelation that has unfolded throughout the book. Where Job fears chaos, God reveals to him gratuity. Where Job fears disorder, God reveals justice. The cries of Job throughout the book are therefore not encounters with chaos but with the love of God who gives preference to the one who suffers. In the same way, the complaints of Job throughout the book are therefore not evidence of disorder but of the justice of God who gives voice to the voiceless. As Gutiérrez argues elsewhere: 'The Lord hides his presence in history, and at the same time reveals it, in the life and suffering, the struggles, the death, and the hopes of the condemned of the earth.'[30] This interplay of hiddenness and revelation is dramatized in the person of Job. In the drama of Job faith can discern the loving and just preference of God for the poor. What he declares at the end of the book has been present throughout: that the revelation of God is hidden and disclosed in the suffering of his servant.

Conclusion

In the lives of Job and Jesus – and the vendor of lottery tickets – the passer-by may only see chaos, confusion and condemnation. As the disciple looks, they are able to discern the uncontainable love and just purpose of the God whom they reveal. The preferential option of the poor is the hermeneutic by which the disciple of Christ might discern the narrative of human history and enter into the drama of its unfolding. In the cacophony of human history, the preferential option for the poor allows the Christian to hear in the cry of Jesus on the cross 'the *cantus firmus*, the leading voice to which all the voices of those who suffer unjustly are joined'.[31]

The preferential option for the poor: reading the human story

Having established *that* the option reveals the unity of this history, I will now explore *how* the preferential option for the poor makes this narrative heard by exploring each of the three concepts that are drawn together in this phrase.

The poor: the relation of history and theology

As I have already demonstrated, Gutiérrez argues that 'history, concrete history, is the place where God reveals the mystery of God's personhood'.[32] As a consequence, the poor in whom God reveals himself are to be considered in the 'density' of their social and political reality.[33] Gutiérrez warns that the 'persons to whom the gospel is proclaimed are not abstract, apolitical beings' but rather they are people who are situated within concrete circumstances of poverty, exclusion and oppression.[34] The implication of this conviction is that a reading of history and an articulation of theology will proceed along the 'new paths' that are opened by human reason such as 'the social, psychological, and biological sciences'.[35] In his earlier writings Gutiérrez emphasizes the importance of such sciences, asserting the particular utility of Marxist historical analysis.[36] He observes that, 'Many agree with Sartre that

"Marxism, as the formal framework of all contemporary philosophical thought, cannot be superseded."'[37] While implicitly seeking to maintain a distinction between the content of Marxist ideology and the use of Marxism as an analytical tool, Gutiérrez argues that theology must make use of such tools if it is to read human history truly and so speak of God faithfully. Asking the question 'What is theology?' he cautions that this question can only be addressed through a consideration of 'modern scientific knowledge', especially as such knowledge concerns psychology, sociology and economics.[38]

This use of Marxist analysis and language has drawn sharp criticism. In 1983 the Congregation of the Doctrine of the Faith rejected what it understood to be 'the uncritical acceptance' of a Marxist reading of the situation in Latin America.[39] The 'Ten Observations on the Theology of Gustavo Gutiérrez' conclude with the warning that the 'recourse to Marxism' found in the theology of Gutiérrez leads it to 'pervert' an otherwise evangelical consciousness of the poor.[40] These observations were followed a year later by the 'Instruction on Certain Aspects of the "Theology of Liberation"'. The 'Instruction' argues that 'since the thought of Marx is such a global vision of reality'[41] it is not possible to distinguish between Marxism considered as an ideology and as an analytical tool because 'no separation of the parts of this epistemologically unique complex is possible'.[42] In a similar way John Milbank argues that the theology of Gutiérrez proceeds through a 'displacing of the Christian meta-narrative' by secular social science in general and Marxism in particular.[43] Milbank and Ratzinger read the theology of Gutiérrez as being fatally flawed by a concession to the autonomy of human reason and the dissolution of theology into a historical narrative constructed through the tools of Marxist social analysis.

These critiques, however, offer an inadequate reading of Gutiérrez and the role that the social sciences play within his theological project. While he calls for an 'ongoing dialogue' with the science of social and psychological analysis,[44] he avers that 'At no time, either explicitly or implicitly, have I suggested a dialogue with Marxism with a view to a possible "synthesis" or to accepting one aspect while leaving others aside.'[45] Gutiérrez emphasizes that the dialogue of theology with the social sciences need not imply a synthesis – much less a conflation – with the presuppositions or ideological structures through which those sciences took shape. It is striking that he calls for a discernment to avoid precisely the kind of displacement about which Milbank warns. Given that science by its nature must proceed through a movement of testing, evaluation and critique, 'to say that something is scientific is to say that it is subject to ongoing discussion and criticism'.⁴⁶ As a consequence Gutiérrez considers the social sciences to be tools in the service of a theological and pastoral project rather than establishing the scaffolding within which that project is to be constructed.⁴⁷ When considering the relation between Marxism and Marxist analysis, Gutiérrez declares that 'The question is a secondary one. In fact, given the situation in which Latin America was living, it seemed to me more urgently necessary to turn to more clearly theological questions.'⁴⁸

This is not to say that the distinction between the two is unimportant or to imply that there are no dangers in the confusion of the two. It does, however, demonstrate the pastoral context and theological focus of the use of such concepts in the theology of Gutiérrez. For Gutiérrez, the social sciences provide tools through which an encounter with the poor might be more clearly understood and more faithfully described. It is, however, the pastoral encounter, called for by a commitment in faith to Christ, that is to provide theology with the datum by which it seeks to speak.

The role of the social sciences within the thought of Gutiérrez is evident in his assertion that theology must address itself to the lived encounters within which it is forged. The conceptual tools that might be used to understand and articulate this encounter are not themselves to determine or define the encounter. Gutiérrez offers an illustration of this dynamic that is worth quoting at length:

> The question therefore that theology must answer is this: If there is a struggle ... how are we to respond to it as Christians? A theological question is always one that is prompted by the content of faith – that is, by love. ... Suppose that analysis were to tell us one day: 'The class struggle is not as important as you used to think.' We theologians would continue to say that love is the important thing, even amid conflict as described for us by social analysis.⁴⁹

The theologian is accountable to the reality that is disclosed in an encounter with the neighbour that is received by faith. The social analysis of this situation is subject to revision and change, but the commitment of love will remain the same. When questioned about what set of tools the theologian might have at his disposal to engage with the unity of history, Gutiérrez responded: 'The question was: "What set of tools is to be used?" I believe I have no other tool than my own personal and pastoral experience.'⁵⁰ Far from seeking to abstract theology into a Marxist metanarrative or dissolve theology into an atheistic and impersonal ideology, he locates theology within the personal encounter with neighbour that is called forth by – and that itself calls forth – faith in Jesus Christ. Tim Noble observes that 'the problem in Latin America is not to decide who the poor are and the urgency of the task militates against over-theorizing', and while this might render a concept of the poor that is 'at best amorphous' it resists the reduction of such a group to one or other ideological construct.[51] The tools of social analysis are, like the other tools at the disposal of the theologian, to be used critically and carefully in the service of the gospel. They are tools to be used in the construction of the new humanity forged in community through Christ. They are not the scaffolding through which this new humanity is to take shape.

Rather than receiving its impulse from an impersonal ideology or finding its form within an atheistic metanarrative, Gutiérrez argues that the preferential option for the poor is called for by the revelation of God in Christ. The preferential option for the poor is described by Gutiérrez as 'a theocentric, prophetic option we make, one which strikes its root in the gratuity of God's love' and that does not ultimately depend on or flow from 'the social analysis we employ'.[52] In his introduction to the revised edition of *A Theology of Liberation* Gutiérrez seeks to clarify that 'in the final analysis an option for the poor is an option for the God of the kingdom whom Jesus proclaims to us'.[53] Observing that 'to be a Christian is to walk, moved by the Spirit, in the footsteps of Jesus', he describes the preferential option for the poor as a following in the path marked out by the incarnation of God in Christ among the poor, oppressed and marginalized.[54] It is the love of God in Christ that draws forth the preferential option and it is the concrete expression of this love that orientates this option to the poor: 'The preference for the poor is based on the fact that God, as Christ shows us, loves them for their concrete, real condition of poverty.'[55] In the incarnation, the love of God is revealed within a context of suffering and exclusion. The flesh by which God comes to the world is a flesh that undergoes deprivation and death. For this reason, the revelation of God in Christ is the revelation of a gratuitous and illimitable love. The incarnation does not proclaim the spiritual superiority of the poor – much less does it sanctify the situation of poverty. Rather, it reveals the freedom, grace and goodness of God. As a consequence, Gutiérrez contends that 'the ultimate basis for the privileged position of the poor is not in the poor themselves but in God, the gratuitousness of God's *agapeic* love'.[56]

The incarnation of Christ reveals that 'the ways of God are not our ways (see Is 55.8)' and so the Christian is called to follow in this 'way' that draws them into a 'free and generous search of those whom society marginalises and oppresses'.[57] The action of God throughout the Bible and the culmination of this revelation in Christ proclaims that 'the least members of history' are in fact 'the first objects of the tender love of the God of Jesus Christ'.[58] Theology must take shape within a preferential option for the poor because the God who is revealed in Jesus of Nazareth is the God who reveals himself in and binds himself to the poor. The historical orientation to the poor is established by the revelation received by faith in the gratuitous love of God in Christ.

The preference: the relation between particularity and universality

According to Gutiérrez, faith in Christ allows the poor to be seen as the site in which the gracious and generous love of God is made known. The preference that is called for by Gutiérrez is to be characterized by this generosity and grace. While the language of preference can be heard to communicate exclusion and division he argues that a preference for the poor is the starting point for a truly universal love. While the argument of Gutiérrez might at first seem counterintuitive, it is central to his conception of the preferential option for the poor. He argues that:

> Universality is not only not opposed to this predilection (which is not to be mistaken for exclusivity) but even requires it in order to make clear the meaning of the universality itself. The preference, in turn, has its proper setting in the call that God addresses to every human being.[59]

To speak of a preference is not to describe a dynamic of exclusion and division. For Gutiérrez, it is to establish the character of the unity in which Christian community is to be forged. Preference does not seek to restrict the universal love of God. It seeks to display the nature of this universal love and the way in which it is to be enjoyed.

In the theology of Gutiérrez, the language of preference must not be heard to express restriction or exclusion. It does not contradict the universal scope of God's love but rather gives meaning to that universal love. The love of God is to be understood as 'becoming concrete in solidarity with human beings – first with the poor and the dispossessed, and then through them with all human beings'.[60] The love of God for the poor reveals and guarantees the love of God for all. A love that is known first among the poor is a love that from first to last will be received and lived in grace. If I might express the argument of Gutiérrez in its simplest form, it is that a love which begins *here* must be a love that reaches *everywhere*. The poor are the place in which the gratuity and generosity of God are to be encountered. For that reason, a preference for the poor secures rather than undermines the universality of God's love. Just as the love of God is made known in the church for the whole world so the poor make known to the church the truth of its God. If the church is to be a sacrament in the world it must receive in the poor the disclosure of what this mission entails. Gutiérrez argues that 'the mediating consciousness of the "other" ... is the indispensable precondition of its own consciousness as a community-sign'.⁶¹ The particular serves and secures the universal. The universal love of God for humanity finds its meaning in the preferential love of God for the poor. As Gutiérrez explains:

> God's love has two dimensions, the universal and the particular; and while there is a tension between the two, there is no contradiction. God's love excludes no one. ... The word *preference* recalls the other dimension of the gratuitous love of God – the universality.⁶²

In what may seem a surprising conclusion, Gutiérrez contends that the language of preference guards the gratuity and the universality of God's love. In the particularity and specificity of the incarnation, God makes known his love to the world. In the preference for the poor that is revealed through the incarnation, God makes known the kind of love that he offers the world. To say that God has a preference for the poor is to establish the grounds by which it is possible to say that God extends his love to all.

The option: the relation between community and conflict

Having considered the characterization of both the poor and the preference, I will turn now to engage with the pastoral orientation that is described by the term 'option'. The preferential option for the poor describes a commitment to the poor which, while involving conflict, nevertheless serves to build the unity of Christian community. In order to understand the option, it is necessary to understand this relationship between conflict, condemnation and opposition on the one hand and solidarity, unity and community on the other.

Gutiérrez draws attention to the particular resonance of the word 'option' when he explains that whereas 'in English, the word merely connotes a choice between two things', the Spanish word 'evokes the sense of commitment' that will involve both a 'solidarity *with* the poor' and 'a stance *against* inhumane poverty'.⁶³ The commitment that is called for by God and that is revealed at the incarnation is not just theoretical. It is to be expressed in a 'commitment to specific people' in the concrete reality of their historical situation.⁶⁴ Such a commitment places the Christian in a context where 'neutrality is impossible' as it 'calls for our active participation'.⁶⁵ The commitment through which Christian community is forged involves the affirmation of life and the rejection of death. It is a confrontation with the stark decision that faces the disciple of Jesus. Drawing on Matthew 6.24 and Luke 16.9–15, Gutiérrez observes that 'The Lord therefore calls upon his disciples to make an uncompromising choice; the words "love" and "hate" underscore the impossibility of compromise and refer to a decision that must be made.'⁶⁶ The life of the disciple is to be lived within the conflict that is described by Jesus – the conflict between God and mammon, between life and death. The community that is formed through commitment is thereby forged in conflict.

The argument of Gutiérrez at this point echoes the logic that I outlined in the previous section. In what might seem to be another surprising move, Gutiérrez argues that this conflictual dynamic is what characterizes a truly inclusive love. Placing discipleship within the context of a 'concrete and conflictual history', he is careful to stress that such conflict is to be understood as expressing rather than excluding love.⁶⁷ The conflict that is called for is not provoked by or in the service of particular political ideologies. It is provoked by pastoral encounters with poverty and serves the building of Christian community.⁶⁸ The character of the option can only be understood when it is viewed through the facets that I have already considered. First, the poor are recognized as the place in which the gratuity of God's love is made known. Then, the preference for the poor is understood as the point from which this love is shared with the world. Having recognized the poor and understood this preference, a commitment to the poor becomes the first step in realizing this love within the world. The conflict that commitment demands builds community because it involves the rejection of death, division and degradation. To stand with the poor is to stand against poverty and for that reason the option is an expression of love.

Acknowledging the potential difficulty that might be encountered in preserving this dynamic, Gutiérrez addresses the question of how Christians are to live the unity of their community in the midst of the conflicts of history. He argues that 'the universality of Christian love is … incompatible with the exclusion of any persons but it is not incompatible with a preferential option for the poorest and most oppressed'.⁶⁹ Far from being incompatible with the universality of Christian love, such an option is a necessary condition for its realization. As the church joins with the 'struggle against the radical causes of social division' it is living its calling to be 'an authentic and effective sign of unity under the universal love of God'.⁷⁰ As the church commits to the poor it lives the graciousness of

God's love and reveals that all are called to its embrace. The option for the poor and the rejection of poverty are the affirmation of universality and the rejection of division. According to Gutiérrez the option must be understood as the call 'to follow Jesus on the path leading to the universal Father'.[71] It is in the historic specificity of Christ that the universal love of God is made known. It is in following in the commitment of Jesus to the poor that the love of the Father for all is made known. Just as Jesus is the way to the Father, so a commitment to the poor is the way to a communion open to all of humanity.

Conclusion

Noble describes the preferential option for the poor as the '*articulus stantis aut cadentis*' of the theology of liberation.[72] It offers the hermeneutic by which the unified work of God to forge a new humanity in community may be discerned and it discloses the way in which this purpose is to be fulfilled. Unfolding throughout history and verified at the incarnation, the commitment of God to the poor offers an encounter with the generosity and gratuity of his love. As the disciple follows Christ in this commitment to the poor, they participate in the work of God by which a new humanity is forged in community. Once humanity can read the narrative of the work of God in history, it is drawn into the unfolding of the story and so participates in its movement towards the climax of communion with God in neighbour.

Notes

1 Gustavo Gutiérrez, 'Option for the Poor' in *Systematic Theology: Perspectives from Liberation Theology: Readings from Mysterium Liberationis*, ed. Jon Sobrino and Ignacio Ellacuría (Maryknoll, NY: Orbis Books, 1996), p. 26.

2 Gutiérrez, 'Option for the Poor', p. 27.

3 John XXIII, 'Pope's Address to World Month Before Council Opened' in *Council Daybook: Vatican II, Sessions 1 and 2*, ed. Floyd Anderson (Washington, DC: The National Catholic Welfare Conference, 1965), p. 19. Quoted in Gutiérrez, 'Option for the Poor', p. 30.

4 Second General Conference of Latin American Bishops, 'Document on the poverty of the Church' in *Liberation Theology: A documentary history*, ed. Alfred T. Hennelly (Maryknoll, NY: Orbis Books, 1990), p. 116. Quoted in Gutiérrez, 'Option for the Poor', p. 26.

5 Gustavo Gutiérrez, 'Remembering the poor: an interview with Gustavo Gutiérrez', *America The Jesuit Review*, https://www.americamagazine.org/faith/2003/02/03/remembering-poor-interview-gustavo-gutierrez (accessed 3.04.2019).

6 Gutiérrez, 'Option for the Poor', p. 26.
7 Rohan M. Curnow, 'Which preferential option for the poor? A history of the doctrine's bifurcation', *Modern Theology* 31, no. 1 (January 2015), p. 43.
8 Curnow, 'Which Preferential Option for the Poor?', p. 58.
9 Rebecca S. Chopp, *The Praxis of Suffering: An interpretation of liberation and political theologies* (Eugene, OR: Wipf & Stock, 2007), p. 62.
10 Gustavo Gutiérrez, *Essential Writings*, ed. James B. Nickoloff (London: SCM Press, 1996), p. 27.
11 Gustavo Gutiérrez, *The God of Life*, trans. Matthew J. O'Connell (Maryknoll, NY: Orbis Books, 1991), p. 80.
12 Gutiérrez, *The God of Life*, p. 84.
13 Gutiérrez, *The God of Life*, p. 85.
14 Gutiérrez, *The God of Life*, p. 90.
15 Gutiérrez, *The God of Life*, p. 91.
16 Gustavo Gutiérrez, *A Theology of Liberation: History, politics, and salvation*, trans. Caridad Inda and John Eagleson (London: SCM Press, 2010), p. 191.
17 Gustavo Gutiérrez, *On Job: God-talk and the suffering of the innocent*, trans. Matthew J. O'Connell (Maryknoll, NY: Orbis Books, 1987), p. 80.
18 Gutiérrez, *On Job*, p. 85.
19 Gutiérrez, *On Job*, p. 84.
20 Gutiérrez, *On Job*, p. 88.
21 Gutiérrez, *On Job*, p. 94.
22 Gutiérrez, *On Job*, p. 80.
23 Gutiérrez, *On Job*, p. 5.
24 Gutiérrez, *On Job*, p. 80.
25 Gutiérrez, *On Job*, p. 97.
26 Gutiérrez, *On Job*, p. 94.
27 Gutiérrez, *On Job*, p. 97
28 Gutiérrez, *On Job*, p. 100.
29 Gutiérrez, *On Job*, p. 79.
30 Gutiérrez, *The God of Life*, p. 90.
31 Gutiérrez, *On Job*, p. 101.
32 Gustavo Gutiérrez, *The Power of the Poor in History*, trans. Robert R. Barr (Maryknoll, NY: Orbis Books, 1983), p. 52.
33 'Theology always sinks its roots in the historical density of the gospel message.' Gustavo Gutiérrez, 'The situation and tasks of Liberation Theology today' in *Opting for the Margins: Postmodernity and liberation in Christian theology*, ed. Joerg Rieger (Oxford: Oxford University Press, 2003), p. 89.
34 Gutiérrez, *The Power of the Poor in History*, p. 62.
35 Gutiérrez, *A Theology of Liberation*, p. 49.
36 For an outline of different phases within the thought of Gutiérrez and a recognition of the importance of 'socio-analytical mediation' in his earlier writings, see Jesús Martínez Gordo, *La Fuerza de la Debilidad: La teología fundamental de Gustavo Gutiérrez* (Bilbao: Instituto Diocesano de Teología y Pastoral, 1994), p. 25.
37 Gutiérrez, *A Theology of Liberation*, p. 53.
38 Gutiérrez, *The Power of the Poor in History*, pp. 56–7.
39 Congregation for the Doctrine of the Faith, 'Ten observations on the theology

of Gustavo Gutiérrez' in *Liberation Theology: A documentary history*, ed. Alfred T. Hennelly (Maryknoll, NY: Orbis Books, 1990), p. 349.

40 Congregation for the Doctrine of the Faith, 'Ten observations on the theology of Gustavo Gutiérrez', p. 350.

41 Congregation for the Doctrine of the Faith, 'Instruction on certain aspects of the "Theology of Liberation"', in *Liberation Theology: A documentary history*, ed. Alfred T. Hennelly (Maryknoll, NY: Orbis Books, 1990), p. 401.

42 Congregation for the Doctrine of the Faith, 'Instruction on certain aspects of the "Theology of Liberation"', p. 402.

43 John Milbank, *Theology and Social Theory: Beyond secular reason*, Signposts in Theology (Oxford: Blackwell, 1990), p. 249.

44 Gutiérrez, *The Power of the Poor in History*, p. 57.

45 Gutiérrez, *The God of Life*, p. 63.

46 Gutiérrez, *The Truth Shall Make You Free*, p. 58.

47 'The tools that are used in an analysis of social reality will vary with time and with the particular effectiveness that they have demonstrated when it comes to understanding this reality and proposing approaches to the solution of problems. It is a hallmark of the scientific method to be critical of the researcher's own premises and conclusions.' Gutiérrez, 'Option for the Poor', p. 25.

48 Gutiérrez, *The Truth Shall Make You Free*, p. 62.

49 Gutiérrez, *The Truth Shall Make You Free*, p. 70.

50 Gutiérrez, *The Truth Shall Make You Free*, p. 23.

51 Tim Noble, *The Poor in Liberation Theology: Pathway to God or ideological construct?*, Cross Cultural Theologies (Abingdon: Routledge, 2014), p. 23.

52 Gutiérrez, 'Option for the Poor', p. 27.

53 Gutiérrez, *A Theology of Liberation*, p. 18.

54 Gutiérrez, 'The option for the poor arises from faith in Christ', *Theological Studies* 70, no. 2 (2009), p. 319.

55 Gutiérrez, *The Power of the Poor in History*, p. 138.

56 Gutiérrez, *On Job*, p. 94.

57 Gutiérrez, *The God of Life*, p. 116.

58 Gutiérrez, *The God of Life*, p. 117.

59 Gutiérrez, *The Truth Shall Make You Free*, p. 14.

60 Gutiérrez, *The Power of the Poor in History*, p. 50.

61 Gutiérrez, *A Theology of Liberation*, p. 232.

62 Gutiérrez, 'Remembering the Poor'.

63 Gutiérrez. 'Remembering the Poor'.

64 Gutiérrez, 'Option for the Poor', p. 325.

65 Gutiérrez, *The Truth Shall Make You Free*, p. 75.

66 Gutiérrez, *The God of Life*, p. 56.

67 Gutiérrez, *The Power of the Poor in History*, p. 38.

68 See for example the clarification offered by Gutiérrez in his revisions to *A Theology of Liberation*. Especially as expressed in the commentary provided in Gutiérrez, *A Theology of Liberation*, p. 245.

69 Gutiérrez, *A Theology of Liberation*, p. 250.

70 Gutiérrez, *A Theology of Liberation*, p. 251.

71 Gutiérrez, *A Theology of Liberation*, p. 252.

72 Noble, *Poor in Liberation Theology*, p. 25.

4

Christ and the Humanity Before Whom We Speak

Over the course of the previous two chapters I have attempted to show that the anthropology of Gutiérrez takes shape within a framework established by his Christology. In this chapter I will examine the stability of this framework in three ways: I will first clarify the role of Christology within the theology of Gutiérrez and then turn to examine two ways in which he renders the identity of Jesus. This identity is rendered through the revelation of Jesus in Scripture and through the relation of Jesus to the world. In other words, Gutiérrez addresses the question of 'Who is Jesus?' by turning to both the Word and the world. I will argue that the portrait of Jesus that emerges within the theology of Gutiérrez tends towards an abstraction that is in tension with the convictions that underpin his anthropological project. In the previous chapter I demonstrated that Gutiérrez takes hold of the incarnation to secure the grace of God on the one hand and the integrity of humanity on the other. In this chapter I attempt to show that, even as Gutiérrez does so, he risks letting the concrete specificity of Jesus slip through his fingers.

Christ and the humanity before whom we speak

The Christology of Gutiérrez does not simply explore what it might mean to speak of God as Father; rather, it seeks to make this truth known to the world so that the world might itself be conformed to this truth. Gutiérrez warns that 'a theology which has as its points of reference only "truths"' which have been established once and for all – and not the Truth which is also the Way – can only be static and, in the long run, sterile'.[1] The vitality of the truth is discovered as it is lived and proclaimed as the way. There is an implication of this conviction that must be considered. If the truth can be discovered and proclaimed along the way, the path traced out for the way must follow the contours of the truth. Gutiérrez seeks to develop a Christology that maintains this relation between the way and the truth and contends that a theology that fails to live in Christ's liberative way is also failing to know the reality of his truth. However, the converse must also be true. The implication of the conviction established by Gutiérrez is this: a methodology that inhibits an account of Jesus in his personal and particular truth will also undermine a conformity to Jesus as the liberative way.

In order to test the consistency of the Christology that takes shape within the theology of Gutiérrez I will draw on a concern raised by David Kelsey. I have shown that he seeks to express in his Christology the concreteness of the historical way of liberation. This begs the question of whether the concrete commitment of the Christian in history finds its counterpart in an account of Jesus in the concreteness of his personal particularity. In short, does the Christology of Gutiérrez credit to Jesus Christ the concreteness and specificity that it calls for from Christians?

If the church is to proclaim the whole Christ, it is necessary to make Christ known in both his ongoing presence and his personal particularity. As the church speaks of the *totus Christus* it distinguishes these realities without separating them. However, I will attempt to show that the theology of Gutiérrez tends to characterize the universal presence of Christ in a way that leads to an occlusion of his personal and concrete particularity.[2] David Kelsey makes explicit and explores the question that is begged by the Christological framework developed by Gutiérrez. Kelsey argues that the 'initial task' of a Christological project is to 'offer a description of Jesus in his unsubstitutable personal identity'.[3] As Kelsey explores different Christological constructions, he evaluates them according to their adequacy for this task. At the centre of this discussion is the way in which these different constructions address 'the formal issue about the conceptual relationship between descriptions of Jesus's identity and Jesus's presence'.[4] Kelsey contends that the Christ of whom we speak must be distinguished – at least formally – from the humanity before whom we speak, otherwise the particularity of the former may be absorbed into the generality of the latter. If the way and the truth are confused, then both will be obscured.

The concern raised by Kelsey may be put to Gutiérrez in order to evaluate the stability of the Christology that plays such an important role within his theological project. At its most simple, the question being put to his theology is this: *Who* is the Jesus in whom God is known as Father in a world that is inhumane? I will consider this question through an exploration of how Gutiérrez portrays the Christ who is present in Scripture and in the world, and in so doing I will aim to draw out a tension that is present in his theology. On the one hand, his theology calls for Christ to be seen in his concrete particularity. On the other hand, his methodology inhibits his expression of Christ's 'unsubstitutable personal identity'.

The Christ who is present in the scriptures

Gutiérrez seeks to develop his Christology within a framework ordered by the norms and narratives of Scripture. He explains that his 'purpose is not to elaborate an ideology to justify postures already taken' and calls for his hearers to 'let ourselves be judged by the word of the Lord'.[5] Arguing that 'the God of the Bible is not the God of philosophers', he calls the theologian to an encounter with 'the God of biblical revelation' as he is made known in Jesus.[6] According to Gutiérrez, the character of this encounter with God in Jesus is shaped by the relation of the reader to the text of Scripture. The two encounters are woven together by Gutiérrez as he explains: 'Encounter with Christ, life in the Spirit, journey to the Father: such, it seems to me, are the *dimensions* of every walking in the Spirit according to the scriptures.'[7] This association is further developed as he compares the dynamic at work in the reading of Scripture to the experience of 'those who approach Jesus' and find themselves challenged by him.[8] The militant stance adopted by Gutiérrez stands on the grounds of an encounter with Jesus that must be normed by the text of Scripture. For him the concrete and historical action in which theology must participate finds its counterpart in the concrete and historical revelation to which theology must respond.

The importance of the biblical text

This concern to develop a Christology that is warranted by the text of Scripture may be clearly heard within the theology of Gutiérrez. He calls for Christology to be developed within a framework that maintains the integrity of the Gospel narratives. Rather than dissolving these narratives into 'collections of somewhat disparate individual literary units (pericopes) like so many beads on a string',[9] Gutiérrez commits himself – and according to a number of commentators even restricts himself – to the integrity of the biblical text. At the start of what is considered to be his most systematic work, *The God of Life*, he seeks to place his theology firmly within a biblical framework. He ends his introduction by explaining: 'My desire is that this book may help readers to know more fully the God of biblical revelation and, as a result, to proclaim the God of life.'[10] Indeed, Rasiah Sugirtharajah critiques the theology of liberation for 'its textualism'[11] and the 'inherent biblicism' of its approach.[12] Far from reading Gutiérrez as developing a Christology abstracted from the biblical narratives, Sugirtharajah opines that 'the authoritative Jesus reconstructed by liberation theology is not the Jesus behind the text, but within the text. His actions are seen as acts of God mediated in solidarity with humanity as depicted in the canonical texts of the New Testament.'[13] In a similar way, Alfredo Fierro objects to what he considers to be a 'pre-critical' methodology in the readings of Scripture that Gutiérrez offers.[14] This evaluation of the hermeneutic deployed by Gutiérrez may arise from his rejection of an 'exegesis that is thought of as "scientific"' and which has the effect of removing the Bible from the hands of the poor.[15] Observing that 'exegetes ... are members of a very exclusive club', Gutiérrez calls for a reading of the Bible that is able to serve the 'proclamation of the good news to the poor'.[16]

This reading of Gutiérrez might be further supported by a recognition of the importance that he places on preserving the 'distance' of the biblical text. Not only does Gutiérrez seek to secure the integrity of the text, he also attempts to respect the otherness of its identity. He argues that 'it is necessary to see that the text is distant' and that 'in approaching this text one must take its otherness into account'.[17] This approach recalls the argument of Hans Frei that an apprehension of the identity of Jesus must take place within a recognition of his 'otherness'. Frei observes that 'to know Jesus, one must indeed know who he is; and before he can be known, he must be able to withdraw from our grasp and turn to us from his own presence'.[18] The Christ made known in Scripture must have an identity and particularity that can speak in judgement over the prejudices and presuppositions established by the reading community. For all the differences that there may be between Frei and Gutiérrez, it is important to hear a resonance in this respect. For Gutiérrez the scriptures and the Christ portrayed by the scriptures have an identity and integrity that must be both 'close and distant' such that 'it is very important to be attentive to the role of challenger that Scripture plays when read in the church'.[19]

Gutiérrez expresses a clear concern to respect the integrity of the biblical text on the one hand and the otherness of the biblical text on the other. Such a distance may give space for the otherness of Jesus in his historical and personal identity to be expressed. However, I suggest that a close reading of Gutiérrez will reveal his Christology to be marked by a tendency towards abstraction that is in tension with the very commitments to which he himself seeks to be accountable. I will aim to bring this tension to the surface through a consideration of the role of biblical narrative within the theology of Gutiérrez.

The narrative of salvation history

While Gutiérrez emphasizes the importance of the concrete and historical reality of the incarnation, this is expressed within a broader framework that inhibits the portrayal of Jesus in his particular and unsubstitutable identity. On the one hand Gutiérrez calls for the incarnation to be considered in its concrete historical context and cautions that 'apart from its historical coordinates the event loses its meaning'.[20] However, the particularity of this moment is caught up in a salvation historical movement that erodes its unique specificity. While Gutiérrez affirms that 'he is a historical fact', Christ is also described as 'in the future of our history', whose second coming is encountered 'in the "today" of the Christian community and of humankind'.[21] The movement from incarnation to parousia is a movement towards a fulfilment of the coming of Christ. Speaking of the fullness of the body that unfolds through history, Gutiérrez comments, 'With the Incarnation we have entered into the fullness of time, though we still have a distance to go; the body of Christ is now present in history.'[22] The incarnation as an event finds its meaning in the coming of the body whose fullness is encountered in history. However important the historical particulars of Jesus may be, the identity of Jesus risks being disclosed less through a person in history and more in the movement of history towards its eschatological end. I do not mean to imply that an emphasis on the ongoing presence of Christ must necessarily be inimical to a presentation of personal particularity. However, Gutiérrez emphasizes the universal and eschatological in a way that risks allowing the historical and particular to recede from view.

This dynamic is especially evident in a sequence where Gutiérrez considers the importance of the resurrection of Jesus. He declares that 'The resurrection uproots him, rips him out of a particular date and time, forces upon us an understanding of the universality of the status of the children of God.'[23] Gutiérrez appears to do more than simply elucidate the universal implications of the unique event of the resurrection. The particular is not the grounds of the universal; rather, it appears to be subsumed into and transcended by the universal. Just as the incarnation of Jesus must look beyond the person of Jesus to find its fullness, the

Christ and the Humanity Before Whom We Speak

resurrection of Jesus defines the identity of Jesus by moving beyond the particularities of his identity. There is an ironic correspondence with the Christological logic outlined by Kelsey. For Kelsey the resurrection of Jesus is 'definitive of who he is'.[24] In a similar way, the treatment by Gutiérrez of the resurrection indicates the identity of Jesus that takes shape within his narrative of salvation and liberation. Whereas for Kelsey the resurrection narratives in the Gospels are central to their portrayal of Jesus in his unsubstitutable personal identity, for Gutiérrez they occasion the subordination of this identity to the ongoing historical process of liberation.

It appears that the narrative of salvation history that unfolds in the theology of Gutiérrez inhibits a portrayal of Jesus in his concrete personality and identity. The diverse particularities of moments within history are absorbed within the unified movement of history. The theology of Gutiérrez appears to be marked by the ambiguities that Kelsey associated with anthropologies that take shape within narratives whose unity is found in their eschatological end. In such constructions, 'finite subjects, at least, are "actual" in the proper sense of the term only at the end of the dialectical process. ... Insofar as the dialectical process is none other than world history, this end is the eschaton.'[25] Where history unfolds as a dialectical process whose unity and energy are derived from its end, then the integrity and identity of the subject is only established at the eschaton. Whether or not this is true for his treatment of humanity as a whole, it appears to characterize the portrayal by Gutiérrez of the person of Jesus in particular. The integrity and the identity of Jesus are not encountered in the narratives of the Gospels; rather, they unfold in the narrative of human history as it moves to an expression and experience of liberative human community.

While this concern might seem to express a particularly Protestant theological sensibility, it is interesting at this point to compare the Christology of Gutiérrez to the 'theological treatise' written by Benedict XVI called *Jesus of Nazareth*.[26] Benedict seeks to convey the identity of Jesus in both its historical particularity and its presence to the church by faith. While he cautions against the limitation of the 'quest for the historical Jesus', Benedict comments that 'exaggerating little, one could say that I set out to discover the real Jesus, on the basis of whom something like a "Christology from below" would then become possible'.[27] There is an intimate relation between the historical and personal identity of Jesus and the ongoing presence of Jesus to the church. This relation depends on the integrity and reality of each. This dynamic of relation-in-distinction is evident in Benedict's explanation that,

Gustavo Gutiérrez and the Liberative Sight of Christ

> I have attempted to develop a way of observing and listening to the Jesus of the Gospels that can indeed lead to personal encounter and that, through collective listening with Jesus's disciples across the ages, can indeed attain sure knowledge of the real historical figure of Jesus.[28]

A 'personal encounter' with Jesus in the present and a 'collective listening' to Jesus with the church across the ages is only possible through a process of 'observing and listening to the Jesus of the Gospels'. In his reflection on the resurrection of Jesus, Benedict observes that the resurrection 'is a historical event that nevertheless bursts open the dimensions of history and transcends it'.[29] Benedict emphasizes both elements of this reality. On the one hand the resurrection establishes 'Christ's transformed body' as the 'place where men enter into communion with God and with one another'.[30] On the other hand Benedict cautions that 'at the same time it must be understood that the resurrection does not simply stand outside or above history' but rather

> as something that breaks out of history and transcends it, the resurrection nevertheless has its origin within history and up to a certain point still belongs there. Perhaps we could put it this way: Jesus's resurrection points beyond history but has left a footprint within history.[31]

According to Hans Boersma, Benedict 'leads his audience into the presence of Jesus, who is at the same time the Jesus of history and the Jesus of the faith of the Church'.[32] There is a distinction between the two that seeks to avoid separation on the one hand and conflation on the other.

In contrast with the dynamic of relation-in-distinction that is evident in the work of Benedict, the Christology of Gutiérrez appears to be characterized by a certain ambiguity. The point at issue here is not the extent to which Kelsey's theology may or may not be hospitable to Roman Catholic emphasis on the ongoing presence of Christ to the world or a traditional construction of the doctrine of the *totus Christus*. However, the questions posed by Kelsey draw to the surface tensions that are present in Gutiérrez's treatment of the theme. Dennis McCann acknowledges the attempt by Gutiérrez to formulate his Christology within the parameters established by credal orthodoxy but argues that he dissolves the definitive event of the incarnation into an ongoing narrative that anticipates and applies this event in the unfolding of human history. According to McCann, the Christology of Gutiérrez rests not on the single assertion that 'the Word became flesh and dwelt among us' (John 1.14), but on a series of assertions that 'in many and various ways God spoke of old to our fathers by the prophets; but in these last days he has spoken to us by a Son' (Heb. 1.1–2).[33]

While McCann emphasizes the presence and importance of both dynamics within the biblical witness, he questions the way in which these dynamics are coordinated by Gutiérrez. For McCann, Gutiérrez allows the particularity of the incarnation and the person of Jesus to be subordinated to the unfolding narrative of revelation and redemption in human history. The coming of Jesus is one moment in a series of 'historic encounters between the divine and human persons' that, while 'culminating in the Incarnation of Christ', find their meaning and purpose beyond the incarnation.[34] Such a reading of history establishes an ambiguity in the identity of the Christ who is made known in this history. The way in which Gutiérrez recounts the narrative of salvation inhibits his portrayal of the very Christ who is to be its central character. McCann asks: 'Is the historical Christ one of the "partial fulfilments" or is he the "total fulfilment"? How can he be both, for a genuinely historical thinker?'[35] The event of the incarnation and the identity of Jesus either express the 'total fulfilment' of the promises of God or take their place among other 'partial fulfilments' of the liberation that is encountered but never completed in history. Gutiérrez seeks to develop a Christology that is normed by and faithful to orthodox credal formulations. However, the ambiguity observed by McCann suggests that this Christology is inhibited by the construction of history within which it is to take place. While Benedict, by contrast, is 'deeply concerned to keep together the realities of history and of faith in a sacramental relationship', I suggest that Gutiérrez conflates the two and in so doing dissolves the former into the latter.[36]

The presence of Christ in the scriptures

Having explored this tension between the particularity of Christ and his presence throughout the course of salvation history, I will now turn to consider the way in which Gutiérrez relates this presence to the biblical text. Kelsey calls for the narratives of the Gospels to be 'construed as having the force of offering identity descriptions of Jesus', warning that when they are not so construed 'one is led to privilege other features of the Gospels than their narrativity'.[37] I suggest that such a movement beyond the scriptural narrative is evident in the theology of Gutiérrez.

Rather than being construed as having the force of identity description, the narratives of the Gospels are construed as directing the attention either *behind* the text to the historical situation that they describe or *before* the text to the contemporary situation of the reader. In this way the scriptures are not the place where Christ is to be encountered but descriptions of this encounter – an encounter witnessed to in the past or an encounter gestured to in the present.

Once again, I am aware that the framing of this question may be shaped by distinctively Protestant theological concerns. Nevertheless, my purpose in posing the question is to explore the extent to which Gutiérrez is at this point consistent with his own convictions. A classical construction of the *totus Christus* offers the text of Scripture as a site where the presence of Christ may be made known. In his reading of the patristic tradition Boersma identifies an exegesis in the church fathers that offers Christ as 'sacramentally present' in the text of Scripture.[38] One way in which Christ discloses his presence in the church today is through an encounter with that unity in the text of the scriptures. Commenting on the 'prosopological exegesis' of the Psalms, Boersma observes that for Augustine, 'the doctrine of *totus Christus* ... meant that in a particular passage Christ could be speaking either in his own person (*ex persona sua*) or in our person (*ex persona nostra*)'.[39] Boersma explains that 'according to the fathers, the church is present in the Psalms because Christ himself is there'.[40] In the preaching of Augustine, for example, the reading of Scripture becomes what Michael Cameron describes as a 'toto-christological exercise'[41] in which listeners encounter 'the speaking Ego of the Bible, who is Christ'.[42] In this reading of the tradition, the presence of Christ in the church today is disclosed in the unity of Christ with the church in the scriptures. Where the text of the scriptures is displaced the call to an encounter with Christ will be undermined.

My contention is that the theology of Gutiérrez has an underdeveloped account of this presence of Christ to the church in the scriptures. The use of the scriptures in his theology inhibits an expression of the objective personal identity of Christ. The objectivity of identity is absorbed into a subjective account of his presence and the personality of identity is abstracted into the conceptual priorities that drive the historical reconstruction.

Christ and the Humanity Before Whom We Speak

The presence of Christ behind *the text*

In his desire to avoid the '"iconization" of the life of Jesus', Gutiérrez calls for an account of Christ to be 'submerged in history'.[43] When the ministry of Jesus is placed within its socio-political context it will be possible to recognize that the 'political is grafted into the eternal' such that 'to preach the universal love of the Father is inevitably to go against all injustice, privilege, oppression, or narrow nationalism'.[44] While an attention to historical context must play a part in the exploration of the portrayal of Christ by the scriptures, it is necessary to ask whether Gutiérrez allows historical reconstruction to displace the narratives that are given in the scriptures.

Evidence for such a displacement may be found through a comparison of the use made of the passion narratives in Kelsey and Gutiérrez. For Kelsey these narratives form an integral part of the portrayal of Jesus in his unsubstitutable individual personal identity. When asking 'Who is this Jesus?' of the Gospels, their narratives answer: 'He is the one who, having had this ministry and, though crucified to death, now lives among us.'[45] In contrast, Jeffrey Siker observes that the passion narratives play a relatively minor role in the theology of Gutiérrez:

> One interesting observation about Gutiérrez's choice of Gospel texts is that he makes very few references to passages dealing with the passion and death of Jesus. Indeed, of the over 900 references to the NT I have been able to identify, Gutiérrez refers to texts from the passion narratives only thirteen times.[46]

Whereas for Kelsey the narrative portrayals of Jesus in the Gospels are inextricably bound to their climax in the passion, it appears that Gutiérrez sets this narrative structure to one side. As he develops his Christology within a narrative or conceptual construction which differs from that encountered in the Gospels, he moves beyond and behind the texts of Holy Scripture in order to offer an encounter with Christ.

The theological method of Gutiérrez at this point shares some of the characteristics of an approach more explicitly articulated by Jon Sobrino. Explaining that 'my starting point is the historical Jesus',[47] Sobrino clarifies that 'we will give preference to the praxis of Jesus over his own teaching and over the teaching of the New Testament theologians concerning his praxis'.[48] The Christology of Sobrino moves behind the text of Scripture to encounter Jesus in the history of his praxis. Furthermore, even within this attention to the praxis of Jesus certain events are given

Gustavo Gutiérrez and the Liberative Sight of Christ

priority over others. In this way even the resurrection of Jesus is an act whose meaning is subordinated to a liberative reading of the work of God in Jesus. It is worth quoting Sobrino's description of his methodology at length:

> Within Christology itself emphasis is placed on the resurrection of Jesus as a paradigm of liberation; but even more insistent is the stress placed on the historical Jesus as the pathway to liberation. It is the historical Jesus who enlightens us with regard to the basic meaning of the task as well as his personal way of carrying it out. Liberation theology is concentrated in Christology insofar as it reflects on Jesus himself as the way to liberation.[49]

It is interesting to observe the correspondence between the treatment of the resurrection as an event and the consideration of Jesus as a person. The resurrection is emphasized only in so far as it serves as a paradigm for liberation. The event is a paradigm of a broader truth. It is one instantiation of a reality from which it derives its true meaning and purpose. In a similar way, there is a tension in Sobrino's call to a reflection on Jesus 'as the way to liberation'. On the one hand there is a concern for the personal and historical particularity of Jesus. However, the person and work of Jesus appear, in this passage at least, to direct attention away from themselves and towards the unfolding narrative of God's liberative plan. The question is whether Jesus may be considered in himself or only 'insofar' as he reveals 'the way to liberation'. The methodology suggested here by Sobrino and evident in Gutiérrez contains this unresolved tension. The Christology of Gutiérrez raises the question of whether Jesus is defined according to a conceptual construct called liberation, or whether the person of Jesus makes possible – and is made known in – a commitment to liberation. Gutiérrez argues for the latter but his methodology risks being structured by the former.

Such a reading of the scriptures moves behind their narratives to encounter a Jesus who takes shape within a history whose unity and meaning is to be found in the movement towards liberation. While Gutiérrez does not articulate his Christology in the explicit and systematic terms of Sobrino, his use of Scripture evidences a corresponding methodology. The encounter with Jesus does not take place in the narrative of Scripture but rather in the historical construction that is shaped by liberative considerations and is discerned beyond and behind the text of Scripture. Colin Greene suggests that liberation theology accentuates the historical Jesus behind the text of Scripture in order to serve its political programme. He observes that 'concentration on the historical Jesus reveals that there is a structural similarity between his situation of religious and political oppression, and the attendant yearning for liberation and the situation that faces people in the Two-Thirds world today'.[50] The history behind the text of Scripture receives its shape from its correspondence to the social and political context of the reader. It is undeniable that such correspondences exist, and that contemporary experience does sensitize the reader to otherwise overlooked realities of the past. However, when history is reconstructed within a framework shaped according to contemporary convictions, the Jesus portrayed within such a history risks being a projection of contemporary concerns rather than a person in their particularity and otherness.

Interestingly, this is a danger against which Gutiérrez himself warns. He cautions that Scripture 'is not a repertory of answers to our questions' but rather 'reads us' as it judges and transforms the community in which it is read.[51] However, by reading Scripture as a testimony to an encounter with Christ rather than the place of an encounter with Christ, that by which the church is to be 'read' or judged or transformed is found not in the text of Scripture itself. It is found in a construction that is to be discerned behind the text of Scripture. However much the authority of Scripture may be affirmed, within this methodology hermeneutics and exegesis are accountable not to the scriptures but to a conceptual construct. It is this construct that gives shape to a history that lies behind Scripture and in which the truth of Scripture is made known. As Frei observes, where such a reading of Scripture proceeds on these terms 'general theory here dictates to, not to say overwhelms, exegesis and subject matter'.[52] It is at this point that the methodology of Gutiérrez must be held accountable to the convictions that he himself develops. He argues for the interdependence of the 'nearness' and the 'distance' of the biblical text, making the important observation that where the distance is not preserved, the nearness cannot be sustained.[53] Where Christology takes shape within a history that lies behind the text and whose form takes shape not from the text but from the contemporary concerns, the risk is that the distance is absorbed into nearness. Such a process risks the danger against which Gutiérrez warns: that Scripture and the Christ it reveals may become 'shackled by our own questions'.[54]

Rather than being construed as having the force of identity description, the narratives of the Gospels are construed as directing attention *behind* the text to the historical situation that they describe. Observing that 'many liberationist Christologies seem to be warranted by a picture of the historical Jesus', Kelsey warns that in such cases, 'it is the historical reconstruction ... that directly norms the Christian adequacy of such claims; the Gospels do so only indirectly by providing the data on which historical reconstruction is based'.[55] When such a historical construction supplants the narratives of the Gospels, the identity that is to be rendered by those narratives is undermined. Where a concept like liberation governs the conceptual scheme within which Jesus is to be made known, his unsubstitutable personal identity 'just slips through the mesh of such theories'.[56] To search for an encounter with Jesus in a history that lies behind Scripture is to make Jesus subject to the concepts according to which such a history is reconstructed. What is encountered in such a history is no longer a person in their unsubstitutable identity but an illustration or instantiation of the concepts according to which this history took shape.

The presence of Christ before *the text*

This movement beyond the scriptures to a construction that is to be discerned *behind* them finds its counterpart in a movement from the scriptures to the context of the reader who stands *before* them. Rather than the scriptures being the space for an encounter with the unsubstitutable personal identity of Jesus, the scriptures direct the reader to their own context as the place where this identity is to be encountered and made known. There is a movement from historical reconstruction on the one hand to contextual reception on the other that passes *through* the text of Scripture rather than finding its focus *in* the text of Scripture. Siker draws attention to this dynamic in his observation that 'the historicity of those who are poor, then, becomes as significant as the historicity of Jesus who was poor, God who has become poor'.[57] The identity of Jesus is found in the circumstances of poverty that lie behind the scriptural narratives and the contexts of poverty in which those narratives are received. The reader is called to discern the reality that lies behind the text so that they might reread the reality of their lives that they have brought before the text.

This dynamic is evident in the characteristic movement by Gutiérrez from the text of Scripture to the context of the reader. He describes the encounter with the scriptures as a 'dialogue between history and history' because they 'give voice to an authentic faith experience' which took place behind the text and so 'shed light on light on our present history' that stands before the text.[58] Recalling the experience of the first disciples as recounted in 1 John 1, Gutiérrez comments: 'What we proclaim (says the writer) is what we have heard and seen and looked upon and touched

Christ and the Humanity Before Whom We Speak

with our hands. These are direct, unmediated experiences that are communicated in order that others too may have the joy of encountering the Lord.'[59] He presents a correspondence between the encounter that John describes and the experience to which disciples today are called. It is important to note that the text of 1 John 1.1–4 particularly emphasizes the primacy of the testimony given by the first disciples. Gutiérrez, however, calls the disciple of today not to a submission to this revelation but rather to an imitation of this experience. The witness of John becomes paradigmatic of the experience of the disciple of Jesus rather than the normative revelation of the identity of Jesus. Ironically, a text that calls its readers to an encounter with Christ in scriptural revelation is used to point the reader beyond Scripture and towards contemporary experience.

The relation established by Gutiérrez is not simply one of application in the life of the community or authority over the life of the community. Rather, the meaning of the scriptures and the identity of the Christ they are to convey are found in the dynamic of their being read and received by this community. Gutiérrez contends that 'Christianity is simply a saga of stories' to which the scriptures contribute one – albeit privileged – voice.[60] Given that 'the story heard gives rise to other tellings', it is in the ongoing life of the Christian community that Scripture finds its meaning and Christ reveals his identity.[61] Once this dynamic is recognized it is possible to appreciate the central role that the parable of the sheep and the goats in Matthew 25 plays within the theology of Gutiérrez. Siker observes that 'Gutiérrez has a relatively clear working canon' within which 'Matt. 25.31–46 is the guiding and paradigmatic text'.[62] The use of this parable by Gutiérrez not only expresses the central concern of his theology but is indicative of the methodology through which this theology takes shape. The scriptural narrative to which he holds his Christology to account is not primarily that of the crucifixion and resurrection, but rather a parable that speaks of the Final Judgement. Instead of forging a Christology within what Kelsey describes as the 'more or less realistic narrative' of the Gospels, Gutiérrez privileges the apocalyptic narrative of a parable.[63] The paradigmatic text through which he develops his theology is privileged not because of its adequacy to render Christ in his personal identity but rather because of its capacity as a story to 'give rise to others that one way or another speak of him and of his witness'.[64] Rather than presenting the relationship between the narrative and the parable as one of context or application, Gutiérrez appears to subordinate the former to the latter. The 'more or less realistic narrative' of the Gospel account is displaced by the apocalyptic narrative of the parable.

As I observe this dynamic within Gutiérrez, I am not seeking to pit the parable against the narrative in which it is found. Nor am I suggesting that there is a tension between the Jesus who speaks the parable and the Jesus of whom the parable speaks. However, when this parable is privileged over the narrative in which it takes place, the unsubstitutable personal identity of Jesus begins to recede.

This dynamic is illustrated in the close relation that Gutiérrez draws between Matthew 5.8 and the parable of Matthew 25. He links the passages in order to disprove 'an alleged Matthean "spiritualism"' and then moves on to use the parable to expound the social and material implication of the beatitude.[65] While such an implication is clearly important, it is interesting that the sight of God that is promised to the pure in heart seems to find its fulfilment not in the concrete person of Jesus but in the ongoing actions of the disciples. Boersma draws attention to the insight of Jonathan Edwards that 'the vision of God is not just *mentioned* in the Beatitudes but actually *takes place* when Jesus preaches them'.[66] Such a reading draws attention to the identity of Jesus in the concrete and unsubstitutable personality that is conveyed in the scripture. The methodology of Gutiérrez, however, directs attention away from Jesus as a concrete person who speaks in and is revealed by the scriptures and towards Jesus as one who is encountered primarily in the experience of liberation.

I do not mean to imply that it is somehow inappropriate for Gutiérrez to highlight and develop the relation between the beatitudes and the parable of Matthew 25. However, it is important to observe the way in which this relation is constructed and the consequence that this has for the rendering of Jesus in his unsubstitutable personal identity. Once again, rather than both the beatitude and the parable contributing to a Gospel narrative that seeks to render the identity of Jesus, Gutiérrez reads the Gospel narrative as a whole – and so the beatitude in particular – within a conceptual structure that is paradigmatically expressed by the parable of Matthew 25. In this way it appears that the Christology developed by Gutiérrez corresponds to those Christologies critiqued by Kelsey which 'develop descriptions of Jesus's identity framed in terms provided by a logically prior and independently formulated description of the mode of Jesus's presence now'.[67] In the specific case of Gutiérrez this 'mode of presence' is encountered within the process of liberation that is testified to by the scriptures, but is only truly encountered in its unfolding throughout the history of humanity.

While Gutiérrez himself calls for an encounter with the distinct personality of Christ that is to be made possible through attention to the otherness of Scripture, his methodology prioritizes the parabolic over

Christ and the Humanity Before Whom We Speak

the realistic. The scriptures do not function to render the unsubstitutable personal identity of Jesus. Instead, as attention is directed beyond the scriptures to the context before the text, the danger is that this identity begins to recede from view.

The Christ who is present to the world

In the previous section I examined the role of the scriptures in the encounter that Gutiérrez calls for with the person of Christ. I will now explore the way in which he coordinates the presence and identity of Christ in their relation to humanity as a whole and the church in particular.

Gutiérrez appears to develop his account of the identity of Jesus within a logically prior framework of his ongoing presence and work. While Gutiérrez proclaims that Jesus 'took on flesh among the poor in a marginal area', the personal is absorbed into the paradigmatic and the particular dissolved into the universal as he continues:

> The God who became flesh in Jesus is the hidden God of whom the prophets speak to us. Jesus shows himself to be such precisely in the measure that he is present to us via those who are the absent, anonymous people of history.[68]

The incarnation is heard to call for an encounter not with Jesus in his unsubstitutable personal identity but in a communion with the neighbour in their present historical reality:

> If we are to dwell in the tent that the Son has pitched in our midst, we must enter into our own history here and now ... If we do so, we shall experience in our flesh the encounter with the word who proclaims the kingdom of life.[69]

As past event the incarnation is treated as a paradigm and example of God's relation to man. As present reality the incarnation speaks of the universality of God's presence to man. Jesus is not marked out as an individual with his own unsubstitutable personal identity, but rather as a paradigm and presence in which we are called to participate.

This emphasis on the universal presence of Christ to humanity is especially pronounced when Gutiérrez considers the ministry of Jesus from the resurrection through the ascension and to the parousia. He does gesture to the ongoing particularity of Jesus in his observation that 'He will understand us, because even today, as he sits at the Father's right hand some of Galilee's dust must still be on his feet.'[70] However, this comment seems to carry more rhetorical than theological weight in his overall argument. That is to say that the post-resurrection ministry of Jesus is predominantly construed by Gutiérrez in terms of a presence that is available universally rather than an identity that is to be understood personally. As has already been demonstrated, when he speaks of Christ 'as the one who is to come' this coming is characterized as 'this openness of history to Christ – in the "today" of the Christian community and of humankind'.[71] The biblical narrative does not therefore find its climax in a person with a unique and unsubstitutable identity, but rather in the fullness of the body that is made known among a liberated humanity. In such a Christology the humanity of Jesus in the particular is dissolved into a presence to humanity in general.

The analysis offered by Kelsey of modern Christologies appears to be an apt description of the methodology deployed by Gutiérrez at this point: 'Modern Christologies tend to focus on explaining in what way Jesus may be said to be present now. Theological addresses to the question of "Who is Jesus?" tend to take the explicit form, "Where is Jesus?"'[72] Within the theology of Gutiérrez the question of the identity of Jesus tends to be supplanted by, and addressed within the context of, considerations of his presence. The scriptures are testimonies to the experience of this presence encountered in the events to be discerned behind the text and lived in the context before the text. Kelsey warns that a 'subtle docetism of a sort persists, even in Christologies done from below' when they are controlled by such a consideration of the presence rather than the identity of Jesus.[73] According to Frei, 'if we begin with the often nagging and worrisome questions of how Christ is present to us and how we can believe in his presence', the irony will be that 'reflection about Christ's presence leads us neither to that presence nor to an understanding of his identity'.[74] To put the question more starkly, it may be asked whether the critique raised by Douglas Farrow in another context may legitimately be applied to Gutiérrez: 'What is sacrificed for the sake of this *Christus praesens*, as Calvin noticed long ago, is his specificity as a particular man. Christ everywhere really means Jesus of Nazareth nowhere.'[75] It is this instability that led Clodovis Boff to reject the methodology that he once advocated.[76] Boff warns that the theology of liberation risks absorbing the particularity of Jesus into his ongoing presence among the poor based on the logic that 'God became poor and so the poor are God'.[77] Where the identity of Christ is subsumed into or subordinated by a conception of the ongoing presence of Christ, this identity loses its personality and integrity. A Christology shaped primarily by considerations of Christ's ongoing presence will render an abstracted account of Jesus in his unsubstitutable personal identity. The emphasis placed by Gutiérrez on the presence of Christ in the unfolding of human history jeopardizes his account of the identity of Jesus. As Farrow observes of the Christology of Sobrino, this approach 'reduces the person to the project' and so renders the identity of Jesus an abstraction.[78]

Conclusion

Gutiérrez opens his argument in *A Theology of Liberation* with the declaration that 'my purpose is not to elaborate an ideology to justify postures already taken ... It is rather to let ourselves be judged by the word of the Lord.'[79] In this chapter I have examined the theology of Gutiérrez in relation to the norms by which he seeks to hold his project to account. The question that I have put to his theology is simply this: *Who is this Jesus in whom God is known as Father in a world that is inhumane?* I contend that the narrative recounted by Gutiérrez risks placing an abstraction at its very heart. By not adequately distinguishing the Christ of whom we speak from the humanity before whom we speak he allows the particularity of the former to be absorbed into the generality of the latter. I argue that his theological project will be more consistent with its own convictions and more robust in the pursuit of its aims if this instability is addressed.

Notes

1 Gustavo Gutiérrez, *A Theology of Liberation: History, politics, and salvation*, trans. Caridad Inda and John Eagleson (London: SCM Press, 2010), p. 56.

2 The intention here is not to engage with or evaluate the theology of the *totus Christus* as a whole, but rather to explore the tensions that exist in the particular construction of this concept within the theology of Gutiérrez. For further consideration of the theme, see Tarsicius van Bavel, 'The "Christus Totus" idea: a forgotten aspect of Augustine's spirituality', in *Studies in Patristic Christology: Proceedings of the Third Maynooth Patristic Conference*, ed. Thomas Finan and Vincent Twomey (Portland, OR: Four Courts Press, 1998), pp. 84–94. For discussion of some possible social and political implications of this doctrine, see Kimberly Baker, 'Augustine's doctrine of the Totus Christus: reflecting on the church as sacrament of unity', *Horizons* 37, no. 1 (2010), pp. 7–24. For a discussion of the ways in which the concept might be received within a Protestant and Reformed context such as that of which Kelsey writes, see J. David Moser, 'Totus Christus: a proposal for Protestant Christology and ecclesiology', *Pro Ecclesia* 29, no. 1 (2020), pp. 3–30.

3 David H. Kelsey, *Eccentric Existence: A theological anthropology*, 1st edn, 2 vols (Louisville, KY: Westminster John Knox Press, 2009), p. 692.
4 Kelsey, *Eccentric Existence*, p. 687.
5 Gutiérrez, *A Theology of Liberation*, p. 1.
6 Gustavo Gutiérrez, *The God of Life*, trans. Matthew J. O'Connell (Maryknoll, NY: Orbis Books, 1991), p. xiii.
7 Gustavo Gutiérrez, *We Drink From Our Own Wells: The spiritual journey of a people* (Maryknoll, NY: Orbis Books, 2003), p. 35.
8 Gutiérrez, *Our Own Wells*, p. 35.
9 Kelsey, *Eccentric Existence*, p. 690.
10 Gutiérrez, *The God of Life*, p. xviii.
11 Rasiah S. Sugirtharajah, *The Bible and the Third World: Precolonial, colonial, and postcolonial encounters* (Cambridge: Cambridge University Press, 2001), p. 240.
12 Sugirtharajah, *The Bible and the Third World*, p. 241.
13 Sugirtharajah, *The Bible and the Third World*, p. 239.
14 Alfredo Fierro, *The Militant Gospel: A critical introduction to political theologies*, trans. John Drury (Maryknoll, NY: Orbis Books, 1977), p. 324.
15 Gustavo Gutiérrez, *The Power of the Poor in History*, trans. Robert R. Barr (Maryknoll, NY: Orbis Books, 1983), p. 18.
16 Gutiérrez, *The Power of the Poor in History*, p. 4.
17 Gustavo Gutiérrez, *The Truth Shall Make You Free: Confrontations*, trans. Matthew J. O'Connell (Maryknoll, NY: Orbis Books, 1990), p. 47.
18 H. W. Frei et al., *The Identity of Jesus Christ, Expanded and Updated Edition: The hermeneutical bases of dogmatic theology* (Eugene, OR: Wipf & Stock, 2013), p. 73.
19 Gutiérrez, *The Truth Shall Make You Free*, p. 47.
20 Gutiérrez, *The God of Life*, p. 85.
21 Gutiérrez, *The Power of the Poor in History*, p. 13.
22 Gutiérrez, *The God of Life*, p. 86.
23 Gutiérrez, *The Power of the Poor in History*, p. 15.
24 Kelsey, *Eccentric Existence*, p. 693.
25 Kelsey, *Eccentric Existence*, p. 107.
26 Benedict XVI, *Jesus of Nazareth: From the Entrance into Jerusalem to the Resurrection. Part Two: Holy Week* (San Francisco, CA: Ignatius Press, 2011), p. xvi.
27 Benedict XVI, *Jesus of Nazareth*, p. xvi.
28 Benedict XVI, *Jesus of Nazareth*, p. xvii.
29 Benedict XVI, *Jesus of Nazareth*, p. 272.
30 Benedict XVI, *Jesus of Nazareth*, p. 274.
31 Benedict XVI, *Jesus of Nazareth*, p. 275.
32 Hans Boersma, 'History and faith in Pope Benedict's *Jesus of Nazareth*', *Nova et Vetera* 10, no. 4 (2012), p. 991.
33 Dennis McCann, *Christian Realism and Liberation Theology: Practical theologies in creative conflict* (Maryknoll, NY: Orbis Books, 2001), pp. 183–4.
34 McCann, *Christian Realism and Liberation Theology*, p. 184.
35 McCann, *Christian Realism and Liberation Theology*, p. 185.
36 Boersma, 'History and Faith', p. 986.
37 Kelsey, *Eccentric Existence*, p. 689.

38 Hans Boersma, *Scripture as Real Presence: Sacramental exegesis in the Early Church* (Grand Rapids, MI: Baker Academic, 2017), p. 278.
39 Boersma, *Scripture as Real Presence*, p. 152. For an introduction to this dynamic in the theology of Augustine, see Michael Cameron, 'The emergence of *Totus Christus* as hermeneutical center in Augustine's *Enarrationes in Psalmos*' in *The Harp of Prophecy: Early Christian interpretation of the Psalms*, ed. Brian E. Daley and Paul R. Kolbet (Notre Dame, IN: University of Notre Dame Press, 2015), pp. 205–26.
40 Boersma, *Scripture as Real Presence*, p. 153.
41 Michael Cameron, 'Totus Christus and the psychagogy of Augustine's Sermons', *Augustinian Studies* 36, no. 1 (2005), p. 65.
42 Cameron, 'Totus Christus', p. 67.
43 Gutiérrez attributes the term 'iconization' to José Comblin. See Gutiérrez, *A Theology of Liberation*, p. 211.
44 Gutiérrez, *A Theology of Liberation*, p. 217.
45 Kelsey, *Eccentric Existence*, p. 650.
46 Jeffrey Siker, 'Uses of the Bible in the theology of Gustavo Gutiérrez: liberating scriptures of the poor', *Biblical Interpretation* 4, no. 1 (1 January 1996), p. 47. It is important to recognize that the identification of biblical allusions may not be quite as simple as Siker suggests and that the precise number of references will have changed in the years since the publication of this article. However, the sheer scale of the ratio demonstrates the ongoing value of his observation.
47 Jon Sobrino, *Christology at the Crossroads: A Latin American approach*, trans. John Drury (Maryknoll, NY: Orbis Books, 1978), p. 3.
48 Sobrino, *Christology at the Crossroads*, p. xii.
49 Sobrino, *Christology at the Crossroads*, p. 37.
50 Colin J. D. Greene, *Christology in Cultural Perspective: Marking out the horizons* (Eugene, OR: Wipf & Stock, 2015), p. 204.
51 Gutiérrez, *The Truth Shall Make You Free*, p. 47.
52 Frei et al., *The Identity of Jesus Christ*, p. 14.
53 Gutiérrez, *The Truth Shall Make You Free*, p. 47.
54 Gutiérrez, *Our Own Wells*, p. 34.
55 Kelsey, *Eccentric Existence*, p. 690.
56 Kelsey, *Eccentric Existence*, p. 691.
57 Siker, 'Uses of the Bible in the theology of Gustavo Gutiérrez', p. 61.
58 Gutiérrez, *The God of Life*, p. xvi.
59 Gutiérrez, *Our Own Wells*, p. 45.
60 Gustavo Gutiérrez, *The Density of the Present: Selected writings*, trans. Matthew J. O'Connell (Maryknoll, NY: Orbis Books, 1999), p. 204.
61 Gutiérrez, *The Density of the Present*, p. 202.
62 Siker, 'Uses of the Bible in the theology of Gustavo Gutiérrez', p. 48. The importance of this text is not only evident in its presence throughout the work of Gutiérrez but also in his explicit declaration that 'no passage of the Gospel has the power of the always startling text of Matthew on the final judgement'. Gutiérrez, *The God of Life*, p. 86.
63 Recall the contention by Kelsey that 'what can describe a person's unsubstitutable personal identity literarily is more or less realistic narrative'. Kelsey, *Eccentric Existence*, p. 691.

64 Gutiérrez, *The Density of the Present*, p. 202.
65 Gutiérrez, *The God of Life*, p. 119.
66 Hans Boersma, *Seeing God: The beatific vision in Christian tradition* (Grand Rapids, MI: William B. Eerdmans, 2018), p. 364.
67 Kelsey, *Eccentric Existence*, p. 687.
68 Gutiérrez, *The God of Life*, p. 86.
69 Gutiérrez, *The God of Life*, p. 84.
70 Gutiérrez, *The God of Life*, p. 100.
71 Gutiérrez, *The Power of the Poor in History*, p. 13.
72 Kelsey, *Eccentric Existence*, p. 686.
73 Kelsey, *Eccentric Existence*, p. 688.
74 Frei et al., *The Identity of Jesus Christ*, p. 20.
75 Douglas Farrow, *Ascension and Ecclesia: On the significance of the doctrine of the Ascension for ecclesiology and Christian cosmology* (Edinburgh: T&T Clark, 1999), p. 12.
76 See, for example, Clodovis Boff, 'Methodology of the Theology of Liberation' in *Systematic Theology: Perspectives from Liberation Theology: Readings from Mysterium Liberationis*, ed. Jon Sobrino and Ignacio Ellacuría (Maryknoll, NY: Orbis Books, 1996), pp. 1–21.
77 'Nesse tranque, a TdL chega, inadvertidamente, a esta perversão: Deus virou pobre, logo, o pobre é Deus.' Clodovis Boff, 'Volta Ao Fundamento: Réplica', *Revista Eclesiástica Brasileira* 68, no. 272 (2008), p. 912. My translation.
78 Farrow, *Ascension and Ecclesia*, p. 210.
79 Gutiérrez, *A Theology of Liberation*, p. 1.

PART TWO

How to Speak of God: Liberation Through Faithful Praxis

5

The Creation of a New Humanity Through Faithful Praxis

In the previous three chapters I have outlined the narrative of human liberation that may be heard in the theology of Gutiérrez. The three chapters that follow will trace out the personal and social transformation through which and towards which this narrative of human liberation moves. Gutiérrez describes this interplay between personal and social liberation by drawing on the concepts of conscientization and praxis developed by Paulo Freire and in this chapter I will explore the relation between these concepts and the role they play within Gutiérrez's theological project. In the next chapter I will offer a more detailed analysis of the praxis that takes shape in his theology before, in the final chapter of Part Two, engaging with a number of questions raised by my analysis.

Conscientization and the creation of a new humanity

Gutiérrez argues that liberation on an institutional and structural level must be accompanied by the personal liberation of real persons in their concrete contexts. Unless the work of liberation takes into account this 'interior dimension' it will be unable to secure true freedom.[1] Gutiérrez draws on the concept of conscientization to both affirm the importance of this personal change and to express its relational and social context:

> In this process which Freire calls 'conscientization' the oppressed reject the oppressive consciousness which dwells in them, they become aware of their situation, and they find their own language. They become, by themselves, less dependent and freer as they commit themselves to the transformation and building up of society.[2]

It is important to note how the language of Gutiérrez carefully traces the interplay between the personal and the social that unfolds within the process of conscientization. The independence and freedom that are described are not to be understood individualistically. Rather, they are achieved and expressed in a commitment 'to the transformation and building up of society'. The process of conscientization at a personal level can only take place when accompanied by a liberative praxis at the social level. In the same way this praxis will only be truly liberative if it is a free and conscious work of concrete persons.

According to Gutiérrez, the new humanity that is created through the liberative work of salvation will be formed through what may be characterized as a social process of conscientization. The forging of a new humanity takes place once 'humankind is seen as assuming conscious responsibility for its own destiny'.[3] This consciousness is truly personal because it is – and only in so far as it is – relational. Gutiérrez describes how the desire for 'an interior freedom'[4] will be fulfilled when the work of liberation achieves the 'ever more total and complete fulfilment of the individual in solidarity with all humankind'.[5] When calling for a society that is 'mindful of this interior liberation', Gutiérrez distances himself from 'the individualist viewpoint which is one of the characteristics of the modern world', and argues instead that his concern is to 'ensure the freedom of *all*'.[6]

For this reason, the gospel calls for a transformation that is at once both deeply personal and extensively social. Gutiérrez speaks of the 'urgent need for a conscientizing evangelism' that will both expose injustice and enact liberation.[7] As this proclamation is received by persons in relation it will transform persons and their relations. As Gutiérrez explains: 'When I suggest that the following of Jesus is a collective adventure I am, of course, not eliminating the personal dimension; on the contrary, I am giving it its authentic meaning as a response to the con-vocation of the Father.'[8] Commenting on this passage, he explains that this description of discipleship as a 'collective adventure' seeks to capture both the personal and social dynamics that are heard in the commission given by Jesus to his church:

> When, in the final verses of Matthew's Gospel, the Lord describes the task to be done he says it is to 'make disciples of all nations.' He obviously means 'of all individuals,' but without disregarding the fact that these individuals belong to human groups, to collectivities.[9]

The call to follow Jesus in discipleship is to be heard as a call to conscientization in community. The proclamation of God as Father in Jesus directs the disciple to know his neighbour as brother and sister in Jesus.

The Creation of a New Humanity Through Faithful Praxis

Personal transformation finds its purpose and meaning in this 'collective adventure' of discipleship. In the same way the 'collective adventure' of discipleship finds its possibility and reality in the lives of persons who have been awakened to the truth of God and their neighbour in the message of Jesus.

The way in which Gutiérrez describes the 'authenticity' of the personal response to Jesus recalls the contention by Freire that, because 'only through communication can life hold meaning', the work of 'authentic thinking' can also only take place 'in communication'.[10] Indeed, for Freire the truth of humanity can only be made known in community. He argues that 'I hold that my own unity and identity, in regard to others and to the world, constitutes my essential and unrepeatable way of experiencing myself as a cultural, historical and unfinished being in the world, simultaneously conscious of my unfinishedness.'[11] A person's unity and identity are forged within their relation to the world and others in an ongoing and ever unfolding dialogue. As a consequence, Freire concludes that 'our being is *being with*' and it is within this relation that person-ality takes shape and is made known.[12] In this way the process of conscientization will involve both a personal and social transformation. Given that 'it is in the intersubjectivity, mediated by objectivity, that my existence makes sense',[13] Freire argues that 'liberating education is a social process of illumination'.[14] To become conscious as a person one must become conscious in community.

McCann claims that in the concept of conscientization, Freire provides the theology of Gutiérrez with the 'distinctive methodological principle' through which his theology takes shape.[15] While it may be overstating the case to identify one thinker or concept as providing a defining or definitive role within the theology of Gutiérrez, it is clear that he draws out and develops the theological implications of Freire's work. For Gutiérrez, consciousness of who we are before God is forged through a consciousness of how we are in relation to our neighbour. To become conscious of the neighbour is to grow towards a consciousness of God. In his reading of Job, he presents the speech of Elihu, despite its conceit and presumption, as a kind of trigger for an increased conscientization in the life of Job. He observes that for Job, 'to go out of himself and help other sufferers (without waiting until his own problems are first resolved) is to find a way to God'.[16] Speaking of God does not begin with certainties or solutions but rather with a solidarity made possible by a consciousness of the suffering neighbour. To speak of God correctly, as Job does in his struggles, therefore involves a conscientization that is both personal in its depth and social in its extent. The proclamation of the gospel creates a consciousness of the truth of God and the truth of neighbour as each are revealed in the other. The God in whom there is 'an encounter with ourselves'[17] is made known in the revelation of Christ who is not only 'the mediator between us and God the Father, but he is also mediator between human beings'.[18] The conscientization that comes through the gospel thus involves a reciprocal movement between the personal and the social and between the human and the divine.[19] By transforming the depths of the human person it extends to the farthest reaches of human society.

Conscientization is a process that takes place within this reciprocal relationship between God and man, and between the personal and the social. This dynamic may be further clarified by observing how both Gutiérrez and Freire relate psychology to social and communal liberation. Tracing the socio-cultural dynamics that have led to the formulation of the theology of liberation, Gutiérrez speaks of the way in which Freud highlighted the importance of the 'individual and intimate dimension' of liberation.[20] Gutiérrez cites the argument of David Cooper that 'if we are to talk about revolution today our talk will be meaningless unless we effect some union between the macro-social and micro-social, and between "inner reality" and "outer reality"'.[21] The concept of conscientization provides a framework within which this union may be expressed. Such a union is an important element in the process of conscientization described by Freire. In the opening sequences of *Pedagogy of Hope*, Freire relates a personal process by which he confronted a painful experience in his childhood and so exposed 'the archaeology of my pain'.[22] The process that Freire describes at the level of personal awakening is then prescribed as a process of social and political liberation. The level of the micro and the macro are brought together when Freire recalls the reaction of Erich Fromm to his educational practice: 'I hear again in my mind something I once heard from Erich Fromm: ... "This kind of educational practice is a kind of historico-cultural, political psychoanalysis"'.[23] The process of conscientization in both Gutiérrez and Freire unfolds both personally and socially; it is a concept that unifies psychological intimacy with public responsibility. As the gospel is heard, an awareness is created of God as Father and our neighbours as his children. This awareness – this conscientization – involves a liberation of the person that is made known in their relations within their community.

The Creation of a New Humanity Through Faithful Praxis

Praxis and the life of a new humanity

Given that this conscientization takes place within community, it must also take shape through praxis.[24] Indeed, given the character of each, it is impossible to understand the one without the other. As Gutiérrez describes the praxis through which this new humanity lives, he first describes a generalized historical praxis before then calling for a specifically liberative praxis and concludes with a characterization of this liberative praxis as a praxis of love.

Historical praxis

As we have seen in Chapter 2, Gutiérrez reads human history as an unfolding of human aspirations for liberation in the historical process.[25] In this process humanity becomes conscious of and assumes responsibility for its power to shape its own destiny.[26] As this consciousness grows there is the possibility of 'the conquest of new, qualitatively different ways of being a human person'.[27] In this language of conquest Gutiérrez subverts a trope of oppressive ideology and ironically adapts it to speak of a liberative movement of history. Reaching a critical point in the industrial revolution, this historical praxis involves 'more than a new consciousness of the meaning of economic activity and political action; there is also a new way of being man and woman in history'.[28] This historical praxis is an ongoing unfolding of the historical process as an ever-growing 'critical awareness' finds expression in the 'permanent effort of those who seek to situate themselves in time and space, to exercise their creative potential, and to assume their responsibilities'.[29] The conscientization of humanity in history will necessarily be accompanied by a historical praxis that will create new conditions, and so new possibilities, for a still greater conscientization and liberation.

The movement to liberation through an ever-unfolding historical praxis is also evident in the pedagogy of Freire. Central to the process of conscientization is the hope given by the awareness of 'my nature as a project'.[30] Men and women are caught up in this historical praxis as they are liberated to see themselves not as static and fixed but rather open to and responsible for historical change. For this reason Freire argues that 'the unfinished character of human beings and the transformational character of reality necessitate that education be an ongoing activity'.[31] The dynamic that Freire identifies within the work of education in general is identified by Gutiérrez in the work of evangelization and gospel proclamation in particular. This word and work make known a faith in God and neighbour that gives hope for historical change to create an ever deeper and ever broader communion of love.

Critics of Gutiérrez such as Daniel Bell have argued that he locates the activity of Christian praxis within an autonomous sphere. In this reading, understanding is presented as distinct from action. For Bell, the praxis in which the disciple is engaged and the revealed word through which this praxis is to be interpreted are presented by Gutiérrez as two autonomous albeit related spheres. This is how Bell reads the interaction of the political and the spiritual in the theology of Gutiérrez:

> The whole process goes something like this: from the Christian practice of faith, which is essentially prayer and commitment to God, theology derives values which it then correlates with the social scientific analysis of reality to come up with a plan for political action.[32]

The consequence of such a schema is that the political realm is ceded to forces such as the state and the market – forces that work the very oppression from which liberation must be sought. However, when Gutiérrez speaks of the praxis through which a new humanity will be formed, he is calling the disciple to a movement that enfolds both action and reflection. As he famously declares in *A Theology of Liberation*, the work of theology is to be characterized as 'a critical reflection on Christian praxis in the light of the Word'.[33]

Gutiérrez clarifies his understanding of praxis in an essay entitled 'Expanding the View' which reflects on *A Theology of Liberation* and was subsequently included as an introduction to the revised edition of his earlier work. He comments that 'in my understanding of it, "praxis" is not reducible to "social aspects" in this narrow sense' and affirms the importance of exploring 'gestures and ways of "being with" that some may regard as having little political effectiveness'.[34] As I will show in more detail when I consider the reading that Gutiérrez offers of Job in the next chapter, the language of praxis involves a presence to God and neighbour in love. This presence – this 'being with' – in its orientation to both God and neighbour will involve both action and reflection. The scope of what Gutiérrez considers to be a truly liberative praxis is evident in a further definition of the theological task that he offers in an article published in the years following the publication of *A Theology of Liberation*. He declares that 'theology is an expression of the consciousness which a Christian community has of its faith in a given moment of history'.[35] It is interesting to note the ways in which this definition corresponds to and clarifies the terms that he deploys in the work published only a few years earlier. The dynamic of critical reflection appears to be drawn here into the language of consciousness and the process of conscientization that this term invokes. In addition, both the concept of praxis and the reflection on this praxis in the light of the Word are expressed as the 'consciousness which a Christian community has of its faith in a given moment in history'. For Gutiérrez praxis describes the concrete life of a Christian community. This life is at once forged in faith and at the same time calls for a continual renewal of that faith in the consciousness – the conscientization – that unfolds through that life. In other words, there are not two separate moments of revelation on the one hand and action on the other. Instead, there is a life forged in faith that becomes itself the force by which that faith is to be renewed. The Christian community in history is a community of action because it is a community of faith. The praxis of the Christian and the Word of revelation do not exist in autonomous spheres that must be brought into relation. Instead, they each inhabit the other. The praxis of the Christian is the praxis of the Word because the Word that they have received is a Word of praxis.

This reading of how Gutiérrez shapes and deploys the concept of praxis in his theology becomes clearer when considered in the context of the use of this concept in the writing of Paulo Freire. Freire argues that a new humanity will only emerge 'in word, in work, in action-reflection'.[36] In order to guard against both 'subjectivism' and 'mechanical objectivism' he contends that 'the praxis by which consciousness is changed is not only action but action and reflection'.[37] As Thomas Pace and Gina Merys conclude, 'Freire's concept of the *word* is action + reflection or *praxis*.'[38] In Freire's thought, praxis cannot be reduced to the action that follows from reflection. It is instead the unity of both. For example, he argues that moments of withdrawal, even retreat, may be appropriately described as praxis. He observes that 'theoretic praxis is what occurs when we take a step back from accomplished praxis ... so as to see it more clearly'.[39] Elsewhere he describes 'the silence of profound meditation, in which men only apparently leave the world, withdrawing from it in order to consider it in its totality and thus remaining with it'.[40] Indeed, for Pace and Merys it is in this very unity of 'theory and practice, between thought and action' that the influence of Freire may be detected in the theology of liberation.[41] When the concept of praxis that takes shape within the theology of Gutiérrez is read within the context of the writings of Freire, it is evident that Gutiérrez considers praxis to be a complex unity of action and reflection, of word and work.

In the language of praxis, Gutiérrez seeks to express the unity of both contemplation and action. Each of these movements animates and informs the other as action provokes contemplation and contemplation demands action. There is a gratuity that gives rise to exigency and an exigency that is animated by gratuity.[42] The distinction of each must be maintained if the reality of either is to be encountered; however, the unity of the two must be proclaimed if either is to be truly understood. This united movement of contemplation and action must not, however, be thought to correspond to one or other side of the relation between faith and works – as if the Word was simply to be received through contemplation and praxis expressed only in actions of obedience. There is a contemplative and active dynamic in each of these elements. Faith is constituted as both a presence to and a love for God. There is both an openness to God as other (contemplation) and a movement towards and reception of God in love (action). In the same way, the encounter with the neighbour in praxis is not simply one of action in solidarity or advocacy. There is a presence to the other (contemplation) that is accompanied by commitment towards the other (action). In both a life of praxis and in the reception of the Word, silence (*callar*) and speech (*hablar*) each form the possibility and reality of the other.[43]

Liberative praxis

If this historical praxis is to work towards the creation of a new humanity it must take the form of a liberative praxis. As humanity is made conscious of its creative power in contexts such as the Enlightenment and Industrial Revolution, the ongoing work of conscientization will expose the need for this historical praxis to take a liberative form. Indeed, when an awareness of the creative potential of humanity does not move to this liberative praxis it can revert to a controlling and mechanistic oppression. Gutiérrez observes that 'to speak of transformation of history from the perspective of dominated peoples and exploited humans, from the perspective of the poor of this world, brings us to see it as a liberating praxis'.[44] Historical praxis is able to become a specifically liberative praxis through a continued openness to community and love. As has already been observed, the 'critical awareness' that is achieved through conscientization and that is expressed in liberative praxis 'is not a state reached once and for all, but rather a permanent effort'.[45] It unfolds in a process that Gutiérrez describes as a 'continuous creation, never ending, of a new way to be human, a permanent cultural revolution'.[46] If praxis is made possible by conscientization, and if conscientization takes place

The Creation of a New Humanity Through Faithful Praxis

in dialogue, then a truly liberating praxis will involve an ever-unfolding movement of ever deeper awareness and ever more effective action. As long as the dialogue remains open so too does the future – and so too does the creative potential of humankind. Liberative praxis is thus the culmination of historical praxis. It is the movement in which historical praxis finds its purpose and life. Where it falls short of liberative praxis, the action of humanity in history will drown out the word that brings conscientization and replace the God of life with idols of oppression and death.

According to Gutiérrez, the work of humanity in history must find expression in a liberative dynamic. The movement of historical action towards liberative praxis may be further clarified when considered in relation to Freire's concept of the 'dialogical man'.[47] Freire argues that conscientization emerges in a process of 'invention and re-invention, through the restless, impatient, continuing, hopeful inquiry human beings pursue in the world, with the world and with each other'.[48] If the truth of a person emerges only in this dialogue with the world, then the truth of a person will remain a dynamic, living and ever-growing reality. Contending that 'only in communication can life hold meaning', Freire argues that the meaning thus achieved *through* communication lives *in* communication. Meaning must remain ever open to the other if it is to retain its truth. The 'dialogical man' is therefore creative in his receptivity. The word that creates the world is spoken as a response to the word that is heard from the neighbour.

What Freire calls for from the 'dialogical man' Gutiérrez hears in Paul's letter to Philemon. When Paul invites Philemon to 'do even more than I say', according to Gutiérrez he 'opens the door to the possibility of limitless work on Philemon's part in the service of his brother, who, in this case, is a man who is not acknowledged to be a human being with all human rights'.[49] Once called to see Onesimus as his brother, Philemon is called to a restless creativity that will restructure his relation to the slave. Paul provokes in Philemon a consciousness of his potential and his responsibility by making it possible for Philemon to recognize in his slave a neighbour and a brother. The liberative praxis called for by Paul does not take shape as a specific programme or series of static rules whose letter might be fulfilled while its spirit is ignored. Instead, there is a call to dialogue – a dialogue with God and a dialogue with neighbour that will lead to ever new expressions of service and love.

The praxis through which a new humanity is to be forged consists in a dynamic of action and reflection and for this reason it must be inspired and energized by the gospel. Gutiérrez explains that 'the praxis on which liberation theology reflects is a praxis of solidarity ... inspired by the gospel'.⁵⁰ The gospel gives life to and finds its life in the praxis to be encountered in the solidarity of Christian community. This is not the movement from idea to application; it is instead the movement between breath and life. The one is the possibility of the other. This relation is not simply a movement from the conceptual to the practical but rather a reciprocal movement in which the one depends on and directs itself to the other. As Freire observes: 'A correct way of thinking knows for example that the practice of critical teaching is not built as if thinking correctly were a mere given. However, it knows that without a correct way of thinking, there can be no critical practice.'⁵¹ What Freire describes here as a correct way of thinking when analysing 'the practice of critical teaching', he labels as faith when he reflects upon his own personal experience. From a personal perspective this interdependence between the gospel message and liberative praxis is evident in the process by which Freire himself developed his educational project. He affirms that, 'all arguments in favour of the legitimacy of my struggle for a more people-oriented society have their deepest roots in my faith'.⁵² The correct thinking that animates critical teaching is encountered in the faith that moved Freire to his struggle to forge a liberated humanity in a transformed society. He does not conceive of a two-step process in which the conceptual is then followed by the practical. They each interpenetrate and animate the other.

There is a similar dynamic in the theology of Gutiérrez. The conscientization that makes possible – and is itself made possible by – praxis allows for the correct thinking through which by faith God is received as Father and the neighbour as brother. The conscientization that comes through the proclamation of the gospel is, according to Gutiérrez, a profoundly spiritual process. As Jesus is proclaimed and encountered it is possible to know that 'here is the testimony to an unconditional life that gives full meaning to a shared filiation, which in its turn is the basis for human fellowship'.⁵³ Through a conscientization to the truth of God and neighbour in the power of the Spirit the Christian community can live the praxis of love by which a new humanity is formed. The work of liberation is far from the differentiated process against which Bell warns. It does not simply take values that are derived theologically and then seek to correlate them to a reality that is analysed scientifically.⁵⁴ The relationship of the gospel to praxis is one of inspiration – where inspiration is understood according to its etymology. It is the relation of breath and life in which the one is the possibility of the other.

The Creation of a New Humanity Through Faithful Praxis

The praxis of love

It is in liberative praxis that historical praxis finds its life, but to be truly liberative this praxis must be lived in love. The praxis that Gutiérrez calls for is to be expressed in the loving relations that take shape within concrete communities. Historical praxis can only come to its fruition when it is a liberating praxis and this liberative praxis is expressed through neighbour love. Gutiérrez explains that 'the liberating praxis, in the measure that it starts from an authentic solidarity with the poor and the oppressed, will be, in short, a praxis of love, of real love, efficacious and historical, towards concrete men'.[55] This praxis of love ensures that the work of liberative praxis remains a humanizing and personal work. In the call to a *praxis* of love, Gutiérrez rejects subjectivism and individualism. In the call to a praxis of *love*, he rejects conceptions of liberation that are mechanistic, deterministic and impersonal. Where liberation is a praxis of love it will flourish and find its form in the diversity and variety of human relationships. Forged in community through love, this praxis will be a restless and creative dynamic expressed differently amid the different contexts in which it lives.

To speak of the praxis of love is therefore to speak of both a personal and a social dynamic. It is, on the one hand, profoundly personal and spiritual. The awareness of God as Father that comes when the proclamation of a conscientizing evangelism is received by faith will lead to a renewed understanding of God, self and the neighbour. The praxis of love is an expression of the spirit of sonship that is at work where God is made known as Father. Gutiérrez comments that

> the liberating commitment signifies for many Christians an authentic spiritual experience, in the original and biblical sense of the term: a living in the Spirit which makes us recognize ourselves as free and creative children of the Father and brothers of all people ('God has sent the Spirit of his Son into our hearts, crying, "Abba! Father!"').[56]

Not only is this praxis of love personal and spiritual, it will (because of this personal and spiritual character) be social and practical. As Jesus makes God known as Father, he makes the neighbour known to us as our brother:

> It is for this reason that it seems to us more authentic and more profound to speak of a praxis of love that takes root in the gratuitous and free love of the Father who made himself a God of history in solidarity with the poor and the dispossessed and through them with all humans.[57]

Gustavo Gutiérrez and the Liberative Sight of Christ

This is neither a mechanistic process of external change nor a retreat into the subjectivism of private and personal improvement. To be truly transformative, praxis must involve both the depths of the personal and the extent of the social. Praxis can only be truly liberative when the gratuity of grace and the exigency of our concrete contexts meet together and find their expressions in love.[58]

Once the praxis of liberation is shown to be truly a praxis of love, the importance of community in the expression of this practice will come more clearly into view. Ecclesiastical communities play a pivotal role in the realization of this praxis of love. When Gutiérrez asserts that 'the gift of sonship is lived in history', he explains that this gift is received and lived in the praxis of 'making brothers and sisters of men and women'.[59] The gospel comes to persons in relations and transforms each by transforming the other. For this reason, he calls for a 'social appropriation of the gospel' amid Christian communities as they form 'groups which announce prophetically a creative and critical church entirely at the service of persons who fight to be persons'.[60] These communities are to be the contexts in which the new humanity is proclaimed, believed, verified and lived. Ecclesiastical communities play a central role in the theology of Gutiérrez as the place in which ways of being human may be forged through the praxis of love. Calling for 'new experiences and new modes of evangelization in the coming together as "Church",' he envisages 'the creation of Christian communities in which the private owners of the goods of this world cease to be the owners of the gospel'.[61] In this way the Christian community in its many and varied forms offers to the world a place in which the praxis of love is made known and transforms the oppressive and idolatrous patterns of the world.

When this social dynamic is overlooked the process of liberation outlined by Gutiérrez will be misunderstood. When Daniel Bell summarizes Gutiérrez's construction of the second level of liberation, he reads him as limiting the personal to the individual:

> The second level, the personal, consists of a 'profound inner freedom.' It is an expression of the inner longing of persons to be the artisans of their own destiny; it marks humankind's assumption of conscious responsibility for its own future. This denotes the realm commonly referred to as the personal, private, or perhaps even the psychological.[62]

While Bell draws his description of this level from the language of Gutiérrez, he appears to abstract this language from the overall structure of his thought. While there is clearly an attention to the personal, private and

The Creation of a New Humanity Through Faithful Praxis

psychological dimensions of human life, these are considered in relation to the social contexts within which they find expression and meaning. It is important to recall not only the interrelation and interdependence of the three levels, but also the relational and interpersonal context of this second level.

Community is the context in which praxis is formulated and expressed. This is evident in the relationship between the different but corresponding definitions of theology that are found in *A Theology of Liberation* and 'Faith as Freedom'. The dynamic described by the term praxis in the former is expressed in the latter as the life of a 'Christian community ... in a given moment of history'.[63] As I have already demonstrated, the praxis of the disciple is the 'collective adventure'[64] embarked upon by 'dialogical man'[65] in his attention to and action with both God and neighbour. The praxis of love to which the disciple is called is realized within communities that have received the Word of the gospel by faith. The importance of the Christian community is further evident in the phrase that I contend is central to the theology of Gutiérrez. Gutiérrez declares that his theology seeks to 'proclaim God as Father in a world that is inhumane'.[66] The work of the theologian to critically reflect on praxis in the light of the Word is here described as the proclamation of God as Father in a world that is inhumane. The relation of God to the neighbour as Father in this latter phrase allows the praxis of the former phrase to be more clearly understood. This praxis is the life of children who have come to know God as Father and so are able to recognize and live towards their neighbour as brother and sister. The praxis called for by Gutiérrez finds its expression in concrete communities of faith.

Having read him as restricting spiritual reflection and political action to distinct and autonomous spheres, Bell contends that liberationists such as Gutiérrez 'remain committed to an apolitical Church and a vision of politics as statecraft'.[67] According to Bell, he characterizes the role of the church as one of reflection, motivation and inspiration. This is then differentiated from the political sphere in which action takes shape from scientific analysis and empirical investigation. Instead of submitting to this 'modern differentiation of life, with its separation of politics and religion', Bell calls for a recognition that a truly liberative community 'must be constructed according to different architectonics'.[68] He points the liberationists to 'examples of ecclesiological reconstruction that may fund resistance to the depredations of the capitalist order'.[69] He seeks to call liberation theology back to the church, to ecclesiology, and ultimately to the 'children of struggle' in their midst, the base communities.[70] It is only if theologians of liberation consider 'the revolutionary practices of the poor in their midst', Bell warns, that there is any possibility that 'their theological vision will be restored'.[71]

Because Bell misreads the relation between contemplation and action in Gutiérrez's theology, he fails to recognize the importance of the ecclesiastical community as the context in which he calls for praxis to be expressed. Once a dual dynamic of action and reflection is heard in Gutiérrez's language of praxis it is possible to recognize the importance of the ecclesial community in its formulation and expression. The action on which theology is to reflect is described by Gutiérrez as 'pastoral action of the Church'.[72] For that reason he defines it as a specifically 'ecclesial praxis'.[73] According to Gutiérrez the work of 'creating the way of being human and being Christian in the present reality of Latin America' will arise out of 'new experiences and new modes of evangelisation in the coming together as "Church"'.[74] The process of 'social appropriation of the gospel' is to be exemplified in specifically ecclesial contexts.[75] While there will be challenges to and ruptures with traditional and institutional expressions of church these 'rebellious communities' are specifically Christian communities in which the structures of society and state are reimagined and remade.[76] Once the character of the praxis called for by Gutiérrez is recognized the context of this praxis is more clearly discerned. The praxis that takes shape within his theology is rooted firmly in the soil of the ecclesial community. It is in the church in its varied expressions that a liberative and loving praxis will flower and flourish.

Conclusion

In this chapter I have outlined the way in which Gutiérrez calls for the creation of a new humanity within the context of social relations and through the outworking of a liberative praxis of love. This concept of praxis involves a unity of action and reflection that takes shape in community and is inspired by the gospel. Having clarified the conceptual framework within which the thought of Gutiérrez unfolds, I will now examine in more detail the steps through which this process of liberation proceeds.

The Creation of a New Humanity Through Faithful Praxis

Notes

1 Gustavo Gutiérrez, *The Truth Shall Make You Free: Confrontations*, trans. Matthew J. O'Connell (Maryknoll, NY: Orbis Books, 1990), p. 133.
2 Gustavo Gutiérrez, *A Theology of Liberation: History, politics, and salvation*, trans. Caridad Inda and John Eagleson (London: SCM Press, 2010), pp. 113–14.
3 Gutiérrez, *A Theology of Liberation*, p. 75.
4 Gutiérrez, *A Theology of Liberation*, p. 69.
5 Gutiérrez, *A Theology of Liberation*, p. 71.
6 Gutiérrez, *The Truth Shall Make You Free*, p. 134.
7 Gutiérrez, *A Theology of Liberation*, p. 130.
8 Gustavo Gutiérrez, *We Drink From Our Own Wells: The spiritual journey of a people* (Maryknoll, NY: Orbis Books, 2003), p. 89.
9 Gutiérrez, *The Truth Shall Make You Free*, p. 49.
10 Paulo Freire, *Pedagogy of the Oppressed*, trans. Myra Bergman Ramos, 30th anniversary edn (New York: Continuum, 2000), p. 64.
11 Paulo Freire, *Pedagogy of Freedom: Ethics, democracy, and civic courage*, trans. Patrick Clarke, Critical Perspectives Series (Lanham, MD: Rowman & Littlefield, 1998), p. 51.
12 Freire, *Pedagogy of Freedom*, p. 58.
13 Paulo Freire, 'Education liberation and the Church', *Religious Education* 79, no. 4 (September 1984), p. 534.
14 Ira Shor and Paulo Freire, *A Pedagogy for Liberation: Dialogues on transforming education* (South Hadley, MA: Bergin & Garvey, 1987), p. 109.
15 Dennis McCann, *Christian Realism and Liberation Theology: Practical theologies in creative conflict* (Maryknoll, NY: Orbis Books, 2001), p. 157. In a similar way Elizabeth Lange observes that 'Freire's influence is readily apparent in the education document of the Medellín Conference (Paiva, 1995) and Gutiérrez incorporated Freire's conscientization process into his treatise on liberation theology (1973) as a pedagogy to animate a new theology.' Elizabeth A. Lange, 'Fragmented ethics of justice: Freire, liberation theology and pedagogies for the non-poor', *Convergence* 31, nos 1 and 2 (January 1998), p. 83.
16 Gustavo Gutiérrez, *On Job: God-talk and the suffering of the innocent*, trans. Matthew J. O'Connell (Maryknoll, NY: Orbis Books, 1987), p. 48. For all of its conceit and presumption, the speech of Elihu appears to function, within the reading offered by Gutiérrez, as a kind of trigger for an increased conscientization in the life of Job.
17 Gutiérrez, *The Truth Shall Make You Free*, p. 51.
18 Gutiérrez, *The Truth Shall Make You Free*, p. 36.
19 'The great principal hermeneutic of the faith and, therefore, the foundation of all theological discourse is Jesus Christ ... That is then the fundamental hermeneutical circle: from man to God and from God to man; from history to faith and from faith to history.' Gustavo Gutiérrez, 'Faith as freedom: solidarity with the alienated and confidence in the future', *Horizons* 2, no. 1 (1975), p. 47.
20 Gutiérrez, *A Theology of Liberation*, p. 69.
21 David Cooper, ed., 'Introduction' in *The Dialectics of Liberation*, Radical Thinkers (Congress on the Dialectics of Liberation, London; New York: Verso, 2015), p. 10. Quoted in Gutiérrez, *A Theology of Liberation*, p. 70.

22 Paulo Freire, Ana Maria Araújo Freire and Robert R. Barr, *Pedagogy of Hope: Reliving Pedagogy of the Oppressed* (London: Bloomsbury, 2014), p. 30.

23 Freire, Freire and Barr, *Pedagogy of Hope*, p. 55.

24 For an exploration of the concept of praxis and the different forms that this concept might take, see Matthew Lamb, 'The theory-praxis relationship in contemporary Christian theologies', *Proceedings of the Catholic Theological Society of America* 31 (1 December 2012) and Daniel Franklin E. Pilario, *Back to the Rough Grounds of Praxis: Exploring theological method with Pierre Bourdieu*, Bibliotheca Ephemeridum Theologicarum Lovaniensium 183 (Leuven: Leuven University Press, 2005). The discussion of praxis in this chapter is not an attempt to explore the topic in itself but rather to clarify the particular form and function of this concept within the theology of Gutiérrez.

25 Gutiérrez, *A Theology of Liberation*, p. 66 and following.

26 Gutiérrez, *A Theology of Liberation*, p. 75.

27 Gutiérrez, *A Theology of Liberation*, p. 71.

28 Gutiérrez, 'Faith as freedom', p. 37.

29 Gutiérrez, *A Theology of Liberation*, p. 114.

30 Paulo Freire and Ana Maria Araújo Freire, *Pedagogy of the Heart* (New York: Continuum, 2007), p. 93.

31 Freire, *Pedagogy of the Oppressed*, p. 72.

32 Daniel M. Bell, '"Men of Stone and Children of Struggle": Latin American liberationists at the end of history', *Modern Theology* 14, no. 1 (January 1998), p. 118.

33 Gutiérrez, *A Theology of Liberation*, p. 57.

34 Gutiérrez, *A Theology of Liberation*, p. 23.

35 Gutiérrez, 'Faith as freedom', p. 26.

36 Freire, *Pedagogy of the Oppressed*, p. 76.

37 Freire, 'Education liberation and the Church', p. 527.

38 Thomas Pace and Gina A. Merys, 'Paulo Freire and the Jesuit tradition: Jesuit rhetoric and Freirean pedagogy' in *Traditions of Eloquence: The Jesuits and Modern Rhetorical Studies* (New York: Fordham University Press, 2016), p. 245. See also the diagram given by Freire that expresses this relation in Freire, *Pedagogy of the Oppressed*, p. 87 n.1.

39 Freire, 'Education liberation and the Church', p. 528.

40 Freire, *Pedagogy of the Oppressed*, p. 76 n. 3.

41 'In other words, liberation theology stresses the importance of a dialectic relationship between theory and practice and between thought and action, ideas that grew out, in large part, from these theologians' reading of Freire.' Pace and Merys, 'Freire and the Jesuit tradition', p. 236.

42 Gutiérrez, *On Job*, p. 88.

43 Gutiérrez, *On Job*, p. xii.

44 Gutiérrez, 'Faith as freedom', p. 37.

45 Gutiérrez, *A Theology of Liberation*, p. 114.

46 Gutiérrez, *A Theology of Liberation*, p. 71.

47 Freire, *Pedagogy of the Oppressed*, p. 79.

48 Freire, *Pedagogy of the Oppressed*, p. 58.

49 Gutiérrez, *The Truth Shall Make You Free*, p. 140.

50 Gutiérrez, *A Theology of Liberation*, p. 22.

The Creation of a New Humanity Through Faithful Praxis

51 Freire, *Pedagogy of Freedom*, p. 43.
52 Freire and Freire, *Pedagogy of the Heart*, p. 104.
53 Gutiérrez, *Our Own Wells*, p. 38.
54 Recall the summary offered by Bell of the structure of praxis that he reads in Gutiérrez, in Bell, 'Men of Stone and Children of Struggle', p. 118.
55 Gutiérrez, 'Faith as freedom', p. 37.
56 Gutiérrez, 'Faith as freedom', p. 39.
57 Gutiérrez, 'Faith as freedom', p. 38.
58 This dynamic recalls the warning of Freire that 'subjectivism or mechanistic objectivism are both anti-dialectical, and thereby incapable of apprehending the permanent tension between consciousness and the world'. Freire, Freire and Barr, *Pedagogy of Hope*, p. 100.
59 Gutiérrez, 'Faith as freedom', p. 54.
60 Gutiérrez, 'Faith as freedom', p. 59. See also the discussion of this term in Gutiérrez, *The Truth Shall Make You Free*, pp. 48–9.
61 Gutiérrez, 'Faith as freedom', p. 58.
62 Bell, 'Men of Stone and Children of Struggle', p. 117.
63 Gutiérrez, 'Faith as freedom', p. 26.
64 Gutiérrez, *Our Own Wells*, p. 89.
65 Freire, *Pedagogy of the Oppressed*, p. 79. I draw here on the language of Freire to capture the dynamic that is expressed at greater length by Gutiérrez. See, for example, his discussion of friendship and openness in Gutiérrez, *A Theology of Liberation*, p. 23.
66 Gutiérrez, *The Power of the Poor in History*, p. 193.
67 Daniel M. Bell, *Liberation Theology After the End of History: The refusal to cease suffering*, Radical Orthodoxy Series (London: Routledge, 2001), p. 70.
68 Bell, *Liberation Theology After the End of History*, p. 71.
69 Bell, 'Men of Stone and Children of Struggle', p. 134.
70 Bell, 'Men of Stone and Children of Struggle', p. 115.
71 Bell, 'Men of Stone and Children of Struggle', p. 135.
72 Gutiérrez, *A Theology of Liberation*, p. 56.
73 Gutiérrez, *A Theology of Liberation*, p. 57.
74 Gutiérrez, 'Faith as freedom', p. 58.
75 Gutiérrez, 'Faith as freedom', p. 59.
76 Gutiérrez, 'Faith as freedom', p. 58. So also Gutiérrez, *Our Own Wells*, p. 22.

6

The Faithful Praxis Through which a New Humanity is Forged

The praxis to which Gutiérrez calls the believer follows the three-fold pattern of 'see-judge-act' that was pioneered by Joseph Cardijn, developed within Catholic Action and later adopted by the Latin American bishops at Medellín in 1968.[1] While this pattern of see-judge-act has been variously understood within the history of Catholic Action, and been critiqued by theologians of liberation, it is a methodology that has allowed practitioners to move beyond the constraints within which it initially functioned. The methodology of Catholic Action gave rise to a pastoral practice that enabled Latin American theologians to offer a new account of the relation between the church and the world.[2]

Gutiérrez calls for the church to see the reality lived by the neighbour who stands before them, to understand the truth given by the God who reveals himself to them and to live in the love of the Spirit who dwells among them. A new and liberative humanity lives in this dynamic as sight, judgement and action give rise to ever clearer vision, ever deeper understanding and ever more effective action on behalf of the neighbour. I will seek to illustrate through his treatment of the life and work of Bartolomé de las Casas how a faithful praxis makes possible – and is made possible by – a sight of the neighbour. In his commentary on Job, Gutiérrez demonstrates how this sight of the neighbour, when received by faith, will involve a conversion to the neighbour. Finally, through his meditations on a truly liberative spirituality in *We Drink From Our Own Wells*, I will consider how this sight and judgement may be expressed in acts of daily commitment.

At each of these points I will engage with distinct critiques of Gutiérrez that have been developed by theologians writing from the perspective of Radical Orthodoxy. I will argue that the objections raised by John Milbank, Daniel Bell and William Cavanaugh misread a number of important dynamics within the praxis to which Gutiérrez calls the church.[3] A thorough engagement with this movement's criticism of liberation theology would take us beyond the purposes of this project. It would require an evaluation of the theological narrative that Radical Orthodoxy recounts, the role that twentieth-century Roman Catholic theology plays within this narrative, and the consequences of these dynamics for the theology of liberation. In this part of the project, I will concentrate my attention on the particular readings that these theologians offer of the work of Gustavo Gutiérrez without broadening the discussion to consider the wider conceptual framework within which these readings take place. I will seek to evaluate the specifics of various criticisms and show that the path of praxis traced by Gutiérrez avoids the pitfalls against which the theologians of Radical Orthodoxy warn.

Bartolomé de Las Casas and the sight of the poor of Jesus Christ

Gutiérrez opens his account of the life and thought of Bartolomé de Las Casas with a consideration of how the sixteenth-century priest might speak into the questions and concerns of the church today. The thesis that he seeks to demonstrate is that the contemporary church may find in Las Casas 'someone driven to proclaim the Reign of God in a fitting manner, through a defence of the life and freedoms of persons in whom his faith enabled him to perceive Christ himself'.[4] While Gutiérrez seeks to avoid 'positing facile equations between eras', he calls the church of today to follow the gaze of Las Casas and so to see the poverty, oppression and suffering that is all around.[5] Las Casas provides a model of how the Christian community is to embark on its work to make the Kingdom of God known in a new and liberated humanity. Just as, four centuries ago, 'in the "afflicted, scourged" inhabitants of these lands, Bartolomé was able to see the presence of Christ himself', in the same way today the Christian must see the neighbour whom they are called to love.[6] In the life and work of Las Casas, Gutiérrez discerns a vision of social reality that transforms faith but is given in the context of faith.

Las Casas and the sight of social reality

Las Casas arrived in the Indies only ten years after the landing of Columbus. In the decades that followed he underwent a transformation from a complacent participant in a violent and exploitative system to one of its most active and vocal opponents.[7] The trigger for this movement from participation to protest was 'his experience of the untimely, unjust deaths of the Indians' which reached a traumatic climax in the massacre of Caonao.[8] According to Gutiérrez, the sight of this suffering unleashed a process of change in Las Casas – a process that sought and was sustained by an ever-clearer sight of the suffering through which it was born.

The work of Las Casas consisted, in large part, of an attempt to share with others this transformative sight of those suffering in the Americas. In order for Las Casas to faithfully judge the situation before him in Cuba, he needed to know 'the complex reality of the Indies'.[9] Gutiérrez argues that it was through 'what we today would call social analysis' that Las Casas was able to 'unmask the "social sin" of his time'.[10] The confrontation between Las Casas and the institutions of church and state unfold as a conflict between contrasting 'visions'. On the one hand there is the abstract vision that allows the victims of violence to recede from sight. On the other hand there is the concrete vision in which the victims and their suffering move into focus. Gutiérrez observes that 'the perspective of the insignificant and oppressed ("whom we see") always withdraws us from the world of abstract principles – from a false pretence of loving "the God who we have not seen"'.[11] It was into this 'world of abstract principles' that Las Casas sought to bring the disruptive and disturbing vision of those who suffered violence, oppression and exploitation. Gutiérrez observes the way in which this conflict played out in the debates between Las Casas and Francisco de Vitoria. According to Gutiérrez, the position of Vitoria is at once understandable and untenable because of his ignorance of the reality of the situation of those suffering in the Indies.[12] It is a position forged through abstractions. The convictions of Las Casas by contrast are marked by the concrete reality he has seen; he gains an entirely different theological perspective: 'Bartolomé's outlook is from within the world of the poor. From among the despised races.'[13] If faithful judgement is to be made and loving action to be taken, then those 'whom we see' must be allowed to intrude on our vision. Las Casas is able to see the world of the poor and see the world with the poor. As with the man born blind, Jesus brings a sight that liberates 'from a false and arrogant notion of religious knowledge'.[14] It is this sight of reality that allows the work of liberation to take place.

Las Casas and the sight of social reality that transforms faith

Once 'those whom we see' enter into our view, this vision will confront and transform a faith that has been sustained among a 'world of abstract principles'. The example of Las Casas shows the way in which this

The Faithful Praxis Through which a New Humanity is Forged

vision of social reality comes before the judgement of faith. As Gutiérrez explains, 'in order for him to be able to judge what is transpiring ... Bartolomé has a need to know the complex reality of the Indies'.[15] A true sight of reality makes possible a faithful judgement. Indeed, apart from the truth of this vision faith itself becomes false. This is evident in the language and imagery used by Las Casas as he describes his own process of conversion. As he is confronted by the implications of what he has seen, the religious system and discourse to which he has committed himself is exposed as idolatry. The massacre witnessed by Las Casas at Caonao disturbs and disrupts his vision of the sacrifice that is offered at mass. In his translation of Ecclesiasticus 34.19–20, Las Casas allows the reality of what he has seen to infuse the text: 'The sacrifice with which they express their reverence is as if, to do honour and service to a father, they were to hack his child to pieces before his eyes.'[16] Having been confronted by the sight of suffering, Las Casas now sees the religious system of which he is part as sustained by exploitation and oppression. For him the mass has become not an offering before God of the sacrifice of Jesus on the cross but an expression of child sacrifice before the idol of human greed.[17] As Las Casas allows himself to be confronted by the reality of the indigenous people around him, he is able to see the truth of the faith that he has professed. It is exposed to have been a lie sustained by abstractions in the service of an idol.

Las Casas and the sight of social reality in the context of faith

The experience of Las Casas as described by Gutiérrez reveals that this sight of social reality not only provides a secure foundation for faith, it also takes place in the context of faith. In one sense, the sight of reality came *chronologically* before the judgement of faith in the conversion of Las Casas. In another sense this sight became a vision of the truth because it took place before – that is, in the *context* of – his Christian faith.

The conversion of Las Casas may be read as exemplifying the 'continuous interaction ... between reflection and concrete commitment – theory and practice' in his work as a whole.[18] While triggered by the traumatic events in Caonao, the conversion of Las Casas unfolds within a context shaped by the liturgy of the church and biblical revelation. It is while 'preparing to celebrate Mass' and revising the sermons that he had preached over the course of Easter that he 'allows himself to be challenged by the biblical passage which calls in question his position in the nascent colonial system'.[19] The language of Gutiérrez at this point offers an insight into how he understands the interdependence of a sight that confronts faith and a faith that provides a context for the discernment of truth in this sight. On the one hand, Las Casas 'allows himself to be challenged' by what he has seen and begun to consider. On the other hand, it is the biblical text that challenges him: 'Scripture and reality are mutually illuminating. They reinforce one another and this relationship produces Las Casas's transformation.'[20] Gutiérrez does not allow for social analysis to be abstracted from faith any more than he allows for faith to be abstracted from social analysis. For sight to give a vision of the truth it must always take place before – that is, in the context of – faith.

The sight of the poor of Jesus Christ: the question of theology and social theory

Milbank argues that the theology of Gutiérrez takes shape within the framework of what he describes as a Rahnerian 'integralism' which 'naturalises the supernatural' and moves towards 'a rapprochement, with the Enlightenment and an autonomous secular order'.[21] According to Milbank, this construction of the relation between nature and grace reduces salvation to an 'empty, formless epistemological transcendence' such that, 'if salvation is to be given content, liberation theology must look to the social realm, which it understands as being over-against the individual and religious'.[22] The theology of liberation is therefore unable to offer an adequate account of either theology or liberation. Milbank outlines this two-fold problem by arguing that for theologians such as Gutiérrez, 'insofar as salvation is "religious", it is formal, transcendental and private; insofar as it is "social", it is secular'.[23] On the one hand, Milbank identifies a tendency to idealize, interiorize and privatize the religious element of salvation. The emphasis on an 'anonymous response' to Christ that is heard in liberation theology is placed by Milbank in tension with a characterization of Christian love as 'a highly complex, learned practice, which Jesus spells out in fully exemplary fashion'.[24] On the other hand, the social element of salvation takes shape in the theology of liberation within a framework established by an autonomous secular order. Milbank argues that 'the claim of political and liberation theology that theology "requires" secular social science, always implies the displacing of the Christian metanarrative'.[25] Within this framework, salvation once understood as a social reality is forced to submit to narratives 'which themselves arose partially as an attempt to situate and confine faith itself'.[26] As a consequence of this two-fold dynamic, the theology of liberation can be neither faithful in its theology nor effective in its political programme.

While the critique developed by Milbank is serious, it is important to question whether the theology of Gutiérrez is indeed characterized by the dual dynamic that he describes. I contend that far from displacing a Christian metanarrative, the liberation that is described by Gutiérrez can only be understood and embraced within such a narrative. This is evident in his description of the role of the Eucharist in the liberative life of the church. Gutiérrez presents the Eucharist as a recapitulation of the biblical narratives of creation and redemption in which the church and the watching world are to find their place. It is a liturgical expression of the interplay between the personal and the political that is at work at every point in the life of believers: 'The Christian Passover takes on and reveals the full meaning of the Jewish Passover. Liberation from sin is at the very root of political liberation. The former reveals what is really involved in the latter.'[27] The reality of political liberation is disclosed within the liturgy of the Eucharist. It is the narrative expressed in this sacrament that provides the context in which the life and purpose of the believer is to be understood.[28] The confrontation of injustice is never to be abstracted from the context of the gospel of Jesus Christ. According to Gutiérrez, this ministry of prophetic denunciation 'is only achieved by confronting a given situation with the reality which is announced: the love of the Father which calls all persons in Christ and through the action of the Spirit to union among themselves and communion with him'.[29] It is only when this gospel is announced that injustice may be denounced. Sight takes place in the context of faith. Liberative mission is a movement that finds its meaning within the narratives of creation and salvation as expressed in both Scripture and sacrament.

Not only is Gutiérrez careful to place his call to liberation within a Christian metanarrative; the work by which this liberation is to be achieved takes its shape from the scriptural and sacramental context from which it drew its motivation. As I have shown, the movement of Las Casas from complicity *in* to a confrontation *of* the injustices of the colonial system took place within the context of his faith. It is while 'preparing to celebrate Mass' that Bartolomé de Las Casas 'allows himself to be challenged by the biblical passage' on which he had been expecting to preach.[30] It is precisely within the context of the 'highly complex, learned practice' of Christian life in the church that Las Casas undergoes a process of conversion and understands the call to liberation. Indeed, Gutiérrez points out that it is the abstractions of social and theological analysis that are deployed to sustain structures of injustice and exploitation. Milbank asserts that 'for nearly all the political and liberation theologians, theology baptizes a universal individualistic ethic, the impulse "of the heart" to love the neighbour'.[31] However, in his reflections on the life and ministry of Las Casas, Gutiérrez warns against the dangers of a theology that functions at the level of such impulses, ideals and abstractions. Indeed, it is the opponents of Las Casas who make of the call to love an abstraction whose instantiation takes shape according to the interests of the state. To take one example, Gutiérrez describes the way in which Sarmiento de Gamboa 'advances a powerful consideration in favour of the conquest of these peoples, and one that he hopes will be regarded as adequate. Love of neighbour has made this conquest a duty.'[32] The sight that Gutiérrez calls for does not seek to dissolve theology into an abstract social theory. Rather, as we have heard, it is the sight of the poor and suffering that will 'withdraw us from the world of abstract principles'.[33] Those whom Las Casas begins to see may have been found outside of the church. Yet Las Casas learned to see within the context of the church. It is in the context of Scripture and sacrament that he learns to see, and moved by that sight, begins to respond.

On Job and the judgement of faith on behalf of the poor

In his consideration of the life and ministry of Bartolomé de Las Casas, Gutiérrez presents a portrait of the 'seeing' to which the judgement of faith is to respond. His meditation on the book of Job illuminates his account of this second step on the path towards a new humanity. According to Gutiérrez, judgement involves a dual encounter with both God and our neighbour. To speak faithfully of one is to speak truthfully of the other. He opens his meditations on Job with the declaration that 'theology is talk about God'[34] but a few pages later explains that the question of 'how are we to talk about God' may also be expressed as another question: 'What words are we to use in telling those who are not even regarded as persons that they are daughters and sons of God?'[35] For Gutiérrez the answer to the one is found by pursuing an answer to the other. It is as we talk faithfully about God that we speak truthfully about our neighbour and as we come to know the truth of our neighbour we are led into the truth of God. The judgement of faith consists in this two-fold truth.

As Gutiérrez follows the theological drama of the book, he traces a movement in which the poor lead Job to God and in which God leads Job to himself. While his reading of the book of Job may be idiosyncratic,

The Faithful Praxis Through which a New Humanity is Forged

it offers a vivid expression of how he understands the relation of sight, revelation and liberative judgement. As Gutiérrez recounts the drama of Job, he presents injustice as that which is seen and grace as that which is revealed. To pretend to know grace without having been truly confronted by injustice is to fall before an idol of abstraction. To pretend to respond to injustice without having been confronted by grace is to fall before an idol of pragmatism. In *On Job* Gutiérrez characterizes the judgement of faith as being based on both that which is seen and that which is revealed. As the believer is led to God by the poor, they are led by God to himself.

The poor lead Job to God

As Job wrestles with the burden of speaking truthfully about God he is confronted by the concrete reality of the poor. In the interchange between Job and his comforters Gutiérrez discerns a movement between 'two types of theological reasoning'.[36] While his friends proceed through abstract reasoning, Job rejects a 'theologizing that does not take account of concrete situations, of sufferings and hopes of human beings'.[37] For the friends, the question of how to speak truthfully about God has a simple, straightforward and theoretical answer. For Job the question is so pressing because the truth of its answer must also account for the truth of the neighbour.

Job is led into the truth of God through a consideration of the truth of the poverty that surrounds him. While this may be an example of one of the more idiosyncratic hermeneutical steps taken by Gutiérrez, it exemplifies what he considers to be a central dynamic within a movement of conversion to the poor. Gutiérrez identifies a 'considerable shift' that takes place in the character of Job when 'the question he asks of God ceases to be a purely personal one and takes concrete form in the suffering of the poor of this world'.[38] As Job comes to recognize that 'poverty and abandonment are not something fated but caused by the wicked', he is able to discern more clearly the truth of both God and his suffering neighbour.[39] Far from such suffering being fated by God it is opposed by him. As God calls his people to care for the poor, he reveals that 'the poor are not persons punished by God ... but rather God's friends'.[40] The world is not governed by a mechanism of reward and retribution. It is instead a place in which God establishes his justice through faithful judgement. As Job shares in the experience of the poor he is able to encounter the truth about God: 'His point of departure was both his own experience and his faith in the living God; it was on that basis that he challenged, and gradually dismantled the doctrine of retribution that his three friends expounded.'[41] As Job seeks to speak the truth about God and his neighbour the judgement that he is to express will be based on this lived encounter with his neighbour. Job discovers that 'to go out of himself and help other sufferers … is to find a way to God'.[42] Job is able to take a step towards faithful judgement as the poor lead him into the truth of God.

Through the poor God leads Job to himself

The experience of the poor is necessary for Job to make a faithful judgement but it is not sufficient. Job recognizes that poverty and suffering are the result of human wickedness and sin and so comes to know God as the friend and father of the poor rather than the author of their poverty. This realization provokes the further question: 'In what sense is God just?'[43]

In his commitment to speak truly of God and his neighbour, Job refuses to judge the one at the expense of the other. Job will condemn neither the innocent nor the just. To judge faithfully he must speak truly of the innocence of his neighbour and the justice of God.[44] Gutiérrez observes that in this way 'his truthfulness leaves him isolated and almost defenceless'.[45] While his commitment to the poor 'provides firm ground for prophetic talk about God', the drama of Job reaches a climax with the realization that 'this kind of talk about God – talk that may be described as "prophetic" – is inadequate'.[46] While the poor may lead Job to the truth of God, it is only as God reveals himself to him through the poor that this truth may be understood. To speak truly of God Job must not only express himself through this prophetic language, he must also learn how to express himself in the language of mystery and contemplation. While Job has seen the truth of his neighbour, he must also encounter the truth of God. He longs for an encounter in which he might see God with his own eyes 'and be able to look upon him as a friend'.[47]

Job has needed to see and speak of the suffering of the poor. He must also hear and receive the revelation of God. It is only as Job comes to see God through his self-revelation that the truth of both God and neighbour may be heard. This encounter with God comes to him first in the revelation that the work of God 'has its origin in the gratuitousness of creative love'.[48] This context of grace allows Job to recognize the work of God's love as God's governance of the world is revealed to take shape through a merciful and humble love. Responding to the revelation of God's creative grace, in 40.4–5 Job confesses his 'littleness' before his Lord. Gutiérrez highlights the striking movement from the confession of

The Faithful Praxis Through which a New Humanity is Forged

Job in 40.4 to the self-revelation of God in 40.9–14. He interprets these verses as revealing that 'God's power is limited by human freedom' such that 'the all-powerful God is also a "weak" God' as he governs the world in a humble and self-limiting love.[49] God leads Job to a confession of his littleness so that Job might recognize the true glory of divine weakness. In his first speech God reveals that 'gratuitousness is the hinge on which the world turns'; in the second speech God reveals his will that 'justice and judgement (*mishpaṭ*, 40.7) be established' in gracious love.[50]

As he marvels at the grace of God revealed in creation and the love of God expressed in his rule Job begins to 'savour the Pauline face-to-face encounter with God'.[51] God works to lead Job into this communion. He does not impose justice on the world in a way that would violate the freedom and integrity of the human because true justice cannot take shape as an impersonal abstraction that is imposed against the will and wish of humanity. It is a communion. As such it is forged through a relationship. As Job is humbled before God, he is able to see the humility of God and so begin to enter into a relationship with him. It was as Job by faith 'flung himself upon the impossible and into an enigmatic future' that he finally 'met the Lord'.[52] Creation and human history are thereby forged in grace and governed by love to lead humanity into a communion with God.

In the reading offered by Gutiérrez, Job is only able to speak truly of God as he learns to speak the language of both prophecy and mystery. As a prophetic concern for the poor leads him on the pathway to God, the mystical encounter with God allows for this journey to reach its fruition. The poor reveal God to Job but it is through divine self-revelation that communion with God is made possible. As the language of prophecy calls for justice its voice must be joined to the language of mystery by which is expressed the grace that gives this justice its meaning. The two movements of the drama of Job combine to lead the reader to join with him in arriving at a faithful judgement of the truth of both God and neighbour. Gutiérrez concludes that 'vision of God (final stage in Job's suit against God) and defence of the poor (a role he discovers for himself because of his own innocence) are thus combined in the experience of Job as a man of justice'.[53] The book of Job as read by Gutiérrez serves to teach its hearers the languages of prophecy and mystery by which they are to speak rightly of God. The two languages 'cross and enrich each other, and finally converge to yield a correct way of talking about God'.[54] As the poor lead Job to God he is able to submit himself to the self-revelation of God who calls him into communion with himself. The truth of the neighbour leads Job into the mystery of God and the mystery of God makes known to Job the truth of his love and grace in history.

Job and the refusal to cease suffering

In this account of faithful judgement it is possible to hear a response to another critique of Gutiérrez that has emerged within the Radical Orthodoxy movement. Daniel Bell criticizes the theology of Gutiérrez for insufficiently addressing what he describes as 'the nature of capitalism as a discipline of desire'.[55] According to Bell, the three levels of liberation delineated by Gutiérrez lead to a 'differentiated vision of life' and an 'insistence upon the independence and autonomy of each of the realms or dimensions'.[56] The result of this differentiation is that the personal and spiritual level is abandoned to capitalism's control of human desire while the public and political level is subjected to the structures of statecraft. Bell argues that in liberation theology 'the state remains the great hope for countering the depredations of the capitalist order', but in so doing, 'liberationists fail to appreciate how savage capitalism ... renders even the "free space" of civil society a form of discipline and control'.[57] This inadequacy finds acute expression in the call to justice that is heard within the theology of liberation. When expressed within this framework the language of justice will be drawn into the service of a desire disciplined by capitalism on the one hand and be subjected to the structures of the state on the other. Bell observes that 'the banner behind which much of capitalism's opposition rallies is "justice"' but he seeks to argue that 'justice so conceived does not accurately describe the therapy that Christianity offers in the hopes of liberating desire from capitalist discipline'.[58] A concept of justice forged within a differentiated vision of life will be unable to offer a path towards liberation. It will rather function as yet another technology through which capitalism is able to further discipline human desire.

In the previous chapter, I sought to demonstrate that, far from insisting on the independence and autonomy of the three levels of liberation, Gutiérrez is concerned to emphasize their interrelation. In the interrelation and interdependence of these levels, his vision of liberation does indeed seek to confront the 'discipline of desire' through which capitalism exerts its control. The structural finds its meaning in the spiritual and the spiritual is lived in the concrete contexts of the structural. Gutiérrez does not insulate the machinations of statecraft from the dynamics of desire. Rather, he affirms both their inner coherence and interdependence.

This interdependence is evident in the vision of justice that emerges in Gutiérrez's meditation on the book of Job. Far from exemplifying a separation between the levels of liberation as Bell argues, the justice that is encountered in the book of Job is made known amid the intimate inter-

The Faithful Praxis Through which a New Humanity is Forged

action of these levels. Gutiérrez discerns at the very heart of the book a drama in which the Lord does, to adopt the language of Bell, draw Job towards a liberation of his desire. It is in the midst of his 'joyous encounter with the Lord'[59] that Job, like the prodigal son, is made to know that he cannot 'confine paternal love within a narrow conception of justice'.[60] It is not that Job is called to abandon his concern for justice. Rather, he must understand the justice of the God who lives rather than that of the idols who bring death. As Gutiérrez observes: 'Grace is not opposed to the quest of justice, nor does it play it down; on the contrary, it gives it its full meaning.'[61] This grace is made known to Job in the midst of a personal encounter in which he is overwhelmed by the love of God. It is his desire for justice that leads him to the Lord, and it is an encounter with the Lord that liberates this desire to seek its satisfaction in his gracious love.

A praxis that fails to address the desires of the human heart is a praxis that will fail to liberate humanity from the structures in which it is bound. The theology of Gutiérrez, as evident in his commentary on the book of Job, weaves together the prophetic language of public denunciation and the mystical language of personal and spiritual transformation. The one is impossible without the other because 'both languages are necessary and therefore inseparable; they also feed and correct each other'.[62] Together they call for an encounter with the Lord that touches and transforms the depths of human desire so that the believer may also say: '"You seduced me, Lord and I let myself be seduced" (Jer. 20.7).'[63]

We Drink from Our Own Wells and the action of life in the Spirit

Gutiérrez ends his meditation on Job by concluding that the truth disclosed through the drama of the text is the same as that which is made known to us by Christ: 'This mystery is the one proclaimed by the dead and risen Son of God. It is the mystery that we come to know when his Spirit impels us to say "Abba! Father!".'[64] As this encounter with God and neighbour evokes a faithful judgement in the believer, they are in turn led into the life of the Spirit. Gutiérrez offers a reflection on this life of loving action in the Spirit in his book *We Drink from Our Own Wells*. According to him, this final step of the pastoral cycle is taken through an encounter with Jesus and lived in the life of the Spirit.

Gustavo Gutiérrez and the Liberative Sight of Christ

Loving action and life from Christ

The life of the believer is forged through an encounter with Christ and this encounter establishes both the origin and the trajectory of that life. It is both source and course. Observing that 'to encounter the Lord is first to be encountered by the Lord', Gutiérrez concludes that it is 'in this encounter we discover ... what the mission is that has been entrusted to us'.[65] The identity of Christ is made known in the character of his mission and so to confess this Christ is to commit to this mission.[66]

An encounter with Jesus forges a new humanity because it is a work of conversion in the lives of individuals and communities by which they turn to each other in love. Gutiérrez argues that 'a conversion is the starting point of every spiritual journey' and that this conversion must involve 'a break with the life lived up to that point'.[67] Observing that 'if we love others, we love them in their social contexts', he concludes that such love will be expressed through a solidarity with others in those social contexts.[68] For this reason 'the sincerity of our conversion to the Lord is to be judged by the action to which this concern leads'.[69] To have turned to the Lord is to be turned to the neighbour. This commitment to the Lord in solidarity with the neighbour 'is a work of concrete authentic love ... The solidarity is not with "the poor" in the abstract but with human beings of flesh and bone.'[70] An encounter with the Lord leads the believer into the mission of the Lord and so into a loving action in solidarity with the poor. It is a break from a life structured by the idolatry of power and greed and the inbreaking of a new life lived in communion with God and the neighbour.

The conversion worked through this encounter with the Lord unfolds in the lives of believers and their communities by grace. Just as the encounter calls the believer into the mission of Jesus, it also places this mission within the context of grace. Calling his readers to a 'realistic and effective' participation in the work of God in history, Gutiérrez cautions that 'the encounter with God results from divine initiative' and for that reason 'creates an impact of gratitude that should permeate the entire Christian life'.[71] If the encounter with Jesus is a gift of grace, then 'gratuitousness is an atmosphere in which the entire quest for effectiveness is bathed'.[72] The believer moves towards the neighbour in love when they are moved by God in his grace. Grace gives life to the work of liberation because grace is the truth of liberation disclosed in the life of Christ. The encounter with the Lord that leads the believer into his mission does so as it envelops the believer in his grace.

The Faithful Praxis Through which a New Humanity is Forged

Loving action and life in the Spirit

As Gutiérrez reflects on the life and loving action of the believer in the third section of *Wells*, he moves from a description of conversion and the requirement for solidarity (chapter 6) to an account of grace as the 'atmosphere' in which this effective action takes place (chapter 7). While these two chapters offer a portrait of the loving action that is forged through an encounter with Christ, the three remaining chapters of the book may be read as a meditation on the life of the Spirit to which this encounter leads. These chapters exemplify the 'collective and incarnate spirituality' that Boff ascribes to the work as a whole.[73] As they call believers to life in the Spirit, they display the unity of both aspects of this phrase: the Spirit is made known in life and life made possible by the Spirit.

The final chapters of *Wells* describe three facets of this life in the Spirit. It will provoke joy in the context of suffering (chapter 8); it will call us to spiritual childhood in concrete contexts of poverty (chapter 9); and it will be lived in both solitude and community (chapter 10). At each point there is a unity of both the exigencies of life and the gracious presence of the Spirit as Gutiérrez renders a portrait of the loving action to which the believer is called. As he describes the joy that will characterize the life of the believer in the Spirit, it is shown to arise out of and lead God's people through the concrete experiences of suffering. It is a 'paschal joy that is proper to a time of martyrdom' that confronts the reality of death with the hope of resurrection.[74] Such a hope is 'in no sense an evasion of concrete history; on the contrary it leads to a redoubling of effort in the struggle against what brings death'.[75] The more that believers are confronted by the realities of suffering and death, the more need they have for the promise and power of the resurrection. Where this hope of the resurrection is encountered in the midst of those realities of suffering and death, the believer and their community are moved to joy. It is in the experience of this 'paschal joy' that 'our fears, doubts and discouragement ... are routed by the power of God's love'.[76] Between the historical reality of suffering and the divine promise of liberation lies 'the road of the "new humankind"'.[77] Where suffering is ignored the call to hope cannot be heard. Where the call to hope is not heard this path to liberation cannot be truly seen.

A life that walks this path of 'paschal joy' will be characterized by a spiritual childhood that is expressed in solidarity with the poor. Gutiérrez argues that the concept of spiritual childhood allows the church to express the integrity of her commitment to spiritual and material poverty: 'Spiritual childhood is one of the most important concepts in the gospel for it describes the outlook of the person who accepts the gift of divine filiation and responds to it by building fellowship.'[78] This interplay between divine filiation and human fellowship is the dynamic by which the believer is to live the call to loving action. According to Gutiérrez, it is only a loving surrender to the Father that will allow an authentic and truly effective service of his children. Filiation leads to fellowship and fellowship is the experience of filiation. It is as the Father shares the Spirit of sonship with his people that they are able to authentically and effectively live a life of loving action.

The path of paschal joy is to be walked by those in whom a spiritual childhood has been born. Gutiérrez concludes *Wells* by showing how this life is born in us both individually and in community. To give oneself to the neighbour in their suffering does not simply mean 'going into that world ... but rather emerging from within it'.[79] To share so intimately in this suffering is to share also in the isolation and loneliness that sufferings bring. Gutiérrez cautions that the call to liberative and loving action must not be heard as a call to 'scattered commitment and an unmitigated activism'.[80] Instead, it is a life that is expressed in and sustained by the Eucharist. It is when the gift of the Eucharist is received by those who share in suffering that the Spirit draws us into its meaning. To share in the Eucharist is to share together in death and resurrection, solitude and community. It is received through the Spirit as the gift of the God who gives himself to us in his Son and calls for us as his children to live in this self-giving love.

In the closing chapters of *Wells*, Gutiérrez reflects on the life in the Spirit that emerges from an encounter with Christ. It is a life of loving action made possible by the power of the Spirit in concrete contexts of commitment to the poor. The loving action of the believer is lived as they walk the path of paschal joy with an attitude of spiritual childhood that is forged in the interplay between community and solitude.

The broken body and the life of Christ

The account of loving action that is expressed in the theology of Gutiérrez provides a response to a further critique that has been developed from the perspective of Radical Orthodoxy. I have engaged with the concerns raised by John Milbank and Daniel Bell, who critique him for failing to be either effectively liberative or faithfully theological. Milbank has objected to the process through which Gutiérrez arrives at a sight of the poor and the oppressed. In the work of Bell there is a criticism of the

The Faithful Praxis Through which a New Humanity is Forged

judgement to which this sight leads. I will now consider the argument of William Cavanaugh that the action called for by Gutiérrez and other theologians of liberation fails to provide a path towards the liberation that they seek.

According to Cavanaugh, Gutiérrez presents social reality as something to be known prior to and apart from faith. In contrast, 'the Christian brings the eyes of faith to the reading of "reality"; she reads the world not as autonomous but as already enfolded in the Christian narrative of the promises of God through Jesus Christ'.[81] A response to this concern is implicit in the arguments that I have developed while engaging with Milbank and Bell earlier in this chapter. I would like at this point, however, to give particular consideration to what Cavanaugh describes as the consequence of the theology of Gutiérrez for the liberative action of the church. Cavanaugh criticizes Gutiérrez for participating in a 'disappearance of the church as a social body' that renders it unable to imagine and inaugurate a truly liberative political reality.[82] This disappearance takes place as the church 'assumes its norms from the political arena and only its abstract motivation from its faith'.[83] While this disappearance of the church cedes social space to the violence of state control, it is in such ecclesial practices as the Eucharist that Christians are called 'to become the true body of Christ, and to bring to light the suffering of others by making that suffering visible in their own bodies'.[84] The united body of Christ encountered in the church and forged through a sharing in the broken body of the Eucharist can offer resistance to the violence of a state that seeks to break the social 'body' in its demand of subjection and its threat of disappearance. It is only through the 'complex set of practices and ways of seeing which are learned in the community of the followers of Jesus' that the church can make visible that which has disappeared and unite that which has been broken.[85]

A thorough engagement with the argument offered by Cavanaugh would need to examine not only his analysis of liberation, but also his account of the influence of Jacques Maritain's thought on the theology of Gustavo Gutiérrez. It is clear that the ecclesiology of Gutiérrez lacks the extended and explicit analysis that is present in the work of Cavanaugh. However, over the course of this chapter and the one that preceded it, I have brought to the surface themes that course through the work of Gutiérrez as a whole. It is interesting that Milbank and Cavanaugh engage primarily with his theology as it is expressed in *A Theology of Liberation*. Furthermore, these engagements appear to treat him as a representative of broader frameworks being explored. When Gutiérrez is read as a representative of Rahner's metaphysic or an expression of

Gustavo Gutiérrez and the Liberative Sight of Christ

Maritain's political theology it is more difficult to be sensitive to the nuance and texture of his work as a whole. A careful reading of texts from different stages of his theological project shows the critique raised by Cavanaugh to be misplaced. Gutiérrez is indeed concerned to make the body visible. As I observed earlier, those whom Las Casas began to see may have been found outside of the church. Yet Las Casas learned to see within the context of the church. As Las Casas contemplated the eucharistic body amid the ecclesial body, he learned to see the suffering bodies around him – and to see in them the broken body of Christ.[86] It is in the context of Scripture and sacrament that Las Casas learns to see, and moved by that sight begins to respond.

Throughout his work, Gutiérrez does indeed call for the world to be read within a metanarrative expressed by sacrament and Scripture. What may be implicit at other points in his theological project finds explicit expression in *We Drink from Our Own Wells*. As Gutiérrez reflects on a life of loving action in the Spirit, he describes a praxis whose meaning is disclosed in the eucharistic life of the church. Rather than abstract liberative praxis from the Christian metanarrative encountered in the life and teaching of the church, Gutiérrez contends that, 'the breaking of bread is at once the point of departure and the point of arrival of the Christian community. ... it is both the expression and the task of the whole church'.[87] In a sequence that resonates with Cavanaugh's conclusion to his book *Torture and Eucharist*, Gutiérrez describes the way in which the practice of the church offers comfort within and strengthens resistance against violence and oppression:

> Against the background of the poverty and exploitation in which the majority of Latin Americans live, against the background of their emaciated, sometimes massacred, bodies, the Spirit deepens in us the meaning of the Eucharist as an act of thanksgiving to the Father for sharing with us the body of the dead and resurrected Christ.[88]

For Gutiérrez, a truly liberative praxis takes place when the church, in the power of the Spirit, lives out their encounter with the Son. Learned and lived within the community of the church, this praxis makes visible the broken and resurrected body of Christ.

The Faithful Praxis Through which a New Humanity is Forged

Conclusion

As Gutiérrez seeks to proclaim God as Father in a world that is inhumane, he calls for a practical commitment to the neighbour that is formed by faith and expressed in love. In this chapter I have traced the movement by which this word is heard and this work unfolds. This movement proceeds along a path from sight through judgement to action. Gutiérrez calls the believer to see the reality lived by the neighbour who stands before them, to understand the truth given by the God who reveals himself to them, and to live in the love of the Spirit who dwells among them. A new and liberative humanity lives in this dynamic as sight, judgement and action give rise to ever clearer vision, ever deeper understanding and ever more effective action on behalf of their neighbour. If believers are to proclaim the truth of God and their neighbour they must be led by God along the path of sight, judgement and action in communion with the humanity to whom and by whom they speak.

Notes

1 For an introduction to Joseph Cardijn's pastoral practice, see Gerard-Rainer Horn, *Western European Liberation Theology: The first wave (1924–1959)* (Oxford: Oxford University Press, 2008), pp. 5–18.

2 For the ways in which the theology of liberation arose out of and moved beyond the theology and practice of Catholic Action, see Horn, *Western European Liberation Theology*, pp. 291–301.

3 While Milbank and Bell may be more self-consciously placing themselves within this framework, I follow Mary Doak in her association of Cavanaugh with the concerns and convictions that find expression within Radical Orthodoxy. Mary Doak, 'The politics of Radical Orthodoxy: a Catholic critique', *Theological Studies* 68, no. 2 (2007), pp. 368–93. Cavanaugh also draws on the analysis of Milbank to summarize his own critique of Gutiérrez. William T. Cavanaugh, *Torture and Eucharist: Theology, politics, and the Body of Christ*, Challenges in Contemporary Theology (Oxford: Blackwell, 1998), p. 180.

4 Gustavo Gutiérrez, *Las Casas: In search of the poor of Jesus Christ* (Eugene, OR: Wipf & Stock, 2003), p. 4.

5 Gutiérrez, *Las Casas*, p. 456.

6 Gutiérrez, *Las Casas*, p. 11.

7 For a chronology of the life and work of Las Casas, see Gutiérrez, *Las Casas*, p. xix.

8 Gutiérrez, *Las Casas*, p. 45.

9 Gutiérrez, *Las Casas*, p. 6.

10 Gutiérrez, *Las Casas*, p. 7.

11 Gutiérrez, *Las Casas*, p. 41.

12 Gutiérrez, *Las Casas*, p. 350.

13 Gutiérrez, *Las Casas*, p. 352.
14 Gustavo Gutiérrez, 'Sermon: Gutiérrez on the liberating of man born blind', *New Blackfriars* 70, no. 826 (April 1989), p. 159.
15 Gutiérrez, *Las Casas*, p. 6.
16 Gutiérrez notes the way in which the Latin translation of the text offered by Las Casas 'is not very literal, but it shows us, by its reinforcement of certain expressions in the original, his own understanding of the text'. Gutiérrez, *Las Casas*, p. 49.
17 Gutiérrez, *Las Casas*, p. 48.
18 Gutiérrez, *Las Casas*, p. 6.
19 Gutiérrez, *Las Casas*, p. 47.
20 Gutiérrez, *Las Casas*, p. 48.
21 John Milbank, *Theology and Social Theory: Beyond secular reason*, Signposts in Theology (Oxford: Blackwell, 1990), p. 207.
22 Milbank, *Theology and Social Theory*, p. 236.
23 Milbank, *Theology and Social Theory*, p. 250.
24 Milbank, *Theology and Social Theory*, p. 240.
25 Milbank, *Theology and Social Theory*, p. 249.
26 Milbank, *Theology and Social Theory*, p. 249.
27 Gustavo Gutiérrez, *A Theology of Liberation: History, politics, and salvation*, trans. Caridad Inda and John Eagleson (London: SCM Press, 2010), p. 235.
28 Gutiérrez, *A Theology of Liberation*, p. 236.
29 Gutiérrez, *A Theology of Liberation*, p. 241.
30 Gutiérrez, *Las Casas*, p. 47.
31 Milbank, *Theology and Social Theory*, p. 239.
32 Gutiérrez, *Las Casas*, p. 411.
33 Gutiérrez, *Las Casas*, p. 41.
34 Gustavo Gutiérrez, *On Job: God-talk and the suffering of the innocent*, trans. Matthew J. O'Connell (Maryknoll, NY: Orbis Books, 1987), p. xi.
35 Gutiérrez, *On Job*, p. xiv.
36 Gutiérrez, *On Job*, p. 27.
37 Gutiérrez, *On Job*, p. 29.
38 Gutiérrez, *On Job*, p. 31.
39 Gutiérrez, *On Job*, p. 32.
40 Gutiérrez, *On Job*, p. 40.
41 Gutiérrez, *On Job*, p. 47.
42 Gutiérrez, *On Job*, p. 48.
43 Gutiérrez, *On Job*, p. 41.
44 Gutiérrez, *On Job*, p. 30.
45 Gutiérrez, *On Job*, p. 38.
46 Gutiérrez, *On Job*, p. 49.
47 Gutiérrez, *On Job*, p. 66.
48 Gutiérrez, *On Job*, p. 69.
49 Gutiérrez, *On Job*, p. 77.
50 Gutiérrez, *On Job*, p. 80.
51 Gutiérrez, *On Job*, p. 84.
52 Gutiérrez, *On Job*, p. 92.
53 Gutiérrez, *On Job*, p. 96.
54 Gutiérrez, *On Job*, p. 94.

55 Daniel M. Bell, *Liberation Theology After the End of History: The refusal to cease suffering*, Radical Orthodoxy Series (London: Routledge, 2001), p. 86.
56 Daniel M. Bell, '"Men of Stone and Children of Struggle": Latin American liberationists at the end of history', *Modern Theology* 14, no. 1 (January 1998), p. 117.
57 Bell, *Liberation Theology after the End of History*, p. 70.
58 Bell, *Liberation Theology after the End of History*, pp. 86–7.
59 Gutiérrez, *On Job*, p. 87.
60 Gutiérrez, *On Job*, p. 90.
61 Gutiérrez, *On Job*, p. 87.
62 Gutiérrez, *On Job*, p. 95.
63 Describing the aftermath of Job's encounter with the Lord, Gutiérrez observes, 'Like Jeremiah in a passage to which reference must be made in any effort to understand the book of Job, Job might have said at this point: "You seduced me, Lord and I let myself be seduced" (Jer. 20.7).' Gutiérrez, *On Job*, p. 87.
64 Gutiérrez, *On Job*, p. 103.
65 Gustavo Gutiérrez, *We Drink From Our Own Wells: The spiritual journey of a people* (Maryknoll, NY: Orbis Books, 2003), p. 38.
66 Gutiérrez, *Our Own Wells*, p. 50.
67 Gutiérrez, *Our Own Wells*, p. 95.
68 Gutiérrez, *Our Own Wells*, p. 101.
69 Gutiérrez, *Our Own Wells*, p. 103.
70 Gutiérrez, *Our Own Wells*, p. 104.
71 Gutiérrez, *Our Own Wells*, p. 107.
72 Gutiérrez, *Our Own Wells*, p. 109.
73 Clodovis Boff, *Feet-on-the-Ground Theology: A Brazilian journey*, trans. Philip Berryman (Eugene, OR: Wipf & Stock, 2008), p. 105.
74 Gutiérrez, *Our Own Wells*, p. 114.
75 Gutiérrez, *Our Own Wells*, p. 118.
76 Gutiérrez, *Our Own Wells*, p. 119.
77 Gutiérrez, *Our Own Wells*, p. 120.
78 Gutiérrez, *Our Own Wells*, p. 127.
79 Gutiérrez, *Our Own Wells*, p. 125.
80 Gutiérrez, *Our Own Wells*, p. 129.
81 William T. Cavanaugh, 'The ecclesiologies of Medellín and the lessons of the base communities', *CrossCurrents* 44, no. 1 (1994), p. 77.
82 Cavanaugh, *Torture and Eucharist*, p. 180.
83 Cavanaugh, 'The ecclesiologies of Medellín and the lessons of the base communities', p. 77.
84 Cavanaugh, *Torture and Eucharist*, p. 281.
85 Cavanaugh, 'The ecclesiologies of Medellín and the lessons of the base communities', p. 77.
86 Gutiérrez, *Las Casas*, p. 47.
87 Gutiérrez, *Our Own Wells*, p. 134.
88 Gutiérrez, *Our Own Wells*, pp. 133–4. In the final paragraphs of his book, Cavanaugh concludes, 'The Eucharist ... creates martyrs out of victims by calling the church to acts of self-sacrifice and remembrance, honouring in Jesus's sacrifice the countless witnesses to the conflict between the powers of life and the powers of death.' Cavanaugh, *Torture and Eucharist*, p. 281.

7

Christ and the Liberation of Humanity Through Faithful Praxis

In the previous chapter I outlined the praxis by which the liberative anthropology of Gutiérrez is to take shape. In this chapter I will ask whether the content and the context of this praxis inhibit the very encounter with God and neighbour in which this praxis is to find its life. According to Gutiérrez, a liberative praxis takes place through an encounter with both God and neighbour in their otherness and concrete particularity. Where the sight of either God or neighbour is obscured, the path to liberation is lost. If Part One of this project concluded with a consideration of the person of Christ, Part Two will now conclude with a consideration of his work. In Chapter 4 I explored the person of Christ as it is rendered by the narrative of human history recounted by Gutiérrez. I now turn in this chapter to explore a tension that emerges between the work of Christ and the praxis called for by Gutiérrez.

This tension will be illuminated by two arguments made by David Kelsey. The first concerns the irreducible and inseparable diversity of the 'canon-unifying' narratives through which Kelsey's anthropology is expressed.[1] The second concerns the irreducible and inseparable loves of God and neighbour that such an anthropology describes.[2] According to Kelsey, the integrity of both God and humanity will only be preserved when the scriptural narratives of God's relation to humanity and the scriptural calls to love of God and neighbour are heard in their unity and diversity. Gutiérrez rejects these distinctions and his account of praxis takes shape within a framework that seeks to proclaim the unity of both God's relations to creation and the loves to which humanity is called. In what follows, I will explore the theological consequences of this methodological commitment by Gutiérrez.

Christ and the Liberation of Humanity Through Faithful Praxis

The context of praxis: the story of salvation

Both Kelsey and Gutiérrez make communion with Christ a defining characteristic of what it is to be human.[3] The question that divides them is how to describe the work of salvation through which this communion is given and received. While Gutiérrez places the movement towards communion within a unified narrative of God's work in creation, salvation and consummation, Kelsey cautions that such a unified narrative obscures the particularity of Christ's work and so the specificity of his identity.

Gustavo Gutiérrez: the universal presence of Christ in the narrative of liberation

As I have shown, Gutiérrez recounts a unified history through which humanity is led into a liberative communion with God and neighbour and, as he recounts the history of liberation, his narrative subsumes the story of salvation into a single plot that moves from creation to eschatological consummation. I outlined this unified narrative in Chapter 2 and in Chapter 3 explored how this narrative is to be discerned. This history finds its origin, purpose and meaning in Christ in whom is revealed the truth of humanity. As Gutiérrez famously contends, 'the fundamental affirmation is clear: there is only one history – a "Christo-finalized" history'.[4] According to Gutiérrez, just as 'the eschatological horizon is present in the heart of the Exodus', so too the work of Christ 'is conceived of as a re-creation and presented in the context of creation'.[5] Salvation unfolds as 'assuming its destiny in history, humankind forges itself'[6] and identifies with the 'movement of human self-generation initiated by the work of creation'.[7]

However, if the story of salvation is told in such a way, there is a danger that the concrete particularity of Christ will be dissolved into a liberating and perfecting presence. It seems that the narrative outlined by Gutiérrez is at least vulnerable to this danger. Tracing a 'twofold process' in which a 'universalization of the presence of God' is matched by 'an internalization, or rather, an integration of this presence',[8] he concludes that 'Christ is the point of convergence of both processes'.[9] As the narrative recounted by Gutiérrez moves from creation to consummation, the distinctive character of Christ and his work tends to recede from view. When he recalls the 'evolution of the revelation of God's presence in the midst of his people', the individual particularity of Jesus appears to give way to a universal presence of God with his people.[10] Gutiérrez describes how 'God became flesh and is present in human history'[11] and when he speaks of Jesus as the 'new tent of meeting' in whom we are all 'called to become one', the Christ in whom humanity finds this unity lives in the actions of humanity in history.[12]

As Gutiérrez draws Christ and humanity together into a unified narrative of liberation, the particularity of Christ and his work tends to be absorbed into the universal identity and action of his people. This tension is evident in Gutiérrez's call for faith in the God 'whom we recognise in his works of rescue and liberation – in his Son become human history'.[13] If God is to be recognized in his works and these works are to be known in his Son, then there must be in Jesus a work that is distinct from and external to the ongoing life and work of his people. However, as I observed in Chapter 4, in his construction of the *totus Christus*, Gutiérrez places such an emphasis on the presence of Christ in his people that it becomes difficult to discern the identity of Christ as a person distinct from his people. If the 'coming of God in the flesh' is characterized as 'his Son become human history', then the personal becomes absorbed into the universal. Where the distinctive work of Christ is obscured, the call to 'recognize' God in Christ is undermined.

In the narrative recounted by Gutiérrez, the person and work of Christ in salvation are absorbed into, and realized through, the life and action of his people as they move towards their eschatological liberation. Little consideration is given to a work that is particular to Christ and little space is left for an identity that is particular to Christ. The narrative of salvation is drawn into the movement from creation to consummation and, as a consequence, the call of Gutiérrez to a faithful praxis is expressed within a context that obscures the distinct and personal work of God in Christ.

David Kelsey: the unique person of Christ in the narrative of salvation

This tension within the theology of Gutiérrez is further illuminated through comparison with the methodology of David Kelsey. Kelsey argues that theological anthropology must have a 'triplex structure' that corresponds to the 'triple plot' of Christian canonical scriptural stories.[14] These three narratives describe the 'three inseparable but irreducibly distinct ways in which God relates to all else'[15] and are woven together in a 'triple helix' around the person of Christ.[16] Where the distinction of these narratives is lost from view Kelsey contends that the work of God particular to each of them is obscured. The relationship of God to humanity must be

Christ and the Liberation of Humanity Through Faithful Praxis

recounted as 'stories of God relating creatively, stories of God relating to draw all else to eschatological consummation, and stories of God relating to all else to reconcile it when it has become estranged from God'.[17] For Kelsey, if anthropology is to be truly theological it must be structured by these relations of God to creation. If theology is to faithfully describe the condition of humanity, these relations of God to creation must be recognized as the context that gives humankind its meaning. When these narratives are separated from each other or subsumed into one another, the integrity of both theology and anthropology begins to unravel.[18] God can only be known according to his relations to creation and humanity can only be known as those to whom God so relates.

These distinctions are used by Kelsey to trace a portrait of Jesus Christ in his concrete particularity. Where the three narratives are reduced into a single- or double-plotted account of God's relation to creation, one or other way of God's relating to creation in Christ will not be properly heard.[19] This unified narrative cannot offer a clear portrait of Christ because it does not clearly recount the work of God in Christ. In particular, unless the work of God in Christ to save is distinguished from the work of God in Christ to create and lead to eschatological consummation, this narrative of salvation, and the identity of Jesus Christ rendered through it, will be occluded. In such tellings, the stories of salvation may simply become 'additional moments of God relating creatively' or perhaps 'symbolic expressions' or 'instrumental moments'[20] in a movement towards eschatological consummation.[21] Only when the distinctive narrative of salvation is clearly heard will the particular identity of Jesus be clearly discerned.

The narrative of salvation as it is recounted by Kelsey unfolds as the work of God in Christ and it is important to note that, for him, the particularity of the person of Christ determines the distinctive quality of this work. Through his reading of the Gospels' narratives, Kelsey argues that 'from beginning to end, these narratives make essential to Jesus's identity that he is uniquely God related'.[22] The narrative of salvation is the story of Jesus, in his unique relation to God, coming to humanity in its estrangement from God. Kelsey summarizes the narrative as a work in which God comes among humanity to be such for humanity that 'God effects an exchange. In solidarity with them in the vicious cycles of their proximate contexts, the triune God takes on their living death and draws them into God's triune life.'[23] The movement of this narrative contrasts the God-relatedness of Jesus with the estrangement of humankind and pivots on the exchange effected by God. The redemption of humanity in their estrangement from God is only possible through Jesus in his unique relation with God. The narrative of salvation is the story of how God 'relates to estranged human beings' in Jesus so that they might share 'in the same status in relation to God that Jesus has in his creaturely humanity'.[24] To use Kelsey's terminology, salvation unfolds eccentrically. As he argues,

> personal bodies' identities flourish when their identities are radically eccentric. Their identities flourish when they are defined as being related to from outside themselves by the triune God's reconciling love in the incarnation of the 'Son sent by the Father in the radical freedom of the Spirit.'[25]

In his person and work Jesus Christ establishes the eccentric identity of humanity reconciled to God.[26] Human beings in their estrangement are – considered apart from their created goodness and eschatological glory – reconciled in Christ. They are, in Christ, *simul justus et peccator*.[27]

Expressed in such a way the distinctively Protestant flavour of Kelsey's account is evident.[28] However, while his concern to distinguish the narrative of salvation in this way might be felt to express a particularly Protestant sensibility, it is a concern that is by no means exclusive to Protestant theology. Cyril O'Regan asks 'whether the most basic structural point of the text, the undecidability and compossibility of inflections of the canonic narrative ... is totally without precedent', and concludes that 'Kelsey's theology in itself is neither systemically open nor closed to Catholic thought'.[29] In order to provide an example of this catholicity O'Regan goes on to suggest that, 'although the evidence is hardly on the surface, I think an argument can be made that there is something like an indirect and highly positive engagement with Aquinas's theocentric and specifically Trinitarian view of creation'.[30] In other words, the tripartite structure of Kelsey's anthropology both accommodates and invites interaction across theological traditions. His anthropology involves what O'Regan describes as his 'embrace of a premodern theological sensibility'.[31] This sensibility arises out of his theological tradition but at the same time opens his work out beyond this theological tradition. In this way the questions raised by Kelsey at the very least call for Gutiérrez to push further into his own tradition. While not seeking to press the theology of Gutiérrez into the system developed by Kelsey, the questions expressed within this system challenge him to be faithful to his own tradition and consistent with his own convictions. These questions may be raised with a distinctively Protestant accent, but they are questions that can be heard expressed within a broadly catholic language. The concerns

Christ and the Liberation of Humanity Through Faithful Praxis

that emerge in conversation with Kelsey invite Gutiérrez to draw on the resources of his own tradition to develop a response.

The sight of the neighbour in the story of salvation

Where the story of salvation is not clearly heard, the work of Christ will not be discerned in its distinctive particularity. What is more, where Christ is not clearly seen, the neighbour cannot truly be known.

I have outlined the way in which Kelsey distinguishes the story of salvation from the stories of creation and consummation in order to express the loving relations that are particular to each. The love in which God works to save humanity in Christ is 'not a love responding to such actual creaturely goodness', nor the eschatological love of 'desiring a blessing for them and giving it in terms set by their creatureliness'.[32] Rather, the story of salvation is the story of God's love for humanity in their estrangement from him.[33] The Christ who in this story is characterized as the agape and grace of God establishes the identity of the humanity to whom he has come to save. The Christ who relates to humanity to reconcile them in their estrangement calls for humanity to be seen now as reconciled in their estrangement. The story of salvation calls humanity to 'an acknowledgement of their shared condition of being in Christ'.[34] Such an acknowledgement will recognize the complexity of this condition. It will accept that in Christ 'it is who they are that is *at once* unlovely and the object of God's love'.[35] The humanity whose identity is found in Christ through the story of salvation – and considered apart from their creational goodness and eschatological transformation – is to be recognized in their 'estrangement from themselves, one another, and God'.[36]

This characterization of human identity as revealed in Christ through the story of salvation differs from the conception of human identity that is forged through the narrative recounted by Gutiérrez. His narrative of liberation moves forward through the commitment to the neighbour in faithful praxis. Human identity is not located eccentrically in Christ but unfolds historically in praxis. As Thomas Lewis observes, within this account of human identity, 'Gutiérrez presupposes a profound unity to the self, such that the fundamental option is manifest in all one's important actions.'[37]

Human identity is realized in the response to grace that calls every person to the work of liberation.[38] Rather than each person with their neighbour being at once estranged and reconciled in Christ, Gutiérrez appears to place each person at a point of decision where they must choose either estrangement or reconciliation with their neighbours in Christ. The identity of humanity in Christ unfolds in their transformation and liberation in history. Union with Christ is not described 'eccentrically' but rather in the actuality of human response. While the 'eccentricity' proposed by Kelsey may be shaped by his Protestant theological commitments, the concern that he expresses must be addressed. I argue that Gutiérrez's construction of human identity tends to obscure the complexity of the concrete conditions of human life. Where the narrative of salvation in Christ is absorbed into a single story of transformation and liberation, the identity of each person in Christ becomes dependent on their relation to the neighbour in Christ. In this way the unified narrative recounted by Gutiérrez inhibits his ability to portray both the particularity of Christ in his distinctive work and the identity of the neighbour in their concrete complexity.

The content of faithful praxis: the response of love

While Gutiérrez calls believers to a faithful praxis the distinctive work of God in Christ recedes from view. This is the consequence of both the context and content of the praxis that he describes. The context of this praxis is a narrative movement from creation to consummation which tends to inhibit an account of the distinctive work of Christ. In a similar way, the content of this praxis is a single love orientated to both God and neighbour which is in danger of obscuring the distinctive and personal love lived by Christ.

Kelsey and the distinction between the two loves

Kelsey argues that the work of Christ in salvation must establish the contours of the love called for by that salvation. Given that the narrative of salvation recounts God's work in Christ to reconcile estranged humanity, the love revealed in this work is 'grace in the strict sense: radically free loving of unlovely creatures'.[39] According to Kelsey the distinctive feature of God's *agape* to humankind is that it is a love for creatures in spite of their unloveliness in their estrangement from God and each other.[40] It is not a love that defines humanity according to creational goodness or eschatological transformation but rather establishes that 'it is who they are that they are at once unlovely and the objects of God's love'.[41] The love by which God acts to save in Christ is thereby to be distinguished from any love that is to be shared within reconciled humanity. This is not to imply that Kelsey's anthropology leaves no space for an imitation of, or participation in, the love of Christ. The importance of such imitation and participation is evident in the call to imagination and anticipation that is heard in Kelsey's book *Imagining Redemption*.[42] His reflections conclude with the observation that 'There is no end to such "living into" God's redemptive relating to us.'[43] The question is how this imitation and participation is construed. In other words, how the agapeic love of Christ is to be lived when transposed from the life of Christ into the life of the believer. Whereas God in Christ moves to a humanity considered in their estrangement, the love called for by this salvation is a love among those who, while estranged, have also been reconciled. The love called for by the work of salvation 'only distantly imitates' the love of God because the people who are loved are already reconciled and 'only Jesus of Nazareth is Christ to their neighbours'.[44] The context in which humanity lives and loves is established by the person and work of Christ. This 'ultimate context is defined as agape and as grace' and, according to Kelsey, 'used strictly, "grace" names the one, Jesus Christ'.[45] The distinctive love of God is found in the distinctive person of Jesus.

Having established the distinctive quality of the salvific love of God in Jesus, Kelsey cautions that the human response called for by this salvation must be two irreducible but intimately related loves for God and neighbour. Within his theology, this difference and relation not only functions to preserve the particularity of Christ in his work. This characterization of the human response to salvation also preserves the particularity of a love for God in Christ. Kelsey argues that the distinction between these loves is determined by 'the intentional object that is definitive of each set'.[46] Given the 'ontological difference' between creator and creation, the love that is directed at each must be different from the other.[47] When the two loves are conflated one or other of these objects will be lost from view. Kelsey warns that when love for God is absorbed into a love for the neighbour, God ceases to become a distinct 'intentional object' of such love: '"God" need have no other function than that of an honorific term used to evaluate and commend the human excellence of "love" for fellow human creatures as something "divine"'.[48] When the two loves are conflated the distinctive otherness of the God who is to be loved in Christ may be lost.[49] If Christ is to be considered as a person who loves and is loved, human love for God and neighbour must be at once 'dialectically interdependent'[50] and 'irreducibly different'.[51]

Gustavo Gutiérrez and the Liberative Sight of Christ

Gutiérrez and the unity of the two loves

I suggest that the love called for by Gutiérrez in his account of praxis is characterized by the conflation that Kelsey describes and suffers from the weakness against which he warns. In this way he illuminates an inconsistency that remains within Gutiérrez's work. With Rahner, Gutiérrez is cautious to distinguish a radical unity from strict identity.[52] He warns of the need to 'keep historical praxis from replacing the gift of grace'[53] and so calls for a recovery of the spirituality that makes possible 'a discourse about God that is both authentic and respectful of its object'.[54] Especially in its later stages, the work of Gutiérrez addresses the concern of critics such as George Hunsinger, who called for a theology of liberation in which 'the precedence given to God's praxis serves to mobilize rather than detract from human praxis' such that it 'might be anchored more securely in a theology of grace'.[55] As Gutiérrez seeks to place praxis in the context of grace, it is important to observe with David Kamitsuka that 'however emphatic he is about human mediation of love for God, he is equally emphatic that the two loves must be distinguished'.[56] While he proclaims the unity of these loves, Gutiérrez emphasizes the importance of their distinction. It is precisely because he so emphasizes the importance of this distinction that it is necessary to consider whether his coordination of these two loves does indeed guard against their conflation.

While Kelsey would affirm with Gutiérrez that 'it is in fact not possible to separate love of God and love of neighbour',[57] he cautions against a construction of this relation in which 'love for God is unavoidably expressed *through* love of one's neighbour'.[58] Arguing that 'it is in the making our neighbours into brothers and sisters that we receive this gift' of adoption as children of God, Gutiérrez concludes that the salvific love of God 'must be enfleshed, incarnated in history – must become history'.[59] As such he characterizes human love as an expression and continuation of the salvific love of God. Locating salvation beyond the person of Jesus and in the action of his people, Gutiérrez declares that 'we become Christians by acting as Christians'.[60] The 'gratuitousness and universality of God's *agapeic* love' are not only the condition of human love but the character of a love expressed in 'a preferential option for the poor' and a 'solidarity with those who suffer'.[61] While salvation is both gift and task, it is not realized apart from its enactment within human relationships.[62] In this way, God's act of giving Christ in love is drawn into and actualized through the human work of receiving the neighbour in love.

The way in which Gutiérrez constructs the relation of Christ to humanity risks obscuring the distinction on which such a relation depends. Once

Christ and the Liberation of Humanity Through Faithful Praxis

again, the concerns expressed by Kelsey are not to be read as a critique of any and all accounts of the unity of the church with Christ in general or as a rejection of the *totus Christus* in particular. Instead, Kelsey's concerns raise questions as to how such a unity is to be construed. This interplay of distinction and relation is evident in Baker's discussion of the *totus Christus*. She explains that 'the individual believers retain their particular identities as members of the Body, but they can no longer be understood apart from one another and Christ'.[63] The doctrine of the *totus Christus* speaks of an intimate union of the believer with Christ that does not lose the particularity of either. By contrast, a conflation of human and divine love will obscure the account of Christ as the one who loves and also inhibit the sight of Christ who is to be loved. While Kelsey portrays the particular personal identity of Jesus by tracing his unique relationship with God, Gutiérrez, by contrast, defines Christ through his relationship with all of humanity: 'God is revealed in history, and it is likewise in history that persons encounter the Word made flesh. Christ is not a private individual; the bond which links him to all persons gives him a unique historical role.'[64]

Strikingly, what is unique in Jesus is not that which makes him distinct. Rather, his uniqueness is the fact that he is present among the whole of humanity. As a consequence, 'our encounter with the Lord occurs in our encounter with others'[65] such that a conversion to Christ not only implies but is constituted by 'a conversion to the neighbour'.[66] Christ is identified with the neighbour to such an extent that Gutiérrez affirms that 'the acceptance of a personal relationship with the Lord' is possible 'in all persons, be they conscious of it or not'.[67] It is not necessary for Christ to be the intentional object of an action for that action to be an expression of a love for Christ. In this way the particularity of Christ as the one who is loved is dissolved into a presence among the neighbour in whom he is loved. When love for Christ is so construed the person of Christ recedes from view.

The theology of Gutiérrez does not simply wrestle with how to make known the God who is hidden in the humility of Jesus. Instead, his theology proclaims that 'Jesus is a hidden God' whose presence must be discerned among those whom the world does not see.[68] Jesus is both 'the hidden God of whom the prophets speak'[69] and the one who himself 'hides his presence in history, and at the same time reveals it, in the life of suffering, the struggles, the death, and the hopes of the condemned of the earth'.[70] As Gutiérrez seeks to make known the Jesus who has revealed himself as hidden in the history of the poor, the stability of his theological project depends on the adequacy of this construction of the relation between Christ and those in whom he is made known. He is clear in the conviction that where Christ is not seen, the truth of humanity may not be known. However, his account of faithful praxis obscures the sight of Christ on which such praxis depends. For Gutiérrez 'a central element of Christian faith' is the historical particularity of the incarnate saviour: 'Jesus Christ, the Son of God made man, one of us in history, a Jew, son of Mary, belonging to a particular people.'[71] A tension between this theological conviction and his methodological commitments has emerged. In his conflation of love to God and love for the neighbour he obscures the particularity of Christ as the one from whom God's love is shared and the one to whom human love is directed.

The sight of the neighbour and the unity of the two loves

Not only does such a coordination of the two loves inhibit the portrayal of Christ in his particular personal identity, it also risks obscuring the sight of the neighbour whom we are called to love. The unity that Gutiérrez ascribes to love of God and love for neighbour does not leave sufficient space for Christ to be known as a distinct intentional object. A characterization of praxis that fails to distinguish Christ will also fail to clearly discern the neighbour.

Kelsey warns that such a distinction is essential if the integrity of the neighbour is to be adequately conveyed. When love towards God is defined by the distinct intentional object of its actions, those who are loved as neighbour will be more clearly discerned in the particularity of their identity. According to Kelsey, 'enactments of practices of prayer protect intentional acts of love-as-neighbour from violating the personal identities of their human intentional objects'.[72]

In a similar way, Gutiérrez underlines the importance of a care for the integrity and particularity of the neighbour. He rejects 'a totalitarian version of history that denies the freedom of the human person'[73] and cautions that 'the neighbour is not an occasion, an instrument for becoming closer to God. We are dealing with real love of persons for their own sake.'[74] However, Gutiérrez draws the presence of Christ into the person of the neighbour in such a way as to obscure the particularity of the neighbour on which such love 'for their own sake' must be based. In fact, the warning expressed by Gutiérrez is in tension with the argument at the end of which it is raised. Observing that 'we meet God in our encounter with others',[75] he argues that 'we love God by loving our neighbour'.[76] This relation is not just inseparable but integral: 'It is not enough to say

Christ and the Liberation of Humanity Through Faithful Praxis

that love of God is inseparable from the love of one's neighbour. It must be added that love for God is unavoidably expressed *through* love of one's neighbour.'[77] Such is the unity of love for God and neighbour that the love expressed to God in the neighbour is itself the grounds of the truth and concreteness of the neighbour.[78] While Kelsey describes a love for the neighbour in Christ, what emerges in the theology of Gutiérrez is a love for Christ in the neighbour. In this construction there is a danger that the particularity and individuality of the neighbour may be displaced by an encounter with the presence of Christ. Gutiérrez asserts that the neighbour is not simply an instrument or occasion. However, his description of the neighbour as mediator of God in Christ appears to overwhelm the particularity of the neighbour with the presence of God in Christ. The danger is that this coordination of love towards God and love for neighbour will inhibit a portrayal of the neighbour in their distinctive particularity.

I contend that the theology of Gutiérrez does indeed suffer from the weakness against which Kelsey warns. His characterization of love for neighbour obscures the sight of that neighbour. If 'human existence in the last instance is nothing but a yes or no to the Lord'[79] then it is hard to see how Gutiérrez can accept 'the possibility of conversion to involve a situation in which we are fundamentally divided between the yes and the no'.[80] If the praxis through which community is formed is the actualization of a commitment, then the community so formed will be closed to those beset by division and contradiction. For Kelsey, the community formed in Christ is characterized precisely in its contradiction. By contrast Gutiérrez calls for a communion in spite of these contradictions. When love for both God and neighbour must be expressed in a resolution of these contradictions then little space is left for an acceptance of the neighbour in their 'estrangement from themselves, one another, and God'.[81] The danger is that such a love to the neighbour will result in 'forcing them into roles and laying on them expectations that they cannot possibly fulfil'.[82] To love Christ in the neighbour risks placing the imperative of personal and communal transformation ahead of the indicative of Christ's reconciliation. This danger is vividly described by Boff as he recalls an incident where a group of priests sought to engage a rural community with political projects:

> I turned around and let loose. 'Hey, folks, for the love of God, let's not put a heavier load on the burden of these poor people than they've already got. Go out there some Sunday, celebrate the Eucharist with a procession out to the fields. Then baptize and marry everyone who

comes forward. ... Let's not start making new demands on top of those they've already got. ... Everything else can come later.'[83]

In the situation described by Boff, space was not provided for a love to God amid the complexities and contradictions of community life. To truly love as neighbour such space must be given to the other – space to express their love to God apart from the commitments and actions to which such a love will inevitably lead.

Conclusion

Gutiérrez calls his readers to a praxis that moves forward in the hope of liberation and which will be characterized by a faith in, and a love for, both God and neighbour. According to him, the path towards liberation is marked at each step by an encounter with God on the one hand and an encounter with the neighbour on the other. The account of this praxis developed by Gutiérrez takes shape within a framework that seeks to proclaim the unity both of God's relations to creation and the loves to which humanity is called. By drawing Gutiérrez into conversation with Kelsey, I have argued that the sight of both Christ and neighbour that is to mark the path of praxis becomes obscured by his methodology. I contend that both the context and content of the praxis called for by Gutiérrez are susceptible to the weaknesses against which Kelsey warns.

Notes

1 David H. Kelsey, *Eccentric Existence: A theological anthropology*, 1st edn, 2 vols (Louisville, KY: Westminster John Knox Press, 2009), p. 460.

2 Kelsey, *Eccentric Existence*, p. 824.

3 Gutiérrez describes 'a reality which is itself indisputable: that all persons are in Christ efficaciously called to communion with God'. Gustavo Gutiérrez, *A Theology of Liberation: History, politics, and salvation*, trans. Caridad Inda and John Eagleson (London: SCM Press, 2010), p. 99.

4 Gutiérrez, *A Theology of Liberation*, p. 151.
5 Gutiérrez, *A Theology of Liberation*, p. 156.
6 Gutiérrez, *A Theology of Liberation*, p. 157.
7 Gutiérrez, *A Theology of Liberation*, p. 158.
8 Gutiérrez, *A Theology of Liberation*, p. 182.
9 Gutiérrez, *A Theology of Liberation*, p. 183.
10 Gutiérrez, *A Theology of Liberation*, p. 178.
11 Gustavo Gutiérrez, *The God of Life*, trans. Matthew J. O'Connell (Maryknoll, NY: Orbis Books, 1991), p. 42.

12 Gutiérrez, *The God of Life*, p. 41.
13 Gustavo Gutiérrez, *The Power of the Poor in History*, trans. Robert R. Barr (Maryknoll, NY: Orbis Books, 1983), p. 20.
14 Kelsey, *Eccentric Existence*, p. 477.
15 Kelsey, *Eccentric Existence*, p. 914.
16 Kelsey, *Eccentric Existence*, p. 897.
17 Kelsey, *Eccentric Existence*, p. 475.
18 For examples of such confusion and its consequences, see Kelsey, *Eccentric Existence*, p. 473.
19 'I suggest that the impetus to plot the canon-unifying narrative in a way that absorbs one or even two of the types of canonical stories of different ways in which God relates to all else into another type of canonical story of a way in which God relates lies in secondary theology's responsibility, and hence interest, to attend constantly to the systematic interrelations among its many proposals. More exactly, it lies in a dangerous choice of strategy to satisfy the pressure of that interest.' Kelsey, *Eccentric Existence*, p. 471. Some examples of these 'dangers' are provided in Kelsey, *Eccentric Existence*, pp. 472–4.
20 Kelsey, *Eccentric Existence*, p. 464.
21 Kelsey, *Eccentric Existence*, p. 465.
22 Kelsey, *Eccentric Existence*, p. 634.
23 Kelsey, *Eccentric Existence*, p. 646.
24 Kelsey, *Eccentric Existence*, p. 1048.
25 Kelsey, *Eccentric Existence*, p. 718.
26 This is not to say that this identity remains external to humanity or is somehow imposed on humanity. By 'defining our ultimate and proximate contexts', the work of God in Christ defines humanity by establishing a truth that is 'intrinsic to who they most basically are'. Kelsey, *Eccentric Existence*, p. 733.
27 Kelsey, *Eccentric Existence*, p. 646.
28 Karen Kilby observes distinctively Protestant and Roman Catholic 'proclivities' towards particular theological paradoxes: 'There is a proclivity towards paradox in the sin/grace opposition in Protestant thought, or at least in one recognizable strand of Protestant thought, and there is a proclivity towards paradox in the nature/grace complementarity of Catholic thought, or at least in what I take to be the better examples of Catholic theology. My proposal is not that there is necessarily a contradiction on either side, but that in both camps we find a tendency to hold certain patterns of thought, certain patterns of affirmation, together, unsynthesised, rather than force them into a single, fully articulable, fully graspable, unity.' Karen Kilby, 'Catholicism, Protestantism and the theological location of paradox: nature, grace, sin' in *Ecclesia Semper Reformanda: Renewal and reform beyond polemics*, ed. Peter De Mey and Wim François, Bibliotheca Ephemeridum Theologicarum Lovaniensium 306 (Leuven: Peeters, 2020), p. 164.
29 Cyril O'Regan, 'Eccentric Existence and the Catholic tradition' in *The Theological Anthropology of David Kelsey: Responses to Eccentric Existence*, ed. G. Outka (Grand Rapids, MI: William B. Eerdmans, 2016), p. 55.
30 O'Regan, 'Eccentric Existence and the Catholic Tradition', p. 65.
31 O'Regan, 'Eccentric Existence and the Catholic Tradition', p. 89.
32 Kelsey, *Eccentric Existence*, p. 705.
33 Kelsey, *Eccentric Existence*, p. 706.

34 Kelsey, *Eccentric Existence*, p. 711.
35 Kelsey, *Eccentric Existence*, p. 706.
36 Kelsey, *Eccentric Existence*, p. 710.
37 Thomas A. Lewis, 'Actions as the ties that bind: love, praxis, and community in the thought of Gustavo Gutiérrez', *Journal of Religious Ethics* 33, no. 3 (September 2005), p. 563.
38 Gutiérrez, *A Theology of Liberation*, p. 149.
39 Kelsey, *Eccentric Existence*, p. 707.
40 Kelsey, *Eccentric Existence*, p. 705.
41 Kelsey, *Eccentric Existence*, p. 706.
42 It is important to note Kelsey's concern to avoid the implication of interiority and subjectivity that these terms might evoke. David H. Kelsey, *Imagining Redemption* (Louisville, KY: Westminster John Knox Press, 2005), p. 70.
43 Kelsey, *Imagining Redemption*, p. 105.
44 Kelsey, *Eccentric Existence*, p. 709.
45 Kelsey, *Eccentric Existence*, p. 623.
46 Kelsey, *Eccentric Existence*, p. 816.
47 Kelsey, *Eccentric Existence*, p. 817.
48 Kelsey, *Eccentric Existence*, p. 862.
49 Kelsey outlines a number of models through which such a conflation might take shape. See Kelsey, *Eccentric Existence*, pp. 813–16.
50 Kelsey, *Eccentric Existence*, p. 827.
51 Kelsey, *Eccentric Existence*, p. 826.
52 Beyer warns that 'it should be clear that Rahner's thesis posits a radical unity, rather than identity of the two loves'. Gerald J. Beyer, 'Karl Rahner on the radical unity of the love of God and neighbour', *Irish Theological Quarterly* 68, no. 3 (September 2003), p. 264. Beyer traces Rahner's use of terms associated with identity and unity and concludes that his work 'clearly attests to his awareness of the distinction. In regard to love of God and love of neighbour, two objects exist, which are co-loved in the same act.' Beyer, 'Karl Rahner on the radical unity of the love of God and neighbour', p. 265 n. 80.
53 Gustavo Gutiérrez, *The Truth Shall Make You Free: Confrontations*, trans. Matthew J. O'Connell (Maryknoll, NY: Orbis Books, 1990), p. 35.
54 Gutiérrez, *The Truth Shall Make You Free*, p. 55.
55 George Hunsinger, 'Karl Barth and Liberation Theology', *The Journal of Religion* 63, no. 3 (1983), p. 263.
56 David G. Kamitsuka, *Theology and Contemporary Culture: Liberation, postliberal, and revisionary perspectives* (Cambridge: Cambridge University Press, 1999), p. 161.
57 Gutiérrez, *The God of Life*, p. 138.
58 Gutiérrez, *A Theology of Liberation*, p. 190. Emphasis original.
59 Gutiérrez, *The Power of the Poor in History*, p. 18.
60 Gutiérrez, *The Power of the Poor in History*, p. 17.
61 Gutiérrez, *On Job*, p. 94.
62 'The saving love of God is a gift, but its acceptance entails a commitment to one's neighbour. Christian life is located between the gratuitous gift and the obligation.' Gutiérrez, *The Truth Shall Make You Free*, p. 36. Gutiérrez argues that the gift of filiation is only received in a life of brotherly love. Reconciliation is not a

Christ and the Liberation of Humanity Through Faithful Praxis

context that has already been given by God and found in Christ. It is a work that is realized in relationships through which liberative communities are formed.

63 Kimberly Baker, 'Augustine's doctrine of the Totus Christus: reflecting on the Church as sacrament of unity', *Horizons* 37, no. 1 (2010), p. 16.

64 Gutiérrez, *A Theology of Liberation*, p. 191.

65 Gutiérrez, *A Theology of Liberation*, p. 192.

66 Gutiérrez, *A Theology of Liberation*, p. 194.

67 Gutiérrez, *A Theology of Liberation*, p. 99.

68 Alexander Nava, *The Mystical and Prophetic Thought of Simone Weil and Gustavo Gutiérrez* (Albany, NY: State University of New York Press, 2001), p. 141.

69 Gutiérrez, *The God of Life*, p. 86.

70 Gutiérrez, *The God of Life*, p. 90.

71 '*Jesucristo el Hijo de Dios hecho hombre, uno de nosotros en la historia, judío, hijo de María, perteneciente a un pueblo determinado. ... el carácter histórico de la Encarnación es un elemento central de la fe cristiana.*' Gutiérrez, '¿Dónde Dormirán Los Pobres?', p. 58 n. 69. My translation.

72 Kelsey, *Eccentric Existence*, p. 822.

73 Gutiérrez, *The Truth Shall Make You Free*, p. 61.

74 Gutiérrez, *A Theology of Liberation*, p. 191.

75 Gutiérrez, *A Theology of Liberation*, p. 183.

76 Gutiérrez, *A Theology of Liberation*, p. 185.

77 Gutiérrez, *A Theology of Liberation*, p. 190. Emphasis original.

78 'That my action towards another is at the same time an action towards God does not detract from its truth and concreteness, but rather gives it greater meaning and import.' Gutiérrez, *A Theology of Liberation*, p. 191.

79 Gutiérrez, *A Theology of Liberation*, p. 149.

80 Thomas A. Lewis, 'Actions as the ties that bind: love, praxis, and community in the thought of Gustavo Gutiérrez', *Journal of Religious Ethics* 33, no. 3 (September 2005), p. 553.

81 Kelsey, *Eccentric Existence*, p. 710.

82 Kelsey, *Eccentric Existence*, p. 823.

83 Clodovis Boff, *Feet-on-the-Ground Theology: A Brazilian journey*, trans. Philip Berryman (Eugene, OR: Wipf & Stock, 2008), p. 82.

PART THREE

Proclaiming God as Father: Liberation and Utopia

8

The Liberation of Utopia

Introduction: the liberation of utopia

In the first part of this project, I explored the context to which Gutiérrez addresses his theology. It seeks to speak into 'a world that is inhumane' and participate in the movement of salvation history towards a new and liberated humanity. In Part Two I traced out the methodology that shapes his 'proclamation of God as Father' in this context. Gutiérrez calls for a liberative praxis of love through which the truth of both God and the neighbour is made known in Christ. Having explored the context and methodology of his anthropology, I turn now in this final part to its content. To put it another way, having discussed the humanity *before* whom Gutiérrez speaks and the humanity *by* whom Gutiérrez speaks, I now turn to the humanity *of* whom he speaks.

In the gospel message of the coming kingdom Gutiérrez hears a call that is at once creative and subversive. According to him the coming of this kingdom involves the 'unceasing search for a new kind of humanity in a qualitatively different society' that is postulated in the 'life and teaching of Jesus'.[1] On the one hand the new humanity of this kingdom will be encountered in the concrete contexts of a 'qualitatively different society'. On the other hand, this kingdom is made known in an 'unceasing search' that resists and subverts any attempt to restrict it to a specific political programme or social structure. To speak of God as Father is to cultivate a vision of this kingdom in the midst of a world that is inhumane.

The context of utopia

Gutiérrez draws on the language and imagery of utopia to express this dynamic of the kingdom. Being both 'subversive to and a driving force of history',[2] he deploys the concept of utopia to 'refer to a historical plan for a qualitatively different society and to express the aspiration to establish new social relations among human beings'.[3] Utopia expresses both a plan to be enacted in history and an aspiration by which this plan is continually to be renewed. According to Gutiérrez, this utopia takes place in the second of the three levels of liberation that he describes. As I have outlined, the first of these levels concerns political structures, while the third addresses the reality of personal sin. It is in the second level of interpersonal relation unfolding through history that the first and third are to meet.[4] As such, this second level is a focal point of the liberative work of God in history. In the different parts of this project I have sought to show the way in which Gutiérrez's anthropology can be seen refracted through this second level of liberation. The first part drew out the new humanity that is forged within this level over the course of salvation history. The second part explored the social relations and liberative praxis by which this humanity is to be forged. This third and final part of the project will outline how the concept of utopia delineates the space in which these relations can take place. Gutiérrez explains that it is 'at this level that are located the plans for a new society, the utopias that spur action in history'.[5] It is a call that can be heard from the future to work towards liberation in the present; and it is a call heard in the present to subject this work to the judgement of the future. Utopia expresses this dynamic in which anticipation and realization both inform and energize each other.

The contours of utopia

As Gutiérrez maps the terrain of this utopia, he traces three contours that give it shape. He outlines 'Its relationship to historical reality, its verification in praxis, and its rational nature.'[6] The first of these characteristics describes the 'prospective character of utopia' through which it becomes a 'dynamic and mobilizing factor in history'.[7] Utopia is not static but an ever-unfolding dialectic that moves between the 'denunciation of the existing order' and 'the annunciation of what is not yet but will be'.[8] This movement of annunciation and denunciation takes place in the context of a commitment to historical praxis without which 'the denunciation will remain at a purely verbal level and the annunciation will be only an illusion'.[9] This commitment to praxis and solidarity with the poor is possible through the conviction that it is a participation in the 'deep meaning of history' through which 'the definitive reality is being built on what is transitory'.[10] Utopia is true rationality because it is consistent with the truth of history. James Nickoloff draws attention to the particular cultural context in which this account of utopia has emerged: 'Three elements characterize utopian thought in Peru's intellectual tradition: a

The Liberation of Utopia

focus on the future, passionate love for the people (the poor), and the search for a meaningful unity within the complexity and constant flux of the popular movement.'[11] While Nickoloff does not draw an explicit connection with the three elements of utopia outlined by Gutiérrez, the correspondence is clear. Utopia is called forth by a future hope, lived in a loving commitment to the poor, and sustained by a faith in the unfolding movement towards liberation. Each of these three characteristics is sustained and energized by the others. They must each shed light on the other if utopia is to be clearly seen.

As Gutiérrez brings his discussion of 'Eschatology and Politics' to an end in *A Theology of Liberation*, he draws these three characteristics together in a single image: 'To hope in Christ is at the same time to believe in the adventure of history, which opens infinite vistas to the love and action of the Christian.'[12] The three characteristics of utopia are here drawn into and defined by the three theological virtues. Hope in Christ sustains a faith in the liberative movement of history that will in turn move the Christian to loving action. This chapter will analyse each of these three facets of utopia as developed by Gutiérrez and at each point I will engage with and evaluate various objections that have been raised to the concept of utopia that takes shape within his theology. The analysis offered in this chapter will establish the foundation for an exploration in the next chapter of some remaining ambiguities that may inhibit the development of a truly liberative utopia in the theology of Gutiérrez.

Hope in Christ: utopian reason

Gutiérrez seeks to recover the concept of utopia from those who might dismiss it as either an unrealistic distraction or an illusory dream. Both those who seek liberation and those who resist any threat to their power and prosperity have been tempted to dismiss the concept of utopia as irrational and ahistorical. The response of Gutiérrez is to counter that utopia 'as we understand it, belongs to the rational order'.[13] According to him, utopia is truly rational because it is truly historical. As Gaspar Martinez observes, when so conceived 'utopia must be rational; that is, must be able to unveil those nonapparent but existent possibilities that represent a quantum leap in the development of sciences and of the understanding of reality in general'.[14] Far from being irrational or ahistorical utopia expresses a conformity to the very structure of history established by God. As Gutiérrez argues, 'There are some who may think that the promise of life in fullness cannot be carried out, but God is not one of them ... That future state is not an illusion but a utopian vision that sets history in motion.'[15] Hope in a future given by God and received in the work of history establishes utopia as truly rational and truly historical.

In what might appear at first to be a paradoxical observation, Gutiérrez argues that in this hope – and the utopia that it envisions – is found the only truly rational response to unjust suffering. The hope of utopia is the only recourse in situations 'when science has reached its limits in its explanation of social reality and when new paths open up for historical praxis'.[16] Where the poor appear trapped in their suffering, Gutiérrez contends that Christian hope refuses to allow such circumstances to be the final word of history. Suffering is true irrationality. Oppression of the poor also sets itself against the purposes of God in history. Declaring that 'Christian hope springs eternal', Gutiérrez sees in 'the situation we are living in Latin America today' a context which 'is perhaps enabling us to experience and to understand in a new way what St. Paul meant when he spoke of "hoping against hope" (Romans 4.18 NAB)'.[17] Amid the irrationality of poverty, suffering and oppression, Christian hope is an encounter with the truth of God's work to establish his purpose in history. Gutiérrez acknowledges that such a hope may appear to make a mockery of suffering and distract from the work of liberation. He acknowledges his own struggles to avoid such distortions:

> One day while preaching from my theoretical hypothesis, a person from my community said, 'You know, you are a great humourist because you speak about the love of God, and you are living in our neighbourhood; you know our lives – we have no work; we have no food; and you say, "Not only does God love you, but you are the first for God."'[18]

When preached as a 'theoretical hypothesis', hope does indeed degenerate into unreality and irrationality. However, the hope that Gutiérrez seeks to describe is forged precisely within the desperation that his parishioner described. He recalls Romero's insistence that 'When I preach, I am always preaching hope', and concludes that 'to welcome the grace of hope is to create resources in history'.[19] Such a hope is not a denial of nor a distraction from the present. It exposes the disorder of the current historical context and calls for this history to be conformed to the order of liberation.

Gutiérrez contends that utopian hope is profoundly practical and rational in its relation to history. This relation to history unfolds in two ways. First, it provides a coherence to history as it discloses the unifying principle and purpose of the historical process. At the same time,

The Liberation of Utopia

however, this utopian hope resists closure within history. It exposes the provisionality of each historical moment and calls for a creative openness to new possibilities for liberation. I will explore each of these dynamics in turn before considering the critique expressed by the then Cardinal Ratzinger concerning the role of hope within the theology of Gutiérrez.

Hope in Christ: recognizing the coherence of history

In order to develop his theology of utopia, Gutiérrez draws on the philosophy of Ernst Bloch. According to him, Bloch seeks to rescue the Marxist project from theoretical abstraction by identifying the importance of hope. Rather than simply considering human relationships in their materiality Gutiérrez calls attention to the dynamic of human 'affections' – among which the most powerful is 'an active hope which subverts the existing order'.[20] Far from inhibiting political action and historical progress, this hope – which Bloch recognizes will often find religious expression – resources such action and makes possible such progress. For Gutiérrez, the philosophy of Bloch provides a framework through which a theology of hope may describe the promise of the future as both forged within and calling forth the struggle to transform the present. In Bloch's work 'hope thus emerges as the key to human existence orientated towards the future, because it transforms the present'.[21] In its disclosure of the unifying principle and purpose of the historical process, hope provides coherence to the apparently chaotic events of human history.

Hope in Christ: resisting the closure of history

While this utopian hope discloses the coherence of history it also secures the openness of history to the ongoing work of liberation. Gutiérrez observes that 'for Bloch what is real is an open-ended process'.[22] In this way, as hope reveals the truth of history, the truth it reveals consists in a creative openness to new possibilities. Hope infuses the utopian vision with a 'creative imagination' that resists closure.[23] From the perspective of this hope, a truly liberative utopia may be contrasted with mere ideology. Ideology simply serves to 'mask' reality and 'fulfils a function of the preservation of the established order'.[24] Without 'historical dynamism and creative imagination', the movement towards liberation will atrophy into a political or religious dogmatism, both of which 'represent a step backward towards ideology'.[25] Gutiérrez decries the 'liberal utopianism' of nineteenth-century Latin America which through the rhetoric of liberty and modernity 'only instituted a more refined exploitation of the Latin American masses – some of whom actually found themselves in conditions worse than that under the old colonial domination'.[26]

Utopia degenerates into such ideology when the historical process suffers closure. This is a susceptibility that is evident in the life and work of Bloch himself.[27] Tom Moylan decries 'Bloch's reduction of utopia's creative potential by means of his uncritical adherence to Soviet ideology'.[28] While Bloch's personal commitments may seem in tension with the logic of his philosophical system, they expose a lacuna in his thought.[29] The concept of hope developed by Bloch would be more robust when placed in the context of 'an external challenge that would have exposed the dialogic contradictions of his work and set its best insights free'.[30] Such an 'external challenge' finds expression in the appropriation of Bloch's thought within the theology of liberation:

> God remains as the signifier of a radical Otherness that empowers humanity to reach beyond its own limits, even beyond the limits of its utopian aspiration. Standing outside humanity, but in partnership with it, the 'God of the Bible' provides an exterior source of radical non-identity that preserves the openness of the liberation process.[31]

The utopia described by Gutiérrez is known in the context of the hope disclosed in Christ. In the life of Christ God reveals his commitment to human history and in the resurrection of Christ God reveals his purposes for human history. There is an interplay of otherness and involvement that maintains an openness of history that is at work within history to lead history towards the liberation of utopia.

Hope in Christ: gift and task

The utopian hope that takes shape in the theology of Gutiérrez has been critiqued for insufficiently attending to the gracious quality of the coming kingdom. According to this criticism, Gutiérrez – especially in his early work – fails to appropriately emphasize that this hope is to be found in the future and received as a gift. A prominent expression of this criticism came in the 'Ten Observations on the Theology of Gustavo Gutiérrez' published by the Congregation for the Doctrine of the Faith in 1983 and the 'Instruction on Certain Aspects of the "Theology of Liberation"' given the year after. The central concern of the first document is that

Gutiérrez 'falls into a temporal messianism and reduces the growth of the kingdom to the increase in justice'.[32] According to the 'Instruction' this tendency leads to the 'absorption' of the Kingdom of God 'into the immanence of human history'.[33] The 'Ten Observations' and the 'Instruction' criticize a perceived reduction of the eschatological to the political through the imposition of Marxist ideology on the life and doctrine of the church. The faith of the church is appropriated by a political discourse and its practice restricted by the immanent horizon. Rather than hope being awaited in the future and received from God, it is to be implemented now through the work of human hands.

Gutiérrez responded to these criticisms in two ways. In an interview given shortly after the publication of these documents, he both acknowledges the need to deepen and clarify his work and at the same time distances it from the description of liberation theology that is offered in these documents.[34] I have already considered the way in which Gutiérrez has denied the dependency on Marx that the documents ascribe to the theology of liberation. He avers that 'there is no question at all of a possible acceptance of an atheistic ideology' in his theology.[35] Far from being restricted to, or seeking a 'synthesis' with, a Marxist framework, Gutiérrez reflects that 'my pastoral practice imposed pressing needs of quite a different kind'.[36] He is adamant that 'the kingdom cannot be identified with historical embodiments of human liberation'[37] and that 'faith does not provide us with a social or political plan'.[38] Prompted by the concrete contexts of pastoral ministry, Gutiérrez makes eclectic use of theoretical resources to envision, empower and enact liberative practice.

The second way in which Gutiérrez responded to these criticisms was to develop his theology in dialogue with them. He reads the documents as 'an invitation to further reflection'[39] and observes that 'the discussion is ongoing, and this is healthy'.[40] In 'Expanding the view', his introduction to the revised edition of *A Theology of Liberation*, Gutiérrez describes 'an important debate' that, despite involving 'some painful moments', has been an 'enriching spiritual experience' through which 'secondary elements have lost the importance they seemed to have at an earlier period'.[41] More recently he has acknowledged the continued need to re-examine and revise the theoretical frameworks through which the theology of liberation takes shape: 'It is true that we must re-evaluate many things: many of the analyses, categories, and propositions enunciated in recent years have become obsolete.'[42] In this dual process of clarification and refinement, Gutiérrez places his thought within a theological framework in which an eschatological hope in Christ leads history on a path to liberation. At the same time this hope and the liberation in which it is expressed are not limited to or defined by the political structures through which the historical process might pass.

Whether these developments are best read as clarification or correction, it is important to recognize the way in which Gutiérrez seeks to place himself in continuity with the tradition and teaching of the church. This claim to continuity is evident in the references to papal pronouncements and historical precedents that are found throughout the exposition of his work that he provides in *The Truth Will Make You Free*. It is a claim that is especially striking as he reflects on the way in which Benedict XVI relates the promotion of justice to the proclamation of the gospel. Gutiérrez observes that 'the road has been long, but its current formulation clearly avoids impoverishing separations as well as possible confusions between the two'.[43] He discerns in the later pronouncement of Benedict a framework that seeks to guard against 'impoverishing separations as well as possible confusions' in a way that corresponds to the structure of his own theological project. Whether it is due to developments in Gutiérrez's theology or in the way in which his theology has been read, the utopian hope that is expressed in his theology finds an echo in the official teaching of Pope Benedict XVI. To observe a correspondence between the frameworks through which hope is described does not imply that the theology expressed within these frameworks shares precisely the same shape. It is, however, important to recognize that the utopian hope envisioned by Gutiérrez is far from the 'temporal messianism' against which the Magisterium warned 30 years ago. It speaks of a gift from God that establishes a task for humanity in a way that is accommodated by the teaching of Benedict XVI.

Conclusion

A truly utopian hope will be continually expressed in and verified by loving praxis. However, before I turn to consider this loving praxis, a question presents itself that I will seek to explore in the following sections of this chapter. If there is now such correspondence between the official teaching of the Roman Catholic Church and the theology expressed by Gustavo Gutiérrez, does space remain for his theology to make an ongoing contribution in the future? Is his theology primarily a call to the church to continually recover and renew the truths to which it holds? Or is it to be a voice that will continually subvert and disrupt any attempt at institutional expression? Does it call the church to remember the truth of its traditions? Or does it offer new wine that requires new theological, ecclesiological and political wineskins? As I outline the next two characteristics of the utopia envisioned by Gutiérrez, I will explore the way in which his theology is confronted by the challenge of its own future.

Love of Christ: the praxis of utopia

The gift that is received in hope must be lived in love. The hope in Christ that characterizes a liberative utopia 'opens infinite vistas to the love and action of the Christian'.[44] This second characteristic of utopia in the theology of Gutiérrez verifies and clarifies the first. Utopia is 'verified in praxis'[45] and it is only in this praxis that utopia can be 'the driving force of history and subversive of the existing order'.[46] I have already explored the concept of praxis in previous chapters, but I will now trace the particular relation between this praxis and the utopia within which a new and liberated humanity finds its form. Having first outlined the creative commitment to the neighbour that is called for by this utopian vision, I will then engage with the criticism that this utopian praxis is inhibited by abstraction and ambiguity.

The praxis of utopia: a creative commitment

Within the utopia described by Gutiérrez this loving praxis is characterized by a creative commitment to the poor. By giving confidence in God's liberative purposes and preventing confusion of these purposes with any one or other political structure, utopian hope establishes the possibility and the responsibility for loving praxis. Christian hope 'not only frees us for this commitment; it simultaneously demands and judges it'.[47] Cautioning that 'one must be extremely careful not to replace a Christianity of the Beyond with a Christianity of the Future', Gutiérrez argues that 'the hope which overcomes death must be rooted in the heart of historical praxis'.[48] It is only in this historical commitment to the poor that utopia finds its concrete life and transcendent truth: 'But for utopia validly to fulfil this role it must be verified in social praxis; it must become effective commitment without intellectual purisms, without inordinate claims; it must be revised and concretized constantly.'[49] The loving praxis that is lived in commitment to the poor keeps utopia from either dissolving into an illusory abstraction or atrophying into ideological dogmatism.

Not only does the praxis called for by utopia involve a commitment to the poor, this commitment is also marked by a creative quality that directs it to concrete encounters with the poor and opens it to new possibilities for action. It is a praxis that seeks a justice beyond the confines established by governments, markets and law courts. It is conformed to the justice of God, 'which transcends the established practice of human justice. It takes into account the deeper needs of human beings.'[50] In such a way, 'the gratuitousness of God's love constantly surprises'.[51] This love not only seeks a justice deeper than that which society so often offers, it conforms itself to a law at once more demanding and more liberating than that which society so often seeks to satisfy. The 'possibility of limitless work' opened up by this creative commitment to the poor would be an impossible burden were it not the expression of a profound and creative love.[52] Nickoloff describes this restless and creative love in a poignant image drawn from the suffering that surrounded Gutiérrez in his pastoral ministry:

> Just as love for a desperately ill child keeps a parent's hope alive and searches constantly for a way out of the crisis, love for the poor of Peru leads the Christian to lift every stone in the search for instances of creativity, initiative, and freedom capable of propelling the poor forward in their struggle for liberation and life.[53]

Love and hope are mutually sustaining and find expression in a desperate and determined search for new ways to share life. For Gutiérrez this creativity and openness are most acutely expressed in the act of forgiveness. In forgiveness from God there is a new life that can be lived in forgiveness towards others. Commenting on the story of Jonah, Gutiérrez observes that 'life and not death is what God desires for all' and concludes that 'to forgive is to give life'.[54] This forgiveness is not simply a personal and private experience. It is given to be shared and in that sharing to resource the forging of new kinds of community. Gutiérrez reads the parable of the talents in Matthew 25 as offering a contrast between two attitudes: 'That of those who pass on to others what they have received from God, and that of those who keep for themselves what the Lord willed to bestow on them.'[55] Forgiveness from God is to be offered to others so that new communities are forged of people who live lives of creative and committed love to those whom the world perceives as being the least deserving.

The Liberation of Utopia

The critique: an abstract account of praxis

The praxis of love that is to be encountered in the utopia envisioned by Gutiérrez has been criticized for being obscured by abstraction. In an earlier chapter I engaged with critiques of this praxis expressed by theologians within the Radical Orthodoxy movement. From the perspective of Radical Orthodoxy, the praxis called for by Gutiérrez was insufficiently theological. I would now like to address the counterpart to this criticism – that the praxis called for by Gutiérrez is inhibited by being *overly* theological. Theologians such as Ivan Petrella have critiqued the theology of liberation for not developing a clear programme within which liberative praxis might be defined and directed.

Petrella criticizes Gutiérrez and other theologians of liberation for not allowing the logic of their argument to take them beyond the constraints of theology. In developing his challenge to the theology of liberation Petrella acknowledges the tension within which it is caught: 'On the one hand it must be given enough specificity so that it actually addresses, rather than glosses over, real oppression and suffering. On the other hand, however, liberation cannot be just a governmental program of immediate assistance.'[56] As it seeks to resolve this tension, he argues that the theology which once allowed reflections on liberation to grow 'is now perhaps that which stifles its future'.[57] For this reason Petrella offers the invitation 'to think about liberation theology without the constraints of the Christian tradition and religion generally'.[58] There are three elements of this vision for liberationist thought: first, it must be wrested free from the 'stranglehold' of the church and the academy; second, it must 'recover politics on a grand scale'; and third, it must not consider capitalism as a 'monolithic whole' but make concrete suggestions for 'piece-by-piece change'.[59] Together these elements call for a greater emphasis on the 'historical project' launched by the theology of liberation.[60] By failing to offer a precise definition of praxis and a political direction to the project of liberation, the theology of liberation risks falling into the very abstraction and alienation against which it warns.[61]

The response: the loving encounter

Where Petrella identifies an enervating abstraction in the praxis called for by the theology of liberation, Gutiérrez would discern a demanding and creative freedom. What is read by Petrella as expressing abstraction is argued for by Gutiérrez in order to establish a personal and concrete context for his account of praxis. It is a praxis that concerns concrete encounters and so is a praxis that is most clearly expressed in the messiness of relationships rather than the synthetic order of political theory.

Gutiérrez acknowledges the danger of speaking of the poor in an 'impersonal way' and warns that there can be no solidarity and no liberative praxis 'if there is no friendship with them and no sharing of the life of the poor'.[62] For this reason the praxis of liberation must take its shape from the neighbour – and the community of neighbours – in which it is to be expressed. The reluctance of Gutiérrez to define or align his account of praxis in terms of particular political movements is an attempt to secure the accountability of praxis to the concrete contexts of the Christian community. To understand this dynamic in his theology it is important to recognize the influence on his thought of two Peruvian writers, José María Arguedas and José Carlos Mariátegui.[63] Both of these writers, in different ways, emphasize the necessary contingency of any political commitment to communities of the poor. Mariátegui, a pioneer in contextualizing Marx within the culture of Latin America, called for attention to 'the wisdom and integrity of the poor as foundational elements for a new order'.[64] Gutiérrez describes this approach as involving a dual commitment – to the work of liberation and to the historical contexts in which that work will take place. Speaking of Mariátegui he observes that 'his socialism was creative because it was fashioned in loyalty. Loyalty to his sources, that is, to the central intuitions of Marx, yet was beyond all dogmatism; he was simultaneously loyal to a unique historical reality.'[65] It is this commitment to each 'unique historical reality' that establishes the space for creative action amid the personal relationships of concrete communities. A true commitment to a specific social and historical context is incompatible with dogmatism.[66] Listening to the poor must be prior to – and the context for – the projection of political programmes.

The dynamic that emerges in the political theory of Mariátegui finds imaginative expression in the novels of José María Arguedas. According to Gutiérrez, the work of Arguedas expresses a 'universality' that is encountered in an experience of intimacy and particularity.[67] It is only from the heart of the poor that a truly liberative humanity can be born. It must be conformed to their experience and proceed according to their possibilities.[68] All visions of liberation must be subject to this experience because even those who are committed to liberation are contaminated by the very oppression they seek to oppose. Arguedas describes a 'dialectic of cleanliness-dirtiness' that attends all human relationships.[69] The image of cleanliness is used to evoke freedom and authenticity whereas dirtiness is the alienation that causes and is caused by greed, exploitation and

The Liberation of Utopia

suffering. Cleanliness is achieved and maintained only through a struggle against the dirtiness that continually threatens to contaminate and corrupt relationships.[70] It is only through a process of purification that relationships of freedom and authenticity may be achieved and this purification takes place in the context of communities of forgiveness and love.[71] Having described this dynamic in the novels of Arguedas, Gutiérrez then introduces its relation to the concept of *'consolar'*. The word *'consolar'* literally means to comfort and console but in the work of Arguedas it is called upon to evoke a work of liberation and the elimination of the causes of suffering.[72] Gutiérrez contrasts the 'consolation' that simply distracts from and ultimately prolongs suffering and the 'consolation' that brings liberation and is encountered in love.[73] This liberative work of 'consolation' can only be carried out by those who have undergone a process of purification that is at once deeply personal and concretely relational. Oppression and alienation are only overcome in the contexts of concrete relationships. It is only in the cacophony of voices that emerge in each community that the call to liberation may be heard. When these voices are heard in love the truth of liberation is disclosed.

The utopian praxis called for by Gutiérrez takes its shape from the exigencies of personal relationships in communities. For this reason, ecclesial base communities are central to his utopian vision. He describes expressions of solidarity with the poor and dispossessed that have taken shape throughout Latin America: 'This is the first flowering at the continental level of what José María Arguedas used to call "the fellowship of the wretched".'[74] These 'fellowships of the wretched' provide the context for a truly liberative praxis. It is in the context of these communities that love receives its definition and direction. Such communities protect both the spiritual and political from the dogmatism that inhibits the work of liberation. The loving praxis of liberation can only be defined, discerned and displayed when it is lived in daily solidarity with the concrete reality of the poor. Gutiérrez warns that if 'the gift of sonship' is to be recognized and received 'we must make it alive daily' amid 'a real identification with the persons suffering oppression' so that it might 'enrich creatively and scientifically, from within, the political processes which have the tendency to get closed in themselves and mutilate authentic human dimensions'.[75] In the place where Petrella discerns a lack of political specificity, Gutiérrez seeks to cultivate a space for continued creativity. The science of social analysis and the political programmes to which they give rise must be subject to the continued process of revision and reconstruction.

The priority of praxis in the theology of Gutiérrez provides not only the context for theological reflection but also for political theorization. In this way it is possible to summarize the response that he might offer to the criticisms raised by Petrella. Each of the three concerns raised by Petrella are addressed in the context of *comunidades de base* and the relationships of loving solidarity that they exemplify. It is these contexts, rather than ecclesiastical or academic institutions, that give utopian praxis its present shape and future direction. In a similar way it is attention to the concrete needs of these communities that will keep liberationists from being led by the concerns that develop among middle-class groups. Finally, far from being paralysed by a monolithic view of capitalism that inhibits gradual and achievable steps towards change, the theology of Gutiérrez calls for these various and variegated communities to be places where liberation is envisioned and enacted in ways that are appropriate to their contexts.

While Gutiérrez may offer a response to the argument developed by Petrella, it appears that his central concern remains. As we have seen, Petrella identifies a tension within the theology of liberation that exists between the need for both resistance to ideological dogmatism on the one hand and practical specificity on the other. Gutiérrez emphasizes the freedom of a praxis that is to be lived in communities of love rather than offering a programme for praxis to be established at the level of political institutions. While he calls for this utopian praxis to be enriched both 'creatively and scientifically', it appears that the latter is absorbed into the former. When addressing the concerns raised by Radical Orthodoxy, I argued that the praxis called for by Gutiérrez took shape within a theological context that kept it from collapsing into immanentism and temporalism. The critique developed by Petrella is that Gutiérrez fails to offer the practical and political direction that his own theology demands. The question is the extent to which an explicit programme is necessary for a liberative community to take shape. While Gutiérrez seeks to evoke a sense of the 'infinite vistas' that are open 'to the love and action of the Christian', Petrella detects the need for a map that might show how such terrain is to be traversed.[76]

The issue that finds expression in this context as a tension between the creative and the scientific will, in the next and final section of this chapter, be explored in terms of the tensions between the denunciation of the present and the annunciation of the future. As Gutiérrez offers his vision for the future, the role of his theology in the forging of this future will depend a great deal on the way in which these tensions are addressed.

Faith in Christ: utopian history

The third perspective that Gutiérrez offers on a liberative utopia is 'its relationship to present historical reality'.[77] The utopian vision that is disclosed through hope in Christ and lived in the love of Christ is sustained by and subject to faith in Christ. It is this faith in Christ that allows the liberative work of Christ to be discerned in the seemingly chaotic unfolding of human history. It is this faith that directs how the believer is to live in hope and love amid the struggle towards liberation in that history.

Faith in Christ the Lord of history

For Gutiérrez, to know God as the Father whose love reaches out to the '*nonperson*' and 'makes us all brothers and sisters' is to respond to Jesus in whom this love is revealed.[78] To recognize the truth of the God who 'comes to us as the God of the poor', it is necessary to 'come to this God through Jesus Christ' in whom is revealed the work of God in history:

> By Jesus's life and death we know that the only justice is definitive justice. But we also know that now is the time to begin building it – from within our concrete, conflictual history, by accepting the kingdom in which the love of God will reign.[79]

Jesus reveals the commitment of God to the liberation of humanity and the call of God to participate in the realization of this work in history. Confronted by the harsh realities experienced by the poor each day, the proclamation that 'the Lord is risen!' reveals that 'death and injustice are not the final word of history'.[80] Both the 'gift of filiation' and the 'fellowship that filiation demands' are revealed in the 'death and resurrection of Jesus Christ' and so it is this faith that allows the truth of history to be received and lived.[81] The hope that Gutiérrez proclaims is not grounded in specific events or developments but is lived out in a loving practice sustained by faith in the love and liberative work of God that is revealed in Christ.

The importance of this faith to the concept of utopia in the theology of Gutiérrez is especially evident in his consideration of martyrdom. In martyrdom there is a testimony to the life to which the Christian is called. Describing the murder of Archbishop Oscar Romero, Gutiérrez declares that at the archbishop's death, 'his blood sealed the covenant he had made with God'.[82] Where there is such conformity to Jesus in such a solidarity with the poor, 'martyrdom (in the broad sense of the term) is the final accomplishment of life'.[83] Martyrdom is the expression of a faith that can see even in death the commitment of God to life. Such faith is expressed in the death of the martyr, and such faith is needed to discern in this martyrdom a testimony to life. Gutiérrez draws on a message given by the bishops of Guatemala in 1981 to express this point. Amid an experience of suffering and death they declare that 'faith makes us realize that the church in Guatemala is passing through a time of grace and positive hope. Persecution has always been an obvious sign of fidelity to Christ and his gospel.'[84] While such martyrdom is never a vocation and always an act of cruelty that must be abhorred, the eyes of faith can see in this death a testimony to life.[85] Such a faith sees in solidarity and suffering with the poor the '*kairos*' that is the 'propitious moment' or 'favourable day' in which 'the Lord becomes present and manifests himself'.[86] For Gutiérrez a mark of true faith – an expression of true spirituality – is found in the solidarity that chooses to suffer with the poor in the confidence that in Jesus, the Lord of history, is the God of the poor.

Faith in Christ lived in history

Utopia is not only sustained by a faith that discloses the truth of Christ as Lord of history; this faith also directs the life of the believer within this history. If Christ is the Lord of history then the relationship of the believer to that history will be marked by the dual dynamic of 'denunciation and annunciation'.[87] There is to be both a rejection of oppression and injustice and a proclamation of life as it exposes the impossibility of what is seen and reveals the necessity of what is still to be. Gutiérrez weaves these two dynamics together so that each will lead to the other. He observes that 'this denunciation is to a large extent made with regard to the annunciation. But the annunciation, in its turn, presupposes this rejection.'[88] On the one hand 'gospel annunciation opens human history to the future promised by God and reveals God's present work', while on the other it expresses a judgement on 'the incomplete and provisional character of any and every human achievement'.[89] The more clearly that the future liberation of God is made known in the present, the more radically will the present moment be criticized and called to be more closely conformed to the liberation that is to come. This interplay constitutes utopian faith as a dynamic that both 'relativizes and radicalizes the building of the human city'.[90] Woven together in this way these two threads become integral to the fabric of the concept of utopia developed

The Liberation of Utopia

by Gutiérrez. It is through this dynamic that the vision of utopian hope is continually and creatively clarified; and it is through this dynamic that the praxis of utopian love is renewed and revised.

The denunciation and annunciation that are expressive of utopian faith must not be understood 'at a purely verbal level' but must instead take place in the context of a commitment to the poor.[91] The faith that discloses the truth of Christ as the Lord of history is the faith that directs the life of the Christian in history. As Gutiérrez concludes: 'In history and only in history is the gift of God believed, loved and hoped for.'[92]

The critique: an insufficiently radical faith

The utopia that takes shape in the theology of Gutiérrez is both sustained by and subject to faith in Christ as the Lord of history. The faith that recognizes the liberative purpose of God *for* history and the liberative presence of God *in* history is expressed in a life that is conformed to these purposes and that participates in this presence. While he describes this life as being characterized by an ongoing process of annunciation and denunciation, he has been criticized for not allowing this dynamic to lead faith itself into the fullness of freedom. Earlier in this chapter I considered Petrella's concern that the utopian praxis described by Gutiérrez is characterized by an abstraction that inhibits its usefulness in the liberative project. At this point I will explore a similar criticism raised by the work of Marcella Althaus-Reid. If Petrella critiques Gutiérrez for not being sufficiently specific and practical, Althaus-Reid objects that his theology is not sufficiently radical. Althaus-Reid argues that the faith to which Gutiérrez calls his readers is restricted by dogmatic and ultimately oppressive structures. Only in a radical and risky faith will the utopia of liberation be found.

In order to unleash what she perceives to be the true radicalism of liberative faith, Althaus-Reid calls for the theology of liberation to recognize and reject the ideological constraints within which it has taken shape. Althaus-Reid argues that liberation theology has become marked by a gap between 'uncontested ideologies and critical reality'.[93] While the theology of liberation has offered a 'message of inclusivity', Althaus-Reid contends that 'the inclusive project affirmed itself by exclusion policies which determined the identity of the poor. The poor who were included were conceived of as male, generally peasant, vaguely indigenous, Christian and heterosexual.'[94] For this reason, Althaus-Reid concludes that 'at best liberation theology's discourse is one of equality but not of difference'.[95]

Gustavo Gutiérrez and the Liberative Sight of Christ

Both the poor and the community to which they are called are defined in a way that is blind to those who problematize categories and transgress boundaries. In this reading, the theology of liberation has failed to become conscious of – much less critique – the fundamental frameworks of social oppression within which it was forged. The theology of liberation is blind to the complexity and variety of those who suffer, instead 'seeing in the institution and structures of heterosexual, *Machista* Latin American society the movement of a *Machista* God, a god of the poor, but a *Machista* one'.[96] This blindness is exemplified for Althaus-Reid in a comment made by Gutiérrez when questioned about the possibility of ordination for women in the church: 'Gutierrez's opinion, predictably, was along the lines that women in Latin America did not care about ordination, but about feeding their children.'[97]

Rather than envisioning a radical liberation, there is a blindness to the very groups who most suffer exclusion, exploitation and oppression. The truly radical faith that works towards this truly radical liberation will be able to see those whom the world ignores. Althaus-Reid argues that 'to take seriously history as a space of faith is ... to recognise the freedom needed to do an Indecent Theology of people's indecent, unruly lives of suffering'.[98] The radicalism of faith must be recovered if the risky path to liberation is to be followed.

According to Althaus-Reid, the limitations of liberation theology find acute expression in its attitude to sexuality. Since the inception of the movement, theologians of liberation have been 'suspicious of ideologically determined definitions such as what theology is, or who is a theologian'; however, she claims that 'it did not occur to them at that time that it was necessary to dismantle the sexual ideology of theology, and for theologians to come out from their closets and ground their theology in a praxis of intellectual, living honesty'.[99] While this sexual ideology remains 'closeted' and unexposed, it continues to exert a power that will distort any theology however liberative its intentions. Rather than taking a risk of faith to accept a scandalous grace, the theology of liberation participates in an economy of repression. Arguing that 'liberation theology knows more about dogmas than about people', Althaus-Reid claims that it 'never took seriously the patterns of love and relationship among the Latin American people'.[100] As a consequence of this it is unable to recognize that 'promiscuity could mean grace, that is, love outside the logic of the law'.[101] Althaus-Reid describes 'a connection between monogamy, monotheism and multinational cartels', and criticizes liberation theology for having 'never challenged this imposed order on the poor, and love among the poor'.[102] It is only by 'unveiling ideologies, including sexual

The Liberation of Utopia

ones', that it is possible to 'keep re-discovering the face of God among us'.[103] Unless it takes the risk of allowing faith the radical freedom to see and lead beyond 'patriarchal and heterosexual ideologies', the utopia envisioned by Gutiérrez cannot be the site of true liberation. A utopia that is decent and straight will only perpetuate oppression, repression and exclusion.

The response: the radicalism of faith in Christ

Before exploring the response that Gutiérrez might offer to this critique it is important to recognize that it is essentially a theological critique. While Petrella seeks to address the lack of practical specificity in the praxis called for by Gutiérrez, Althaus-Reid is questioning the very theological framework in which his conception of utopia takes shape. For Petrella the theology of liberation must recognize and recover the inner dynamic of its own theology that seeks to break free from the theology in which it first found expression. Petrella describes his project in this way: 'I propose to reflect on liberation theology by moving beyond liberation theology. I want to separate liberation theology's main ideas from theology.'[104] Even as Petrella calls for a liberation beyond the boundaries of theology, there is a confidence that the theology of liberation when correctly read provides the impulse for this movement. The theology itself has within it the inner dynamism to break free from itself. By contrast, Althaus-Reid is suspicious of assumptions that are woven into the very fabric of the theology of liberation. For Althaus-Reid it is not possible to call the theology of liberation to be faithful to its own insights when it is blinded by the sexual ideologies in which it was formed. As a consequence, Althaus-Reid appears less concerned to offer practical proposals for political change than she is to radically subvert the conceptual structures in which such proposals might be expressed.

The theological focus of the critique developed by Althaus-Reid is evident in her concern for the Christology that both shapes and is expressed in a response to the poor. Gutiérrez clearly emphasizes the concern expressed at Puebla for women as those who are 'doubly oppressed'.[105] However, Althaus-Reid contends that if the Christ of theology is a Christ of repression and exclusion, the liberation expressed by such a theology will itself be restricted and exclusive. However laudable its intentions, the theology of liberation is betrayed at its very beginnings by the Christology to which it conforms: 'It is the coherence of life shown in heterosexual Christology which takes the role of legislating the symmetry of theology.

Such symmetry always rules out indecent corners.'¹⁰⁶ While Althaus-Reid acknowledges that the theology of liberation has produced a 'methodological rupture in Christology', she contends that it 'has been and still is part of the present hegemonic discourse'.¹⁰⁷ In place of this restricted and restrictive Christology Althaus-Reid calls for the production of 'an efficacious Christology with our creative imagination, nurtured by our own historical experiences'.¹⁰⁸ The work of liberation theology may only truly begin once Christ has been liberated from theology. While Althaus-Reid describes herself as 'more interested in orthopraxis than in orthodoxy', she is concerned to critique the orthodoxy that inhibits and undermines the orthopraxy that she seeks.¹⁰⁹

In contrast to this Christological suspicion, the theology of Gutiérrez expresses a confidence that a historic Christology, when truly understood, provides a structure in which a truly liberative theology might be expressed. He acknowledges that each historical moment will call for a renewed vision of this Christ and the liberation that is disclosed in him. It is however *this* Christ in whom such a liberation may and must be sought. A creative openness in history is accommodated within and secured by the Christ who is revealed in the scriptures and the teaching of the church. In describing the unity of personal and political liberation, Gutiérrez comments that 'the methodological approach here is inspired by the Council of Chalcedon'.¹¹⁰ According to him, this approach 'arises from the conviction that the gratuitousness of God's love is all-embracing' and leads to an expression of both 'God's call and the free response of human beings'.¹¹¹ Within this Chalcedonian framework, Gutiérrez is able to accept that any one or other expression of liberation theology will be entangled in dogmas and ideologies from which it must be freed. At the same time, he is confident that this structure sets free a continual dynamic of critique, revision and renewal.

This Christological structure gives Gutiérrez the confidence that the inevitable limitations of his theology will be exposed and addressed over time. It also implies an alternative to the project developed by Althaus-Reid. As I have demonstrated earlier, the specificity and particularity of Christ establish the motivation and model for the historical commitment called for by the theology of Gutiérrez. He formulates his theology within a series of convictions and commitments that Althaus-Reid does not share. As is evident in his response to the concerns expressed by the Congregation for the Defence of the Faith, Gutiérrez places his work within a clear historical, theological, and ecclesial framework. He welcomes the call of the Magisterium to a 'deepening and a clearer formulation of these themes'¹¹² and acknowledges that in the process 'we must re-evaluate

The Liberation of Utopia

many things'.[113] He seeks for his theology to take shape within a framework that is discerned within biblical revelation and its interpretation in the community of the church. By contrast, Althaus-Reid calls for a vision of Christ that destabilizes and problematizes these frameworks. It is a Christology that comes through a creative response to lived experience rather than one formed through 'just following thirty something years of his life which have been reduced to less than thirty something minutes of reading in the Gospels'.[114] It is clear that Gutiérrez would also reject a reductionistic and simplistic engagement with the witness of Scripture. However, it is the specificity of this life and the historicity of the gospel witness that calls liberation to a specific and historical expression. The contours of the liberation that is to be announced are established by the Christ by whom this liberation is proclaimed.

While Althaus-Reid might denounce this Christ and this liberation as being constrained within a particular sexual ideology, it is important to ask what annunciation accompanies her denunciation. In the theology of Gutiérrez 'the denunciation is to a large extent made with regard to the annunciation', and this annunciation concerns the incarnate Christ who is made known in the testimony and ministry of the church.[115] While it is unfair to say that the denunciation expressed by Althaus-Reid is devoid of a corresponding annunciation, this annunciation must remain unstable and uncertain. Althaus-Reid explains that 'we do not know definitely if the critical Christology of hope which we propose is feasible or not, or if in achieving efficacy it would cease to be Christology'.[116] Her theology must question even its own feasibility. Even the 'christological resymbolization' that takes place within this theology must be continually revised and, if necessary, abandoned along the way marked out by the radical freedom of faith.[117] However, if there is only the radical freedom of faith it is hard to see how the works of this faith can be examined, evaluated and revised. It is this radical faith that becomes an end in itself rather than the liberation that it is called to serve.

Conclusion

The utopia envisioned by Gutiérrez is characterized by a hope that discloses the liberative purpose of history; a love that directs liberative praxis in history; and a faith that sustains a liberative commitment to history. This utopia is a dynamic process that calls for the participation of Christians in history as they conform themselves to the promises of God for history. Gutiérrez concludes his exploration of the theme of utopia by declaring that 'to hope in Christ is at the same time to believe in the adventure of history, which opens infinite vistas to the love and action of the Christian'.[118] In each part of this utopian process, I have shown that his Christology is central to his utopian vision. This utopia unfolds through a hope in Christ that leads to an expression of a love of Christ which is sustained by a faith in Christ. As I engaged each of the criticisms developed in response to the theology of Gutiérrez, I considered how the Christology of Gutiérrez framed his response. The stability of the utopia that Gutiérrez constructs in his theology thus depends on the adequacy of the Christological framework by which it is secured and within which it takes shape. As I have shown throughout this project, the liberative vision of Gutiérrez depends for its clarity and coherence on the Christological proclamation through which it finds its focus. In the next chapter I will turn to a closer consideration of this Christology and its relation to the utopia envisioned by Gutiérrez.

Notes

1 Gustavo Gutiérrez, *A Theology of Liberation: History, politics, and salvation*, trans. Caridad Inda and John Eagleson (London: SCM Press, 2010), p. 216.
2 Gutiérrez, *A Theology of Liberation*, p. 218.
3 Gutiérrez, *A Theology of Liberation*, p. 217.
4 For an overview of these levels and a response to various criticisms, see Gustavo Gutiérrez, *The Truth Shall Make You Free: Confrontations*, trans. Matthew J. O'Connell (Maryknoll, NY: Orbis Books, 1990), pp. 128–40.
5 Gutiérrez, *A Theology of Liberation*, p. 135.
6 Gutiérrez, *A Theology of Liberation*, p. 218.
7 Gutiérrez, *A Theology of Liberation*, p. 219.
8 Gutiérrez, *A Theology of Liberation*, p. 218.
9 Gutiérrez, *A Theology of Liberation*, p. 219.
10 Gutiérrez, *A Theology of Liberation*, p. 223.
11 James B. Nickoloff, 'Church of the Poor: The ecclesiology of Gustavo Gutiérrez', *Theological Studies* 54, no. 3 (September 1993), p. 521.
12 Gutiérrez, *A Theology of Liberation*, p. 224.
13 Gutiérrez, *A Theology of Liberation*, p. 219.
14 Gaspar Martinez, *Confronting the Mystery of God: Political liberation and public theologies* (New York: Continuum, 2002), p. 131.
15 Gustavo Gutiérrez, *The God of Life*, trans. Matthew J. O'Connell (Maryknoll, NY: Orbis Books, 1991), p. 93.
16 Gutiérrez, *A Theology of Liberation*, p. 219.
17 Gustavo Gutiérrez, *The Power of the Poor in History*, trans. Robert R. Barr (Maryknoll, NY: Orbis Books, 1983), p. 72.
18 Gustavo Gutiérrez, 'A hermeneutic of hope', *The Center for Latin American Studies, Vanderbilt University – Occasional Papers* 13 (September 2012), p. 6.

19 Gutiérrez, 'A hermeneutic of hope', p. 9.
20 Gutiérrez, *A Theology of Liberation*, p. 201.
21 Gutiérrez, *A Theology of Liberation*, p. 201.
22 Gutiérrez, *A Theology of Liberation*, p. 201.
23 Gutiérrez, *A Theology of Liberation*, p. 219.
24 Gutiérrez, *A Theology of Liberation*, p. 220.
25 Gutiérrez, *A Theology of Liberation*, p. 222.
26 Gutiérrez, *The Power of the Poor in History*, p. 187.
27 Jack Zipes, 'Traces of hope: the non-synchronicity of Ernst Bloch' in *Not Yet: Reconsidering Ernst Bloch*, ed. Jamie Owen Daniel and Tom Moylan (London: Verso, 1997), pp. 1–14.
28 Tom Moylan, 'Bloch against Bloch: the theological reception of Das Prinzip Hoffnung and the liberation of the utopian function', *Utopian Studies* 1, no. 2 (1990), p. 42.
29 Moylan observes that 'Bloch still argues against the closure to which he himself has fallen prey.' Moylan, 'Bloch against Bloch', p. 45.
30 Moylan, 'Bloch against Bloch', p. 47.
31 Tom Moylan, 'Denunciation/Annunciation: The radical methodology of liberation theology', *Cultural Critique* 20 (Winter 1991–2), p. 56.
32 Congregation for the Doctrine of the Faith, 'Ten Observations on the Theology of Gustavo Gutiérrez' in *Liberation Theology: A documentary history*, ed. Alfred T. Hennelly (Maryknoll, NY: Orbis Books, 1990), p. 349.
33 Congregation for the Doctrine of the Faith, 'Instruction on Certain Aspects of the "Theology of Liberation"' in *Liberation Theology: A documentary history*, ed. Alfred T. Hennelly (Maryknoll, NY: Orbis Books, 1990), p. 408.
34 Gustavo Gutiérrez, 'Criticism will deepen, clarify liberation theology' in *Liberation Theology: A documentary history*, ed. Alfred T. Hennelly (Maryknoll, NY: Orbis Books, 1990), p. 423.
35 Gutiérrez, *The Truth Shall Make You Free*, p. 61.
36 Gutiérrez, *The Truth Shall Make You Free*, p. 63.
37 Gutiérrez, *The Truth Shall Make You Free*, p. 15.
38 Gutiérrez, *The Truth Shall Make You Free*, p. 43.
39 Gutiérrez, *The Truth Shall Make You Free*, p. 87.
40 Gutiérrez, *The Truth Shall Make You Free*, p. 86.
41 Gutiérrez, *A Theology of Liberation*, p. 7.
42 Gustavo Gutiérrez, 'Memory and prophecy' in *The Option for the Poor in Christian Theology*, ed. Daniel G. Groody (Notre Dame, IN: University of Notre Dame Press, 2007), p. 32.
43 Gustavo Gutiérrez, 'Option for the Poor' in *Systematic Theology: Perspectives from Liberation Theology: Readings from Mysterium Liberationis*, ed. Jon Sobrino and Ignacio Ellacuría (Maryknoll, NY: Orbis Books, 1996), p. 324.
44 Gutiérrez, *A Theology of Liberation*, p. 224.
45 Gutiérrez, *A Theology of Liberation*, p. 218.
46 Gutiérrez, *A Theology of Liberation*, p. 219.
47 Gutiérrez, *A Theology of Liberation*, p. 223.
48 Gutiérrez, *A Theology of Liberation*, p. 203.
49 Gutiérrez, *A Theology of Liberation*, p. 222.
50 Gutiérrez, *The God of Life*, p. 111.

51 Gutiérrez, *The God of Life*, p. 115.
52 Gutiérrez, *The Truth Shall Make You Free*, p. 140.
53 James B. Nickoloff, 'A future for Peru? Gustavo Gutiérrez and the reasons for his hope', *Horizons* 19, no. 1 (Spring 1992), p. 35.
54 Gutiérrez, *The God of Life*, p. 40.
55 Gutiérrez, *The God of Life*, p. 36.
56 Ivan Petrella, *The Future of Liberation Theology: An argument and manifesto* (Aldershot: Ashgate, 2004), p. 16.
57 Ivan Petrella, 'The futures of Liberation Theology' in *Radical Christian Voices and Practice: Essays in honour of Christopher Rowland*, ed. Zoë Bennett and David B. Gowler (Oxford: Oxford University Press, 2012), p. 202.
58 Petrella, 'The futures of Liberation Theology', p. 201.
59 Petrella, *The Future of Liberation Theology*, p. 149.
60 Petrella, *The Future of Liberation Theology*, p. 11.
61 Although expressed from a different perspective, it is helpful to recall the concern raised by Stanley Hauerwas: 'At the beginning of *A Theology of Liberation* Gutiérrez explains why liberation is the primary theme of his theology. It is the term that best expresses in our times "the struggle to construct a just and fraternal society" ... The great difficulty with this kind of claim is its fatal abstractness.' Stanley Hauerwas, 'Some theological reflections on Gutiérrez's use of "liberation" as a theological concept', *Modern Theology* 3, no. 1 (October 1986), p. 69.
62 Gutiérrez, *A Theology of Liberation*, p. 23.
63 While European theology and philosophy have clearly left their mark on the theology of Gutiérrez, Cadorette observes that 'no one has influenced his thinking more than two fellow Peruvians: José María Arguedas and José Carlos Mariátegui'. Curt Cadorette, *From the Heart of the People: The theology of Gustavo Gutiérrez* (Oak Park, IL: Meyer Stone Books, 1988), p. 67.
64 Cadorette, *From the Heart of the People*, p. 76.
65 Gutiérrez, *A Theology of Liberation*, p. 112.
66 Gutiérrez, *A Theology of Liberation*, p. 222.
67 Gustavo Gutiérrez, 'Entre Las Calandrias' in *Arguedas: Mito, Historia, Religión y Entre Las Calandrias*, vol. 48 (Lima: Centro de Estudios y Publicaciones, 1982), p. 261.
68 Gutiérrez, 'Entre Las Calandrias', p. 262.
69 Gutiérrez, 'Entre Las Calandrias', p. 258.
70 Gutiérrez, 'Entre Las Calandrias', p. 257.
71 Gutiérrez, 'Entre Las Calandrias', p. 259.
72 Gutiérrez, 'Entre Las Calandrias', p. 263.
73 Gutiérrez, 'Entre Las Calandrias', pp. 265-6.
74 Gustavo Gutiérrez, *We Drink From Our Own Wells: The spiritual journey of a people* (Maryknoll, NY: Orbis Books, 2003), p. 21.
75 Gustavo Gutiérrez and Richard Shaull, 'Freedom and Salvation: a political problem' in *Liberation and Change*, trans. Alvin Gutiérrez (Atlanta, GA: John Knox Press, 1977), p. 85.
76 'To hope in Christ is at the same time to believe in the adventure of history, which opens infinite vistas to the love and action of the Christian.' Gutiérrez, *A Theology of Liberation*, p. 224.
77 Gutiérrez, *A Theology of Liberation*, p. 218.

78 Gutiérrez, *The Power of the Poor in History*, p. 193.
79 Gutiérrez, *The Power of the Poor in History*, p. 209.
80 Gutiérrez, *Our Own Wells*, p. 1.
81 Gutiérrez, *Our Own Wells*, p. 71.
82 Gutiérrez, *A Theology of Liberation*, p. 40.
83 Gutiérrez, *A Theology of Liberation*, p. 41.
84 Gutiérrez, *Our Own Wells*, p. 116.
85 Gutiérrez, *Our Own Wells*, p. 117.
86 Gutiérrez, *The God of Life*, p. 101.
87 Gutiérrez, *A Theology of Liberation*, p. 218.
88 Gutiérrez, *A Theology of Liberation*, p. 218.
89 Gutiérrez, *A Theology of Liberation*, p. 244.
90 Gutiérrez, *A Theology of Liberation*, p. 381 n. 48.
91 Gutiérrez, *A Theology of Liberation*, p. 219.
92 Gutiérrez, *A Theology of Liberation*, p. 244.

93 Marcella Althaus-Reid, Ivan Petrella and Luiz Carlos Susin, eds, 'Class, sex and the theologian: reflections on the liberationist movement in Latin America' in *Another Possible World: A selection of the contributions to the First World Forum on Theology and Liberation*, Reclaiming Liberation Theology (World Forum on Theology and Liberation, London: SCM Press, 2007), p. 26.

94 Althaus-Reid, 'Demythologising liberation theology: reflections on power, poverty and sexuality, in *The Cambridge Companion to Liberation Theology*, ed. Christopher Rowland, 2nd edn (Cambridge, UK; New York: Cambridge University Press, 2007), p. 125.

95 Marcella Althaus-Reid, 'On wearing skirts without underwear: "Indecent Theology challenging the liberation theology of the pueblo". Poor women contesting Christ', *Feminist Theology* 7, no. 20 (January 1999), p. 42.

96 Marcella Althaus-Reid, *Indecent Theology: Theological perversions in sex, gender and politics* (London: Routledge, 2000), p. 22.

97 Althaus-Reid, *Indecent Theology*, p. 133.
98 Althaus-Reid, *Indecent Theology*, p. 163.
99 Marcella Althaus-Reid, *The Queer God* (London: Routledge, 2003), p. 2.
100 Althaus-Reid, 'Demythologising liberation theology', p. 127.
101 Althaus-Reid, 'Demythologising liberation theology', p. 127.
102 Althaus-Reid, 'Demythologising liberation theology', p. 128.
103 Althaus-Reid, 'Demythologising liberation theology', p. 132.

104 Ivan Petrella, 'Liberation theology undercover', *Political Theology* 18, no. 4 (19 May 2017), p. 326.

105 Gustavo Gutiérrez, 'Gustavo Gutiérrez' in *Teólogos de La Liberación Hablan Sobre La Mujer*, ed. Leonardo Boff and Elsa Tamez (San José, Costa Rica: Departamento Ecuménico de Investigaciones, 1986), p. 52. My translation.

106 Althaus-Reid, *Indecent Theology*, p. 102.
107 Althaus-Reid, 'Wearing skirts without underwear', p. 40.
108 Althaus-Reid, *Indecent Theology*, p. 118.
109 Althaus-Reid, 'Wearing skirts without underwear', p. 51.
110 Gutiérrez, *The Truth Shall Make You Free*, p. 122.
111 Gutiérrez, *The Truth Shall Make You Free*, p. 123.
112 Gutiérrez, 'Criticism Will Deepen', p. 423.

113 Gutiérrez, 'Memory and prophecy', p. 32.
114 Althaus-Reid, *Indecent Theology*, p. 118.
115 Gutiérrez, *A Theology of Liberation*, p. 218.
116 Marcella Althaus-Reid, 'Do not stop the flow of my blood: a critical Christology of hope amongst Latin American women', *Studies in World Christianity* 1, no. 2 (October 1995), p. 146.
117 Althaus-Reid, 'Do not stop the flow of my blood', p. 157.
118 Gutiérrez, *A Theology of Liberation*, p. 224.

9

Liberation and the Humanity that 'Is Not Here'

Introduction: eschatology and the Christ who is not here

In each of the Gospels, the reality of the resurrection is first made known through a confrontation with the empty tomb. The narratives render the absence of Christ as the grounds for hope in him. The absence of *his* body becomes the hope for *every* body – and the whole of creation. As I outlined in the previous chapter, the eschatology of Gutiérrez proclaims a hope in the liberation that is disclosed in Christ. This hope is made known by Christ in the contexts of suffering and oppression where its absence is most acutely felt. In these contexts, hope in Christ leads to an expression of love for Christ which in turn is sustained by a faith in Christ. In the darkness of the tomb, a confrontation with the reality that 'he is not here' becomes the possibility of knowing the hope that 'he is risen'.

As Gutiérrez develops and defends his theological project, Christology is central to his utopian vision and in order to explore the eschatological terrain that he maps out it will be necessary to check these Christological bearings. In previous chapters I have argued that the anthropology developed by Gutiérrez is inhibited by the Christology through which it takes shape. At the close of Part One, I argued that the particularity of Christ in his person receded from view. At the end of Part Two, I argued that the specificity of Christ in his work was obscured. In this final chapter I will draw these two threads together and contend that the attempt by Gutiérrez to speak of a liberated humanity is inhibited by an underdeveloped account of the resurrected Christ in his personal and physical particularity.

This chapter will begin with a consideration of how Gutiérrez relates liberative hope to human history, before moving on to examine the personal and physical quality of the hope that he proclaims. At each stage I will argue that his Christology makes his eschatology vulnerable to the very abstractions against which he warns. In order to offer a vision of a humanity who may speak of God as Father, the one who returned to the Father and will return from the Father must be clearly seen.

When will God be known as Father? Hope for history

As Gutiérrez recounts the unified history of salvation and creation, the Kingdom of God is characterized as both a present reality and a future hope. He identifies the tension of this eschatological 'now and not yet' in the ministry of Jesus and wrestles with this tension in his own attempt to envision the future of liberation.

The relation of the kingdom to human history: 'Now and not yet'

In his theology, Gutiérrez presents the Kingdom of God as at once intimately bound to human history and fundamentally distinct from human history. On the one hand, he presents biblical eschatology as an 'intrahistorical reality' whose progress is marked by 'social realities implying a historical liberation'.[1] Eschatology is known in history and unfolds through history. However, when Gutiérrez speaks of eschatology as an 'intrahistorical reality' he is cautious not to restrict or reduce the eschatological to the historical. The unfolding of God's eschatological purposes takes place as each stage of promise and fulfilment calls forth new promises which anticipate further fulfilment. The eschatological promises of God find 'partial fulfilments through liberating historical events, which are in turn new promises marking the road towards total fulfilment'.[2] For Gutiérrez, therefore, the eschatological promises of Scripture address themselves to, but resist closure within, the events of history: 'The eschatological prophecy refers therefore to a concrete event and *in* it to another fuller and more comprehensive one to which history must be open.'[3] The kingdom unfolds throughout history by proclaiming to each moment of history a fullness that still awaits. While 'the historical, political liberating event *is* the growth of the Kingdom and *is* a salvific event', Gutiérrez cautions that 'it is not *the* coming of the Kingdom, not *all* of salvation', but must rather be understood as 'the historical realization of the Kingdom and, therefore, it also proclaims its fullness'.[4] The eschatological is known within but is not to be confused with the historical. Far from being limited to or restricted by history, the eschatological purposes of God are what give history its impulse towards the future.

Liberation and the Humanity that 'Is Not Here'

The proclamation of the Kingdom of God must be characterized by this relation to and distinction from human history. Both the possibility of the 'now' and the promise of the 'not yet' must be heard in a faithful proclamation of the kingdom. In this way the proclamation of the kingdom proceeds through the dynamic of denunciation and annunciation that I explored in the previous chapter. Gutiérrez calls for a 'denunciation of the existing order' that takes place within the context of an 'annunciation of what is not yet, but will be'.[5] Each is described as informing and enriching the other. He argues that 'eschatological promises are clearly being fulfilled in history' but calls for a relation to that history which is marked by 'a permanent detachment'.[6] This detachment is marked by and makes possible a hope in the eschatological promises of God as they unfold throughout history. While it is necessary to be attentive to 'the ambivalence that marks every historical development', such caution about historical developments must never slip into cynicism towards them: 'To thwart them out of fear that history might repeat itself would be to display too mean-spirited an analysis of the situation and a lack of hope in the God who makes all things new (see Rev. 21.5).'[7] The 'not yet' calls the Christian to discern the promise and possibility of the future in the 'now'. A hope for a future in which all things are made new leads to a commitment to the history from which this future is born.

According to Gutiérrez, the teachings of Jesus offer a model for how this tension is to be understood and expressed. As Jesus proclaims his kingdom the historical and political are placed into an eschatological context through which their true meaning is revealed. Drawing on the work of Oscar Cullmann, Gutiérrez traces this relationship in a comparison between the ministry of Jesus and the Zealot movement. He argues that 'the Zealots were not mistaken in feeling that Jesus was simultaneously near and far away'.[8] The nearness is felt in the historical and social reality that is proclaimed in the kingdom. The distance is the hope to which these historical realities point.[9] The preaching of the kingdom is characterized by a 'universality and totality' through which the liberation of Israel is placed 'on a deeper level, with far reaching consequences'.[10] There is no conflict between the political and the spiritual nor is there a conflation of the historical and the eschatological. Instead, in the preaching of Jesus 'the political is grafted into the eternal'.[11]

This language of grafting expresses the tension that Gutiérrez is concerned to preserve. While he draws on observations made by Cullmann, he rejects the way in which Cullmann coordinates the relation between the spiritual and the political, the historical and the eschatological. Gutiérrez reads in Cullmann an 'insistence on personal conversion as opposed, in a certain sense, to the need for the transformation of structures'.[12] A concern for conversions arises from the conviction of the impending advent of the kingdom. In contrast, a commitment to the transformation of social structures is characteristic of a hope in the kingdom whose coming is delayed. For Gutiérrez this schema separates personal conversion from its political implications. The two are placed in opposition with one replacing or having priority over the other. According to Gutiérrez, the conclusion drawn by Cullmann 'is based on Jesus's words but tends to diffuse or debilitate the tensions between the present and the future which characterizes his preaching of the Kingdom'.[13] The present and the future are to be neither conflated nor placed into conflict. Instead, the tension between the two must be preserved. Historical commitment deepens the eschatological hope by which it is at the same time critiqued. This critique gives rise to a new stage of historical commitment which is then refined through further eschatological critique.

Proclaiming the kingdom that is 'not yet'

The tension that Gutiérrez identifies in the teaching of Jesus makes itself felt in his own attempt to both cast a vision for the future and keep that future from being captured by the present. The kingdom cannot be 'planned or predesigned' and it is precisely in being unknown within history that it offers a radical hope for history.[14] Gutiérrez argues for a sensitivity to 'the ambivalence that marks every historical moment';[15] the cultivation of an attitude of 'permanent detachment' in the midst of historical commitment;[16] and an acceptance of an 'ignorance' that refuses to be restricted by the realities of the present.[17]

As Gutiérrez proclaims the 'not yet' of the kingdom, it is important to ask what hope is offered to those who live, suffer and die in the 'now'. On the one hand, the kingdom comes in history. As Gutiérrez describes the 'historical pilgrimage' of the people of God he acknowledges that 'its successes, its omissions, and its errors are our heritage. They should not, however, delimit our boundaries. The People of God march on, "accounting for their hope" toward "a new heaven and a new earth".'[18] On the other hand, each moment of this history is characterized by ambivalence and ambiguity. As history moves forward, it is important to ask whether those who suffer today are at risk of being left behind. As Benedict XVI observes, in any consideration of the relation of hope to history, 'The question unavoidably arises that Adorno so clearly posed: What kind of reconciliation is it that only counts for those who come after? What about us? What about the victims of injustice throughout history?'[19] In a similar way, Kelsey draws attention to certain anthropological questions that arise when creation, salvation and consummation are drawn together into a single narrative. For Kelsey, such a narrative begs the question of when the truth of humanity is actually to be achieved: 'Can eschatological consummation be understood simply as the final actualization of the goal of creation without the consequence that the movement from beginning to end just *is* God's creative act and that only at the eschatological state is the "creation" truly actual?'[20] If the actuality of humanity is only achieved at the end of a historical process, then this begs the question of the status of the humanity that is encountered within the unfolding of this historical process. There is a danger that while 'the People of God march on', there are those who never see the historical moment to which the painful process – characterized as it is by 'its omissions and its errors' – is to lead. Even if history lives now 'on the verge of human epiphany, "athropophany"', it is important to ask what hope this offers to those whose suffering and death have led history to such a moment. It is important to ask whether, amid the 'not yet' of the kingdom, there is a hope to be received by those who live, suffer and die 'now'.

Proclaiming the kingdom that is 'now'

Gutiérrez seeks to guard his theology against the risks associated with an evolutionary view of salvation history in a number of ways. First, he emphasizes the present reality of the kingdom. He argues that 'the term "eschatological" does not refer solely to the end of history; it also implies a clear-sighted attention to the present'.[21] Distinguishing between '*chronos* and *kairos*', Gutiérrez associates the coming of the kingdom with the second of these concepts and its reference 'not so much to an hour or a date as to the element of human density'.[22] As he considers the proclamation of the kingdom in Mark 1.14–15, he observes that in this passage 'a *kairos* has arrived and not simply that a date set in advance has been reached'.[23] The coming of the kingdom is not to be understood chronologically; rather it is

> if I may coin a word 'kairologically' at hand and in the process of being brought to completion ... This twofold aspect is captured in the term 'eschatology,' which refers to both the future and to the historical present or, in other words, to an event that is already present but has not yet attained to its full form.[24]

The successive stages of human history are not simply subordinated to a future moment within history. Rather, the kingdom disclosed in Christ is 'kairologically' present to each moment. The past and present are not subsumed within an impersonal process. The future proclaimed in the kingdom makes the neighbour present in their concrete and historical particularity.

Not only does Gutiérrez describe the nearness and presence of the kingdom to each historical moment, but he also draws on the concept of memory to describe the way in which each historical moment is present before God. Gutiérrez argues that 'far from being an abstract category, or from being limited to a tiresome chronological succession, time becomes, thanks to memory, a space where we encounter the face of Jesus, the Son of God made flesh, and a space for encounter with others'.[25] This memory 'is a present that has its fount in the always active and ever-faithful love of God' because 'the God of the Bible is a God who remembers'.[26] If the character of God is made known in his faithfulness, the life of his people will be marked by remembering. The life of God's people involves hearing the call to 'make God's memory our own' and so to make present in history those whom history might otherwise forget.[27]

In this way Gutiérrez echoes the language of Benedict who, following Augustine, draws on 'the concept of memory' as a model for how time in its passing may be interiorized and so 'is given a continuing existence, a sort of eternity'.[28] This dynamic is exemplified in the cross. The self-giving of Christ on the cross is not only a gift given in time, but also 'in the giving of self over to the Father, transcends time and at the same time draws time into itself'.[29] The cross makes known the presence of God to each successive moment of human history. The past is not simply a stage in the service of some future state, it is always present before God. This remembering is both what makes possible the proclamation of the kingdom and what the proclamation of the kingdom makes possible. As the people of God make the memory of God their own, the forgotten of history are made present and are called to remember their own dignity before God: 'The option for the poor is a contribution that empowers them to take ownership of their own voice by proclaiming the Gospel's challenge to remember their human dignity as daughters and sons of God.'[30] The kingdom is the rule of the God who remembers and so it cannot be made present when the poor and suffering are absent. For Gutiérrez, a conception of history as an impersonal evolutionary process is inimical to the call of the kingdom to make present and remember those who are forgotten and left behind. As he recounts a narrative of God's Kingdom unfolding through the successive stages of human history, he seeks to protect this narrative from degenerating into the account of an impersonal movement towards a future goal. The concepts of *kairos* and memory are deployed by Gutiérrez to express the relation of time and eternity as they come together in the Kingdom of God. The coming kingdom is present to each moment of history and each moment of human history is present before God.

As Gutiérrez seeks to proclaim the presence of the kingdom to the present realities of suffering and oppression, his conviction is that resurrection hope is only truly encountered in the darkness of the empty tomb. In other words, the proclamation of the kingdom is most clearly heard when the tension between annunciation and denunciation – the now and the not yet – is carefully preserved. James Ashley argues that the structure of mystical theology provides a framework through which this dynamic can be understood. The annunciation and denunciation that characterize the proclamation of the kingdom correspond to a tension that is characteristic of the mystical encounter with God. Ashley explains:

> The *via negativa* does not replace the *via positiva* or render it superfluous but complements it. The two together combine to open up a space within which the mystery of God can be found for the one willing to risk the itinerary it proposes.[31]

As mystical theology proceeds through an experience of the interplay between presence and absence – knowledge and ignorance – so in liberation theology there is a 'contemplation in historical action' in which socio-political action is the locus for a kind of mystical union with God.[32]

Ashley observes that both mystical and liberation theologies depend on a tension in which presence and absence are experienced together. One is not supplanted by the other, rather, each is the context through which the other is to be understood: 'Affirmation and denial, constructed in tension with one another, open up the space in which the mystery of God can be disclosed.'[33] The option for the poor and a commitment to struggle within history places the Christian into the heart of what Ashley describes as 'the tensive moment' in which the truth of the kingdom may be encountered.[34] Just as the mystical sight of God will be experienced amid darkness and ignorance, so too the liberative sight of the kingdom will be disclosed in sites of suffering and oppression.

An apocalyptic orientation sustains a commitment to history in which resurrection hope is known in the midst of suffering and death. Ashley observes that this dynamic is developed by Gutiérrez by 'drawing a parallel with the imagery of the dark night' that is such an important a feature of the mystical tradition.[35] His liberation theology draws on the mystical tradition of the church to argue that 'the hope of resurrection ... is experienced in this life ... in the "dark night" of labouring with the victims, of solidarity with those who suffer'.[36] Gutiérrez describes the 'two fold experience of the Christian' in which 'a new face-to-face encounter with the Lord' is made possible 'in the blackest depth of "the dark night of injustice"': 'John of the Cross speaks of the "frightful night" through which one must pass, but he also says that the desert is "the more delightful, savorous, and loving, the deeper, vaster, and more solitary it is".'[37] The 'permanent detachment' and 'ignorance' to which Gutiérrez calls the Christian must not be confused with uncertainty or equivocation. They describe instead a willingness to enter more deeply and painfully into this desert and to accept the darkness of this night. The emphasis on ignorance and ambiguity in the theology of Gutiérrez weaves a mystical and apophatic texture into his proclamation of the kingdom. Sustained by apocalyptic hope, the Christian is able to enter into the darkness and desert of suffering confident that in such moments the truth of Christ is made known.

Conclusion

While Gutiérrez is attentive to the tension that must characterize a proclamation of the kingdom, his treatment of this tension raises the question of whether the kingdom can ever be encountered beyond this 'tensive movement'. While the option for the poor and a commitment to historical struggle are the site of kingdom proclamation in the present, it is important to ask whether the kingdom proclaimed by Gutiérrez offers a sight of the history that lies beyond both poverty and struggle. If fulfilment always gives way to further promise, is history only ever the place of promise and never of final fulfilment? Does the kingdom express more than an ever-receding hope? Is the kingdom rendered unknowable and ambiguous if it can only be expressed apophatically? Is it always asymptotically related to human history? Where and when will it be possible to speak of God as Father in a world that has been made humane? It is to these questions that I now turn.

Liberation and the Humanity that 'Is Not Here'

Where will God be known as Father? Hope for every body

The Gospel narratives present not only an encounter with the darkness of the tomb. They attest to the light in which the resurrection hope is disclosed. The hope of the resurrection is known in the absence of Christ's body and so eschatology bears the shape of the Christology in which it is expressed. A theology that speaks of Christ in his concrete particularity has the resources to describe his eschatological kingdom in a way that avoids the danger of an abstraction from history or an idolatrous identification with history. As such it is important to examine the relationship between Christology and eschatology in the theology of Gutiérrez and ask whether 'darkness or absence' remain always an 'ineluctable part' of his proclamation of the kingdom. Having recognized the importance of the historical within the eschatology of Gutiérrez it is important to ask if this is accompanied by an emphasis on the personal and physical quality of resurrection hope. I will argue that his account of the resurrection of Jesus inhibits his attempt to proclaim a liberation that is both personal and physical.

The resurrection of Christ and personal liberation

The theology of Gutiérrez draws the resurrection into an intimate relationship with history. The history of death and lament is also a history of resurrection and rejoicing as each intensifies the other and together characterize an encounter with the kingdom. While resurrection hope is woven into the experience of human history, Gutiérrez emphasizes the reality of the resurrection that is lived in the life of the believer and the believing community. However, he tends to characterize the resurrection as a hope that is corporate and historical rather than particular and personal. In his reflection on Job 19, he cites Job's desperate cry of faith: 'After they have pulled my flesh from me, and I am without my flesh, I shall see God.'[38] Gutiérrez goes on to draw out the present and historical implications of this hope. It is 'the experience of near death' that brings Job to a vision of 'the God who ("at the end") will not allow him to be destroyed in the world of injustice and loneliness'.[39] The chapter that follows on from this reflection begins with the observation that 'Job's hope is not in vain: his desire to see God and to speak to God is fulfilled' and that this fulfilment takes place within history 'for it is there that God grants self-revelation'.[40] While the commentary offered by Gutiérrez understandably has in view the theophany that takes place at the climax of the book, it is interesting that little attention is given to the implication in Job's cry that there is a hope that lies beyond both life and death. It is important to acknowledge with Gutiérrez that Job 19.25-27 'has come down to us in a form that makes the reading difficult and therefore susceptible of substantially different translations'.[41] However, in the translation adopted by Gutiérrez there is at the very least the suggestion of an encounter with God that may be hoped for after death – a body that might see God even 'after they have pulled my flesh from me'. While he describes Job being brought near to death in his commentary on these verses, there is little consideration of this hope beyond death. In the narrative of the book, the hope of Job expressed in chapter 19 finds a fulfilment in the life of Job – but the language of chapter 19 at the very least raises the question of a further hope to which this historical encounter might point. Job's hope in 'the God who ("at the end") will not allow him to be destroyed' is so striking because it looks beyond even the experience of destruction.[42] It may be that Gutiérrez is, at this point and in a way that is common within the field of Old Testament scholarship, simply being cautious to avoid a projection of New Testament categories onto an Old Testament text. What is striking, however, is that this reticence to speak of a personal and physical resurrection remains, as we shall see, even in his exploration of the resurrection in the New Testament.

While Gutiérrez emphasizes life in the midst of death, he does not develop the idea of a resurrection life that liberates from personal and physical death. The emphasis that is evident as he reflects on the book of Job is also present in his consideration of a liberative spirituality in *We Drink from Our Own Wells*. In this work, Gutiérrez explores the theme of resurrection as it is expressed especially in 1 Corinthians 15. The central concern of this chapter is the reality of the resurrected life of Christ and the believer after death, but the exposition of this chapter offered by Gutiérrez centres on the resurrected life of the believer and the community of faith *before* personal death. He explains that 'a "spiritual body"' is one belonging to a person who 'walks according to the Spirit', and observes the way in which Pauline theology characterizes 'the body as capable of living a definitive kind of life'.[43] This emphasis on the present reality of resurrected life in the Spirit appears to absorb the corresponding Pauline teaching on the future resurrected life that lies beyond death. Gutiérrez takes the 'dialectic of *death/life* in Paul's theology' to be the 'key to an understanding of Christian existence' and so concludes that 'The body that has been freed from forces of death will lead a life in the Spirit. "Flesh and blood cannot inherit the kingdom of God" (1 Cor. 15.50), but the liberated body can.'[44] Gutiérrez takes a sequence that addresses the life of Christ and the believer after death and applies it to the life of the believer in the present. A sequence that explores eschatological transformation is drawn into a description of historical liberation. As he develops these reflections in this section of his book he draws heavily on the work of Rudolf Bultmann. It is interesting that his comments on 1 Corinthians 15.50 are accompanied by a note in which a different emphasis is evident in the exegesis of Bultmann. In the note, Gutiérrez cites the observation of Bultmann that 'Paul cannot conceive even of a future human existence after death "when that which is perfect is come" as an existence without *soma* – in contrast with the view of those in Corinth who deny the resurrection.'[45] While the exegesis of Bultmann emphasizes 'a future human existence after death', the argument of Gutiérrez centres on the life of the Christian and the community of faith in the present. The Kingdom of God is to be inherited by the liberated body as it – as they – walk by the Spirit in history.

In his consideration of the resurrection in the book of Job and in the theology of Paul, Gutiérrez draws out the emphasis on the lived reality of the resurrection that is present in these texts. What is striking, however, is the paucity of his engagement with the reality of resurrected life that lies after and beyond the death of the individual. I am not suggesting that the theology of Gutiérrez is inimical to or incapable of such a consideration. It is important however to observe his reticence to develop such a consideration. In his theology the resurrection is most commonly either drawn into the life of the believer or opened into the ongoing life of the church. In both cases a question remains concerning the hope held out to individuals as they consider their physical death.

While Gutiérrez warns against turning Jesus into 'an abstraction, a symbol, a cipher' and characterizes the incarnation as 'an irruption that smells of the stable', the 'realism' that he seeks to convey in his account of the incarnation seems not to be carried over into his account of the resurrection.[46] By failing to consider sufficiently the personal and material reality of the resurrection after death, Gutiérrez inhibits his own articulation of the historical and political implications of the resurrection in the present. The answer to the question 'What about us?' must be heard in the empty tomb. It is heard in the claim staked by the resurrection on the body that has died and will be raised.

The resurrection of Christ and physical liberation

If the previous stage of my argument considered the characterization of the person in the eschatology of Gutiérrez, this section will focus more precisely on the role of the body. What follows therefore is a consideration of the same theme from a different perspective. In the previous section I explored the problem of death and questioned whether the eschatological hope offered by Gutiérrez was sufficiently *personal*. In this section I will turn to the challenge of martyrdom and ask if this hope is adequately *physical*. I will argue that, in a context where theology has traditionally accentuated the otherness of Christian hope, Gutiérrez emphasizes ongoing historicity.

The stark reality of a corpse demands a response that is personal, and this response is heard in the empty tomb of Jesus. As a hope that is personal it is also a hope that is physical. If it is to be a hope for everybody, it must be a hope for every *body*. The problem of death raises the question of how each person is related to the eschatological kingdom and the challenge of martyrdom accentuates this question. It provokes a question that specifically concerns the body. The question of how every *body* is related to this eschatological hope.

Gutiérrez writes movingly of the martyrdom that has characterized the experience of the church in Latin America. He observes that the 'furrows' being ploughed by the presence of the poor in the Latin American church 'are watered at times with the blood of witnesses (martyrs) to that preferential love of God for the poor' which in a 'land of premature and unjust death' is bearing fruit in 'an ever-stronger assertion of the right to life and to the joy of Easter'.[47] As Gutiérrez reflects on the contemporary experience of martyrdom, he argues that 'the present-day Latin American experience of martyrdom bids us all turn back to the major sources of all spirituality: the blood-stained experience of the early Christian community'.[48] By drawing a connection between martyrdom in present-day Latin America and the 'blood-stained experience of the early Christian community', Gutiérrez discerns in the sufferings of the contemporary church the seeds of hope. Amid the experience of death he seeks to proclaim the hope of resurrection. He declares that, 'solidarity, prayer, and martyrdom add up to a time of salvation and judgment, a time of grace and stern demand – a time, above all, of hope'.[49] Martyrdom becomes a proclamation of the hope to which the believer lays claim by faith. In the context of martyrdom and suffering the church must be attentive to the hope of those who suffer and are martyred if it is to grow and be sustained in its faith. For Gutiérrez, the church must draw on the resources of its eschatological hope if its faith is to be sustained in the midst of suffering and martyrdom.

While Gutiérrez places the contemporary context of martyrdom in continuity with the historical experience of the early church, it is interesting to note the emphasis that he places on the vindication of the martyr in history. Reflecting on Jesus' challenge that following him involves 'taking up the cross', Gutiérrez observes that while this 'can be a rich metaphor', it also expresses 'a shocking reality'.[50] The reality of which the disciples were aware at the time of Jesus is a reality that is experienced by the church in Latin America. However, when he turns to consider the resurrection hope that is the counterpart to faithfulness in death, his language moves from the personal to the historical and from the physical to the spiritual. As he describes those 'who have determined to put themselves behind Jesus and follow him, paying the price of rejection, of calumny, or even of the surrender of their own lives', he recalls the hope that is held out to those who take up the cross: 'Those who lose their life for the Lord and the gospel will save it. The following of Jesus is oriented to the horizon of resurrection, definitive life.'[51] It is important to examine the language of Gutiérrez at this point. The promise of salvation and resurrection is expressed in terms of 'definitive life'. The language that is associated here with the hope of the resurrection is deployed later in the book to describe how the hope of the resurrection is lived out in the life of the believer. The believer living in the power of the Spirit is 'a "spiritual body"' that is 'capable of living a definitive kind of life'.[52] The definitive life that is promised to the martyr is discerned in the commitment to liberation lived by the church. Gutiérrez follows the tradition in his confidence that 'the blood of martyrs gives life to the ecclesial community'.[53] There is, however, little evidence of the tradition's concern for the life given to the body of the martyr in the resurrection. While he declares that 'fidelity unto death is a wellspring of life', this life is associated more with the body of the church in history than with the body of the martyr at the resurrection.[54]

What is interesting to note is that while Gutiérrez draws attention to the 'reality' that is expressed in the call to the cross, he accentuates the richness of resurrection as a theological image rather than material and personal reality. Both cross and resurrection may serve, to use the language of Gutiérrez, as 'a rich metaphor'. It is interesting, however, that the emphasis he places on the realism of the former is not evident in his consideration of the latter. This dynamic is evident in the reflections on martyrdom that are developed in *The Power of the Poor in History*. In one particular sequence, Gutiérrez speaks of 'the latter-day martyrs of

Gustavo Gutiérrez and the Liberative Sight of Christ

Latin America' and comments that 'it is through the critical experience of the empty tomb that the followers of Jesus today, like his friends of yesterday, come to grasp the fulness of the life and of the risen Christ who conquers all death'.[55] He goes on to marvel that 'rarely have so many deaths enriched a people and a church with such life' and, drawing on the imagery of Ezekiel 37, proclaims that, 'The living God is with his people. His Spirit lives in our dead and fills them with life. And now he raises up a whole people.'[56]

The reflections of Gutiérrez shift from the personal and material to the corporate and historical. The empty tomb of Christ finds its counterpart not in the resurrection of the body that suffered martyrdom but in the body of the church enlivened and sustained by the testimony of this martyrdom. The life that the Spirit gives to the body of the dead is evident in the people that are raised up by their witness and example. This is not to say that it is inappropriate to expound the spiritual, historical and ecclesiastical implications of the resurrection. However, while Gutiérrez draws out both metaphorical and 'realistic' readings of the cross, his treatment of the resurrection is so focused on the metaphorical that the physical and material become obscured.

The consideration of martyrdom emphasizes a continuity with the early church, but this continuity makes evident the discontinuities – or at the very least developments – in his discourse of martyrdom.[57] While it is important not to impose an artificial homogeneity onto the martyrology of the early church, an emphasis on the personal and material resurrection of the body is a prevalent theme of its discourse.[58] Douglas Farrow draws on Tertullian's treatise on the resurrection in order to explore how the doctrine of the resurrection of the body was forged in the context of martyrdom. In his treatise Tertullian offers 'not simply an apology for a dogma to which the pagan mind is ill-disposed'; rather, he develops 'a defence of the body, without which there can be no defence of either man or God as revealed in Jesus Christ, nor any exposition of eternal life'.[59] Farrow observes that 'Tertullian makes the martyrs his clients in the case for bodily continuity' and illustrates this argument of Tertullian with the following quotation from his treatise:

> For how absurd, and in truth how unjust, and in both respects how unworthy of God, for one substance to do the work, and another to reap the reward: that this flesh of ours should be torn by martyrdom, and another the crown.[60]

Liberation and the Humanity that 'Is Not Here'

The experience of martyrdom accentuates the personal and material reality of the resurrection. The same flesh destroyed by martyrdom is restored in and receives its recompense through its resurrection from the dead. The resurrection hope that is proclaimed in the context of martyrdom consists not only in the life that the martyr's death will bring to the church. It consists in the life that will be brought to the torn flesh of the martyr's body. On the basis of this historical analysis, Farrow draws a conclusion that, while polemical in its expression, nonetheless demands consideration. In so far as the church continues to 'insist on adherence to a literal reading of the creed's "on the third day he rose again in accordance with the scriptures"', Farrow argues that 'the symbolist readings of various liberationist and modernist theologians are disavowed'.[61] Gutiérrez would surely reject the dismissal of his theology as 'symbolist'. However, I have demonstrated that the physicality of eschatological hope remains at the very least underdeveloped in his thought. While the resurrection has a historical, cosmic and ecclesial scope, the personal and bodily resurrection of Christ provides its controlling centre. In the context of martyrdom, the church has traditionally made the body of the martyr a site in which the future hope is to be seen. The hope of the martyr is the hope revealed in the empty tomb. It is the hope that the same body that suffered death and shame will be the same body that receives life and vindication.

It may seem churlish to press for greater theological precision in the context of such a painful pastoral situation; however, it is precisely the gravity of the situation that indicates the need for further theological reflection. If the theology of Gutiérrez is to be true to its own liberative commitments, then it must follow in the tradition of the early church and cultivate what John Thiel describes as an 'eschatological imagination'.[62] In contrast with an eschatology that 'becomes a kind of "immanentology" in which talk about the life to come is really taken to be talk about life in the present',[63] Thiel claims that, 'a "thick" eschatology – one that exercises the eschatological imagination more rigorously – can be much more effective in portraying "the assurance of things hoped for, the conviction of things not seen" (Heb. 11.1)'.[64] This is not necessarily to follow Thiel in every aspect of how this eschatological imagination is to be expressed. It is one thing to emphasize that there is a real hope for the physical body. It is another to delineate precisely what must be imagined for this future hope to make itself felt in the present.[65] Thiel does helpfully raise the question of the integrity of this eschatological hope, however this integrity is to be conceived. Farrow delineates some of the historic parameters within which such an imagination is to be elaborated. The four points offered by Farrow as a summary of 'Christian thinking about the resurrection' begin by asserting that 'the resurrection is understood first as a human event, an event for the man Jesus'[66] before moving on to observe that 'second, and by extension, the resurrection is understood as a political event'.[67] Farrow's movement from the physical to the political is persuasive. The resurrection of Jesus defines the resurrection as a bodily reality, and it is as primarily a bodily reality that the resurrection has a political scope. Farrow explains that if the resurrection is not bodily it can have no political meaning, since political authority *is* authority over the body. But if the resurrection is bodily, then no social or political sphere is exempt from the judgement passed by God.[68]

Especially given the emphasis of Gutiérrez on the physicality and the reality of the incarnation, the argument developed by Farrow poses an important question for his theology. It is the question of whether the attention paid by Gutiérrez to the physicality of Christ in his incarnation is carried into a recognition of the physicality of Christ in his resurrection. According to him, to reflect on the reality of the body of Jesus in his incarnation is to hear the call of God to liberation. In the same way, a recognition of the physicality of Jesus in his resurrection is surely to find this call confirmed. The claim of the resurrection over politics and history passes through the reality of the resurrection as disclosed in the body. If the theology of Gutiérrez is to resource a truly liberative eschatology, then it must more clearly proclaim the personal and physical particularity of the hope that is offered in the resurrection.

Conclusion

In order to explore the eschatological terrain that is mapped out by the theology of Gustavo Gutiérrez, I began by examining the concept of the Kingdom of God that takes shape in his theology before moving on to examine the personal and physical quality of the hope that he proclaims. In previous chapters I have argued that the anthropology developed by Gutiérrez is inhibited by the Christology through which it takes shape. At the close of Part One I argued that the particularity of Christ in his person receded from view. At the end of Part Two I argued that the specificity of Christ in his work was obscured. In this final chapter I have argued that the attempt by Gutiérrez to speak of the eschatological reality of a liberated humanity is inhibited by an underdeveloped account of Christ in his personal and physical resurrection.

While Gutiérrez attempts to express the distinction in relation of history and eschatology, his theology evidences a tendency to absorb the latter into the former. In my analysis of the concept of the Kingdom of God in his theology, I explored the concern of Gutiérrez to maintain the tension of this relation. However, by examining his account of the resurrection of Jesus, I exposed the instability of this relation. As I explored the problem of death I questioned whether the eschatological hope offered by Gutiérrez was sufficiently personal, and as I considered the challenge of martyrdom I asked if this hope was adequately physical. I argued that, in his eschatology, the personal identity of the risen Jesus tends to be absorbed into the unfolding of history and the physical character of the risen Jesus tends to be expressed in terms of the ongoing life of the church. A more robust eschatology will need to take shape within the framework of a more stable Christology – a Christology that offers an adequate account of the Jesus who is personally and physically risen from the dead. The empty tomb receives its meaning from the particularity of the person whose body is absent, and it is the absence of this person and this body that establishes the resurrection hope which is to be proclaimed.

Notes

1 Gustavo Gutiérrez, *A Theology of Liberation: History, politics, and salvation*, trans. Caridad Inda and John Eagleson (London: SCM Press, 2010), p. 166.
2 Gutiérrez, *A Theology of Liberation*, p. 165.
3 Gutiérrez, *A Theology of Liberation*, p. 162.
4 Gutiérrez, *A Theology of Liberation*, p. 176. Emphasis original.
5 Gutiérrez, *A Theology of Liberation*, p. 218.
6 Gutiérrez, *A Theology of Liberation*, p. 166.
7 Gustavo Gutiérrez, *The Truth Shall Make You Free: Confrontations*, trans. Matthew J. O'Connell (Maryknoll, NY: Orbis Books, 1990), p. 116.
8 Gutiérrez, *A Theology of Liberation*, p. 216.
9 Gutiérrez, *A Theology of Liberation*, p. 217.
10 Gutiérrez, *A Theology of Liberation*, p. 216.
11 Gutiérrez, *A Theology of Liberation*, p. 217.
12 Gutiérrez, *A Theology of Liberation*, p. 215.
13 Gutiérrez, *A Theology of Liberation*, p. 215.
14 Gutiérrez, *A Theology of Liberation*, p. 167.
15 Gutiérrez, *The Truth Shall Make You Free*, p. 116.
16 Gutiérrez, *A Theology of Liberation*, p. 166.
17 Gutiérrez, *A Theology of Liberation*, p. 167.
18 Gutiérrez, *A Theology of Liberation*, p. 84.
19 Joseph Cardinal Ratzinger, 'The end of time' in *The End of Time?: The provocation of talking about God: Proceedings of a meeting of Joseph Cardinal Ratzinger, Johann Baptist Metz, Jürgen Moltmann, and Eveline Goodman-Thau in*

Ahaus, ed. Tiemo Rainer Peters, Claus Urban, and James Matthew Ashley (New York: Paulist Press, 2004), p. 22.

20 David H. Kelsey, *Eccentric Existence: A theological anthropology*, 1st edn, 2 vols (Louisville, KY: Westminster John Knox Press, 2009), p. 904.

21 Gustavo Gutiérrez, *The God of Life*, trans. Matthew J. O'Connell (Maryknoll, NY: Orbis Books, 1991), p. 92.

22 Gutiérrez, *The God of Life*, p. 100.

23 Gutiérrez, *The God of Life*, p. 101.

24 Gutiérrez, *The God of Life*, p. 102.

25 Gustavo Gutiérrez, 'Memory and Prophecy' in *The Option for the Poor in Christian Theology*, ed. Daniel G. Groody (Notre Dame, ID: University of Notre Dame Press, 2007), p. 20.

26 Gutiérrez, 'Memory and Prophecy', p. 20.

27 Gutiérrez, 'Memory and Prophecy', p. 22.

28 Ratzinger, 'The end of time', p. 24.

29 Ratzinger, 'The End of Time', p. 24.

30 Gutiérrez, 'Memory and Prophecy', p. 31.

31 J. Matthew Ashley, 'Apocalypticism in political and liberation theology: toward an historical Docta Ignorantia', *Horizons* 27, no. 1 (2000), p. 42.

32 Ashley, 'Apocalypticism in political and liberation theology', p. 37.

33 Ashley, 'Apocalypticism in political and liberation theology', p. 38.

34 Ashley, 'Apocalypticism in political and liberation theology', p. 40.

35 James Matthew Ashley, *Interruptions: Mysticism, politics, and theology in the work of Johann Baptist Metz*, Studies in Spirituality and Theology 4 (Notre Dame, IN: University of Notre Dame Press, 1998), p. 193.

36 Ashley, *Interruptions*, p. 194.

37 Gustavo Gutiérrez, *We Drink From Our Own Wells: The Spiritual Journey of a People* (Maryknoll, NY: Orbis Books, 2003), p. 131.

38 Gustavo Gutiérrez, *On Job: God-talk and the suffering of the innocent*, trans. Matthew J. O'Connell (Maryknoll, NY: Orbis Books, 1987), p. 64.

39 Gutiérrez, *On Job*, p. 66.

40 Gutiérrez, *On Job*, p. 67.

41 Gutiérrez, *On Job*, p. 64. The translator clarifies that the passage as it is cited in this sequence 'is translated from the author's Spanish text'. Gutiérrez, *On Job*, p. 121 n. 9.

42 Gutiérrez, *On Job*, p. 66.

43 Gutiérrez, *Our Own Wells*, p. 67.

44 Gutiérrez, *Our Own Wells*, p. 68.

45 Rudolf Bultmann quoted in Gutiérrez, *Our Own Wells*, p. 154 n.30.

46 Gutiérrez, *The God of Life*, p. 85.

47 Gutiérrez, *Our Own Wells*, p. 2.

48 Gutiérrez, *Our Own Wells*, p. 23.

49 Gutiérrez, *Our Own Wells*, p. 25.

50 Gutiérrez, *Our Own Wells*, p. 51.

51 Gutiérrez, *Our Own Wells*, p. 51.

52 Gutiérrez, *Our Own Wells*, p. 67.

53 Gutiérrez, *Our Own Wells*, p. 23.

54 Gutiérrez, *Our Own Wells*, p. 23.

55 Gustavo Gutiérrez, *The Power of the Poor in History*, trans. Robert R. Barr (Maryknoll, NY: Orbis Books, 1983), p. 89.

56 Gutiérrez, *The Power of the Poor in History*, p. 90.

57 For an example of such developments, see the reflections published in Johann Baptist Metz, Edward Schillebeeckx and Marcus Lefébure, eds, *Martyrdom Today*, Concilium 163 (Edinburgh; New York: T&T Clark; Seabury Press, 1983) and also T. Okure, J. Sobrino and F. Wilfreld, eds, *Rethinking Martyrdom*, Concilium (English Language Edition) (London: SCM Press, 2003).

58 Paul Middleton observes that 'beliefs and practices varied in the early Church in regard to martyrdom, a fact frequently overlooked.' Paul Middleton, *Radical Martyrdom and Cosmic Conflict in Early Christianity*, Library of New Testament Studies 307 (London: T&T Clark, 2006), p. 5. For an exploration of some of the difficulties of delineating martyrological discourse, see Middleton, *Radical Martyrdom and Cosmic Conflict in Early Christianity*, pp. 1–15.

59 Douglas Farrow, 'Resurrection and Immortality' in *The Oxford Handbook of Systematic Theology*, ed. John Webster, Kathryn Tanner and Iain R. Torrance (Oxford: Oxford University Press, 2009), p. 216.

60 Farrow, 'Resurrection and Immortality', p. 217.

61 Farrow, 'Resurrection and Immortality', p. 226.

62 John E. Thiel, 'For what may we hope? Thoughts on the eschatological imagination', *Theological Studies* 67, no. 3 (September 2006), pp. 517–41. See also his expanded reflection on this theme in John E. Thiel, *Icons of Hope: The 'Last Things' in Catholic imagination* (Notre Dame, IN: University of Notre Dame Press, 2013).

63 Thiel, 'For what may we hope?', p. 519.

64 Thiel, 'For what may we hope?', p. 525.

65 See the cautions raised by Kilby in Karen Kilby, 'Eschatology, suffering and the limits of theology' in *Game Over?: Reconsidering Eschatology*, ed. Christophe Chalamet et al. (Berlin: De Gruyter, 2017), pp. 279–92.

66 Farrow, 'Resurrection and Immortality', p. 219.

67 Farrow, 'Resurrection and Immortality', p. 220.

68 Farrow, 'Resurrection and Immortality', p. 220.

10

Conclusion

What we have is a theological reflection – vigorous at some moments, hesitating at others, but always in progress – at the service of the proclamation of God's love for each and every person, especially for the poor of his time. This is the material of the pages to follow.[1]

The introduction that Gutiérrez provides to his study of Bartolomé de Las Casas serves as a fitting summary of his own life and ministry. Over the course of this project, I have sought to develop a faithful account of this proclamation and a careful examination of this reflection. I have presented the theology of Gustavo Gutiérrez as an attempt to answer the question that he himself has raised: the question of how to speak of God as Father in a world that has been made inhumane. In this way I have sought to develop both an analysis of Gutiérrez that is attentive to the fundamental structures of his own thought and an examination of his theology that is consistent with these convictions. He poses an anthropological question to which he offers a Christological response and the contribution of this project has been to listen to this question, hear his response, and then evaluate his answer.

Hearing the Christological anthropology of Gustavo Gutiérrez

By framing Gutiérrez's theology as an attempt to speak of God as Father in a world that is inhumane, I have been able to characterize his theology as an anthropological project and trace out the Christological framework within which this project takes shape.

Reading the theology of Gutiérrez as a response to 'a world that is inhumane' has allowed me to identify the anthropological dynamic that gives unity to his theological project. The liberation he proclaims is a process through which God works in history to forge a new humanity and attention to this theme has allowed for the unity of his theological project to come into view. In Part One I considered the problem of a

Conclusion

world that is inhumane and the call for liberation that can be heard in the preferential option for the poor. In Part Two I explored the way in which this humanity was to be forged through a truly liberative praxis. The final part presented the vision of a liberated humanity that is offered by Gutiérrez in his concept of utopia. In this way his theology finds its unity in his attempt to proclaim and participate in the work of God to create a new and liberated humanity.

This anthropological perspective not only made it possible to recognize the overall shape of Gutiérrez's theology, but it also provides a context within which the distinct parts of his project could be read. Gutiérrez seeks to express the unity of various theological dynamics whose relations are often presented in terms of tension or contradiction. Attention to the unity of Gutiérrez's theology allowed for its 'unities' to be discerned. In Part One, I outlined the narrative of salvation history recounted by Gutiérrez. In this context he emphasizes both the gratuity of grace and the freedom of human response. His characterization of the relationship between nature and grace seeks to emphasize the sovereign and gracious work of God to create a new and liberated humanity. However, this emphasis on divine grace provided warrant for an emphasis on human freedom and responsibility. Rather than place the two in tension or conflict Gutiérrez presents the two in a dynamic and mutually defining relation. In Part Two I considered the liberative praxis called for by Gutiérrez and drew attention to the dynamic that structures the relationship between faith and works. Once again, the relationship is not one of tension or contradiction. Instead, there is a unity-in-difference of silence and speech; reflection and action; and the mystical and the prophetic in which each is the context and consequence of the other. In the final part I described the interrelation of politics and eschatology in the liberative utopia that is envisioned by Gutiérrez and showed that, once again, he presents the two concepts in such a way as to convey both the integrity of each in distinction and the harmony of the two together in relation. History moves towards liberation through both denunciation and annunciation. Each new stage of history makes possible a vision of the future by which it is to be judged and to which it is called to move. This opens up a new stage that will in turn be renewed through the same dynamic of future hope.

As I outlined the shape of Gutiérrez's theology its Christological form became evident. Christology provides both the focus and the framework for his anthropological project. On the one hand, the unified work of God to create a new and liberated humanity finds its focus in Christ. For Gutiérrez, Christ is the humanity before whom we speak; Christ is the humanity through whom we speak; and Christ is the humanity of whom we speak. In the option for the poor Christ reveals the neighbour and the neighbour reveals Christ. In liberative praxis, Christ gives the sight, establishes the judgement and directs the action through which a new humanity is forged. In his vision of utopia, Gutiérrez presents Christ as the promise, received by faith, that moves humanity in love towards their future hope. At each point his anthropology finds its focus in Christ.

Not only does Christology provide the focus for the anthropology of Gutiérrez, Christology also establishes its framework. The work of God to forge a new humanity unfolds through the dynamics of unity-in-difference that I have described. For Gutiérrez the incarnation not only reveals the content of liberation, it also makes known the context through which that liberation takes place. The incarnation establishes the framework that guards against separation on the one hand and confusion on the other, such that in the liberation of humanity, nature and grace, faith and works and politics and eschatology are to be distinguished but not separated. For Gutiérrez the incarnation of God in Jesus establishes the structure by which God works in history in order to liberate humanity.

Examining the Christological anthropology of Gustavo Gutiérrez

This process of exposition and analysis established the ground for a further step of evaluation and critique. By reading the theology of Gutiérrez from an anthropological perspective I drew attention to its Christological focus and framework and so argue that Christology offers a key point at which his theology may be engaged. An evaluation and critique of Gutiérrez that begins with individual themes within his work is at risk of engaging only with a distortion of these themes. These themes will be more fruitfully and faithfully read when they are placed within the context through which they find their coherence. To understand the way in which Gutiérrez characterizes the preferential option for the poor, liberative praxis and utopian hope, it is important not to start with these themes as if they were freestanding theological constructs. The liberation proclaimed by Gutiérrez has a Christological focus and takes shape within a Christological framework and so these themes must be examined and evaluated within this context.

The Christology that emerged from my examination of Gutiérrez became the point at which I engaged with an evaluation of his theology. In this project I asked whether the Christology of Gutiérrez was able to

Conclusion

sustain the weight that his anthropological project calls for it to bear and over the course of the three parts of the project I examined and evaluated the way in which he characterizes the person, work and presence of Christ. In this way, I have sought to offer a critical engagement with Gutiérrez that is consistent with his own fundamental convictions. By making the fundamental structure of his thought evident I aimed to expose and identify the internal inconsistencies that make this structure unstable. In order to explore these questions, I drew Gutiérrez into conversation with the theological anthropology developed by David Kelsey. In Part One of this project, I put to Gutiérrez two questions that emerge from within this conversation with Kelsey. The first question concerned the Christological consequences of recounting the work of God in creation, salvation and consummation as a single united narrative. The second question concerned the relationship between the identity of Jesus in history and his presence to history. Both of these questions led me to ask whether Gutiérrez attributes to Christ the concrete particularity on which his anthropology depends. While the liberative work of God unfolds in history through concrete encounters in community, the person of Jesus lacks the very particularity and specificity in which such historical encounters take place. The characterization of Jesus in the theology of Gutiérrez tends towards the abstract and impersonal. Within the framework he himself established, the questions of 'Who is God?' and 'What is man?' cannot be adequately addressed if the question of 'Who is Jesus?' is not clearly and concretely answered.

After two chapters exploring the theme of praxis, I concluded Part Two by examining the way in which Gutiérrez presents the work of Christ. Once again, in this part of the project I drew him into conversation with Kelsey and argued that he tends to obscure the particularity of Christ's work. I argued that both the context and content of the praxis called for by Gutiérrez are susceptible to weaknesses against which Kelsey warns. By placing liberative praxis in the context of a unified narrative of creation, salvation and consummation, the work of Christ is absorbed into the transformation actualized in a life of liberation. By characterizing the love that is lived by humanity in Christ as a unity of love towards God and love towards neighbour, the distinctive identities of both Christ and the neighbour recede from view and the path of faithful praxis becomes obscured. The account of this praxis developed by Gutiérrez takes shape within a framework that seeks to proclaim the unity of God's relations to creation and the unity of the loves to which humanity is called; however, this methodology risks obscuring the sights of both Christ and neighbour on which his account of praxis depends.

Having examined the person and work of Christ in Parts One and Two I turned in the final part to an examination of his presence. In this final chapter I asked 'where' and 'when' God would be known as Father by a liberated humanity. I argued that his ability to answer this question is inhibited by his account of the presence of the risen Christ to human history. As I explored the problem of death, I questioned whether the eschatological hope offered by Gutiérrez was sufficiently personal and, as I considered the challenge of martyrdom, I asked if this hope was adequately physical. I argued that, in Gutiérrez's eschatology, the personal identity of the risen Jesus tends to be absorbed into the unfolding of history and the physical character of the risen Jesus tends to be expressed in terms of the ongoing life of the church. While Gutiérrez attempts to express the distinction in relation of history and eschatology, his treatment of Christ and his resurrection evidences a tendency to absorb the latter into the former.

My examination of the Christology that takes shape within – and gives shape to – Gutiérrez's anthropology seeks to follow the contours of his own convictions. I have asked whether his Christology is able to sustain the weight that his theological project calls for it to bear and, over the course of this project, I have drawn attention to certain key weaknesses that inhibit the development of his liberative anthropology. These weaknesses offer points at which the theology of Gutiérrez may be developed and deepened in the future. In order to proclaim God as Father in a world that is made inhumane he seeks to proclaim the truth of both God and humanity in the Son. This proclamation will be clarified when the person, work and presence of Jesus are themselves made known in their concrete and personal particularity.

Conclusion: final words and an unfinished work

In the introduction to this book, I outlined a series of stages through which the development of Gutiérrez's theology could be traced. Gutiérrez is now in his tenth decade, and it may be that we are approaching the start of a new stage in the development and reception of his theology. It is the stage at which his theological work may be viewed and evaluated as a whole and so a stage in which it may be deepened and developed by a new generation. It seems fitting to conclude this study of Gutiérrez with the words that he uses to open his preface to the English edition of his biography of Bartolomé de Las Casas:

Conclusion

There are figures in history – few, to be sure – who leap the barriers of time to become the contemporary of all ages. These are people who immerse themselves so deeply in their own age that they remain relevant long after historical anecdotes and others of their own time are simple memories of the past. In their lives they combine a commitment to the immediate present with vision of the future, achievement and failure, intense action and original reflection, covenants and protests that transcend death.[2]

It is too soon to say whether Gutiérrez will himself join Las Casas as one of these figures. However, in his theological reflection and his pastoral action Gustavo Gutiérrez profoundly shaped the church in which he has ministered and the communities in which he has served. In his commitment to this church and to these communities his voice will continue to offer a valuable contribution to all those who wish to proclaim God as Father in a world that has become inhumane.

Notes

1 Gustavo Gutiérrez, *Las Casas: In search of the poor of Jesus Christ* (Eugene, OR: Wipf & Stock, 2003), p. 15.
2 Gutiérrez, *Las Casas*, p. xv.

Bibliography

Althaus-Reid, Marcella, 'Do not stop the flow of my blood: A critical Christology of hope amongst Latin American women', *Studies in World Christianity* 1, no. 2 (October 1995), pp. 143–59.
———, *Indecent Theology: Theological perversions in sex, gender and politics*, London: Routledge, 2000.
———, 'On wearing skirts without underwear: "Indecent Theology challenging the Liberation Theology of the pueblo". Poor women contesting Christ', *Feminist Theology* 7, no. 20 (January 1999), pp. 39–51.
———, *The Queer God*, London: Routledge, 2003.
———, 'Demythologising Liberation Theology: Reflections on Power, Poverty and Sexuality' in *The Cambridge Companion to Liberation Theology*, edited by Christopher Rowland, 2nd edn, pp. 123–36. Cambridge Companions to Religion, Cambridge, UK; New York: Cambridge University Press, 2007.
Althaus-Reid, Marcella, Ivan Petrella and Luiz Carlos Susin, eds, 'Class, sex and the theologian: reflections on the liberationist movement in Latin America' in *Another Possible World: A selection of the contributions to the First World Forum on Theology and Liberation*, Reclaiming Liberation Theology, London: SCM Press, 2007, pp. 23–38.
Ashley, James Matthew, 'Apocalypticism in political and liberation theology: Toward an historical Docta Ignorantia', *Horizons* 27, no. 1 (2000), pp. 22–43.
———, *Interruptions: Mysticism, politics, and theology in the work of Johann Baptist Metz*, Studies in Spirituality and Theology 4, Notre Dame, IN: University of Notre Dame Press, 1998.
Baker, Kimberly, 'Augustine's doctrine of the Totus Christus: reflecting on the Church as sacrament of unity', *Horizons* 37, no. 1 (2010), pp. 7–24.
Bañuelas, Arturo J., ed., *Mestizo Christianity: Theology from the Latino perspective*, Eugene, OR: Wipf & Stock, 2004.
Bavel, Tarsicius van, 'The "Christus Totus" idea: a forgotten aspect of Augustine's spirituality' in *Studies in Patristic Christology: Proceedings of the Third Maynooth Patristic Conference*, edited by Thomas Finan and Vincent Twomey, Portland, OR: Four Courts Press, 1998, pp. 84–94.
Bell, Daniel M., *Liberation Theology After the End of History: The refusal to cease suffering*, Radical Orthodoxy Series, London: Routledge, 2001.
———, '"Men of Stone and Children of Struggle": Latin American liberationists at the end of history', *Modern Theology* 14, no. 1 (January 1998), pp. 113–41.
Benedict XVI, *Jesus of Nazareth: From the Entrance into Jerusalem to the Resurrection. Part Two: Holy Week*, San Francisco, CA: Ignatius Press, 2011.

Bibliography

Beyer, Gerald J., 'Karl Rahner on the radical unity of the love of God and neighbour', *Irish Theological Quarterly* 68, no. 3 (September 2003), pp. 251–80.

Boersma, Hans, 'History and faith in Pope Benedict's Jesus of Nazareth', *Nova et Vetera* 10, no. 4 (2012), pp. 985–91.

———, *Scripture as Real Presence: Sacramental exegesis in the Early Church*, Grand Rapids, MI: Baker Academic, 2017.

———, *Seeing God: The Beatific Vision in Christian tradition*, Grand Rapids, MI: William B. Eerdmans, 2018.

Boff, Clodovis, *Feet-on-the-Ground Theology: A Brazilian journey*, translated by Philip Berryman, Eugene, OR: Wipf & Stock, 2008.

———, 'Methodology of the Theology of Liberation' in *Systematic Theology: Perspectives from Liberation Theology: Readings from Mysterium Liberationis*, edited by Jon Sobrino and Ignacio Ellacuría, Maryknoll, NY: Orbis Books, 1996, pp. 1–21.

———, 'Volta Ao Fundamento: Réplica', *Revista Eclesiástica Brasileira* 68, no. 272 (2008), pp. 892–927.

Brackley, Dean, *Divine Revolution: Salvation and liberation in Catholic thought*, Eugene, OR: Wipf & Stock, 2004.

Cadorette, Curt, *From the Heart of the People: The theology of Gustavo Gutiérrez*, Oak Park, IL: Meyer Stone Books, 1988.

Cameron, Michael, 'The emergence of *Totus Christus* as hermeneutical center in Augustine's *Enarrationes in Psalmos*' in *The Harp of Prophecy: Early Christian interpretation of the Psalms*, edited by Brian E. Daley and Paul R. Kolbet, Notre Dame, IN: University of Notre Dame Press, 2015, pp. 205–26.

———, '*Totus Christus* and the psychagogy of Augustine's sermons', *Augustinian Studies* 36, no. 1 (2005), pp. 59–70.

Cavanaugh, William T., 'The ecclesiologies of Medellín and the lessons of the base communities', *CrossCurrents* 44, no. 1 (1994), pp. 67–84.

———, *Torture and Eucharist: Theology, politics, and the Body of Christ*, Challenges in Contemporary Theology, Oxford: Blackwell, 1998.

Chopp, Rebecca S., *The Praxis of Suffering: An interpretation of liberation and political theologies*, Eugene, OR: Wipf & Stock, 2007.

Congregation for the Doctrine of the Faith, 'Instruction on Certain Aspects of the "Theology of Liberation"' in *Liberation Theology: A documentary history*, edited by Alfred T. Hennelly, Maryknoll, NY: Orbis Books, 1990, pp. 393–414.

———, 'Ten Observations on the Theology of Gustavo Gutiérrez' in *Liberation Theology: A documentary history*, edited by Alfred T. Hennelly, Maryknoll, NY: Orbis Books, 1990, pp. 348–50.

Cooper, David, ed., 'Introduction' in *The Dialectics of Liberation*, Radical Thinkers, London; New York: Verso, 2015, pp. 7–12.

Curnow, Rohan M., 'Which preferential option for the poor? A history of the doctrine's bifurcation', *Modern Theology* 31, no. 1 (January 2015), pp. 27–59.

Doak, Mary, 'The politics of Radical Orthodoxy: a Catholic critique', *Theological Studies* 68, no. 2 (2007), pp. 368–93.

Elizondo, Virgil, 'Mestizaje as locus of theological reflection' in *Mestizo Christianity: Theology from the Latino perspective*, edited by Arturo J Bañuelas, Eugene, OR: Wipf & Stock, 2004, pp. 5–27.

———, 'Jesus the Galilean Jew in Mestizo theology', *Theological Studies* 70, no. 2 (May 2009), pp. 262–80.

Farrow, Douglas, *Ascension and Ecclesia: On the significance of the doctrine of the Ascension for ecclesiology and Christian cosmology*, Edinburgh: T&T Clark, 1999.

———, 'Resurrection and Immortality' in *The Oxford Handbook of Systematic Theology*, edited by John Webster, Kathryn Tanner and Iain R. Torrance, Oxford: Oxford University Press, 2009, pp. 212–35.

Fierro, Alfredo, *The Militant Gospel: A critical introduction to political theologies*, translated by John Drury, Maryknoll, NY: Orbis Books, 1977.

Frei, H. W., J. B. Davis, M. Higton and M. A. Bowland, *The Identity of Jesus Christ, Expanded and Updated Edition: The hermeneutical bases of dogmatic theology*, Eugene, OR: Wipf & Stock, 2013.

Freire, Paulo, 'Education liberation and the Church', *Religious Education* 79, no. 4 (September 1984), pp. 524–45.

———, *Pedagogy of Freedom: Ethics, democracy, and civic courage*, translated by Patrick Clarke, Critical Perspectives Series, Lanham, MD: Rowman & Littlefield, 1998.

———, *Pedagogy of the Oppressed*, translated by Myra Bergman Ramos, 30th anniversary edn, New York: Continuum, 2000.

Freire, Paulo and Ana Maria Araújo Freire, *Pedagogy of the Heart*, New York: Continuum, 2007.

Freire, Paulo, Ana Maria Araújo Freire and Robert R. Barr, *Pedagogy of Hope: Reliving Pedagogy of the Oppressed*, London: Bloomsbury, 2014.

Greene, Colin J. D., *Christology in Cultural Perspective: Marking out the horizons*, Eugene, OR: Wipf & Stock, 2015.

Gutiérrez, Gustavo, 'A Hermeneutic of Hope', *The Center for Latin American Studies, Vanderbilt University – Occasional Papers* 13 (September 2012).

———, *A Theology of Liberation: History, politics, and salvation*, translated by Caridad Inda and John Eagleson, London: SCM Press, 2010.

———, 'Appendix B: An Interview with Gustavo Gutiérrez December 8, 2009' in *An Immigration of Theology: Theology of context as the theological method of Virgilio Elizondo and Gustavo Gutiérrez*, by Simon C. Kim, Eugene, OR: Wipf and Stock, 2012.

———, 'Criticism will deepen, clarify liberation theology' in *Liberation Theology: A documentary history*, edited by Alfred T. Hennelly, Maryknoll, NY: Orbis Books, 1990, pp. 419–24.

———, '¿Dónde Dormirán Las Pobres?' in *El Rostro de Dios En La Historia*, by Javier Ihuiñiz, Felipe Zegarra, Gustavo Gutiérrez, Manuel Díaz Mateos, Jorge Alvarez Calderón, Yolanda Díaz, Amparo Huamán, Rolando Ames and Luis Fernando Crespo, CEP 175, Lima: Pontificia Universidad Católica del Perú, Departamento de Teología, 1996, pp. 9–69.

———, 'Entre Las Calandrias' in *Arguedas: Mito, Historia, Religión y Entre Las Calandrias*, Vol. 48, Lima: Centro de Estudios y Publicaciones, 1982.

———, *Essential Writings*, edited by James B. Nickoloff, London: SCM Press, 1996.

———, 'Expanding the view' in *Expanding the View: Gustavo Gutiérrez and the*

Bibliography

future of Liberation Theology, edited by Marc H. Ellis and Otto Maduro, translated by Matthew J. O'Connell, Eugene, OR: Wipf & Stock, 1990, pp. 3–36.

———, 'Faith as freedom: solidarity with the alienated and confidence in the future', *Horizons* 2, no. 1 (1975), pp. 25–60.

———, 'Gustavo Gutiérrez' in *Teólogos de La Liberación Hablan Sobre La Mujer*, edited by Leonardo Boff and Elsa Tamez, San José, Costa Rica: Departamento Ecuménico de Investigaciones, 1986, pp. 51–9.

———, *Las Casas: In search of the poor of Jesus Christ*, Eugene, OR: Wipf & Stock, 2003.

———, 'Memory and Prophecy' in *The Option for the Poor in Christian Theology*, edited by Daniel G. Groody, Notre Dame, IN: University of Notre Dame Press, 2007, pp. 17–38.

———, *On Job: God-talk and the suffering of the innocent*, translated by Matthew J. O'Connell, Maryknoll, NY: Orbis Books, 1987.

———, 'Option for the Poor' in *Systematic Theology: Perspectives from Liberation Theology: Readings from Mysterium Liberationis*, edited by Jon Sobrino and Ignacio Ellacuría, Maryknoll, NY: Orbis Books, 1996, pp. 22–37.

———, 'Remembering the poor: an interview with Gustavo Gutiérrez', *America*, https://www.americamagazine.org/faith/2003/02/03/remembering-poor-interview-gustavo-gutierrez, accessed 3.04.2019.

———, 'Sermon: Gutiérrez on the liberating of man born blind', *New Blackfriars* 70, no. 826 (April 1989), pp. 158–60.

———, *The Density of the Present: Selected writings*, translated by Matthew J. O'Connell, Maryknoll, NY: Orbis Books, 1999.

———, *The God of Life*, translated by Matthew J. O'Connell, Maryknoll, NY: Orbis Books, 1991.

———, 'The option for the poor arises from faith in Christ', *Theological Studies* 70, no. 2 (2009), pp. 317–26.

———, *The Power of the Poor in History*, translated by Robert R. Barr, Maryknoll, NY: Orbis Books, 1983.

———, 'The situation and tasks of liberation theology today', in *Opting for the Margins: Postmodernity and Liberation in Christian Theology*, edited by Joerg Rieger, Oxford: Oxford University Press, 2003, pp. 89–103.

———, *The Truth Shall Make You Free: Confrontations*, translated by Matthew J. O'Connell, Maryknoll, NY: Orbis Books, 1990.

———, 'Two theological perspectives: Liberation Theology and Progressivist Theology', in *The Emergent Gospel: Theology from the underside of history: Papers from the Ecumenical Dialogue of Third World Theologians, Dar Es Salaam, August 5–12, 1976*, edited by Sergio Torres González, Maryknoll, NY: Orbis Books, 1978, pp. 227–55.

———, *We Drink From Our Own Wells: The spiritual journey of a people*, Maryknoll, NY: Orbis Books, 2003.

Gutiérrez, Gustavo and Richard Shaull, 'Freedom and salvation: a political problem' in *Liberation and Change*, translated by Alvin Gutiérrez, Atlanta, GA: John Knox Press, 1977, pp. 2–94.

Hauerwas, Stanley, 'Some theological reflections on Gutiérrez's use of "liberation" as a theological concept', *Modern Theology* 3, no. 1 (October 1986), pp. 67–76.

Horn, Gerard-Rainer, *Western European Liberation Theology: The first wave (1924–1959)*, Oxford: Oxford University Press, 2008.

Hunsinger, George, 'Karl Barth and Liberation Theology', *The Journal of Religion* 63, no. 3 (1983), pp. 247–63.

John XXIII, 'Pope's Address to World Month Before Council Opened' in *Council Daybook: Vatican II, Sessions 1 and 2*, edited by Floyd Anderson, Washington, DC: The National Catholic Welfare Conference, 1965, pp. 18–21.

Kamitsuka, David G., *Theology and Contemporary Culture: Liberation, postliberal, and revisionary perspectives*, Cambridge: Cambridge University Press, 1999.

Kelsey, David H., *Eccentric Existence: A theological anthropology*, 1st edn, 2 vols, Louisville, KY: Westminster John Knox Press, 2009.

———, *Imagining Redemption*, Louisville, KY: Westminster John Knox Press, 2005.

Kilby, Karen, 'Catholicism, Protestantism and the theological location of paradox: nature, grace, sin' in *Ecclesia Semper Reformanda: Renewal and reform beyond polemics*, edited by Peter De Mey and Wim François, Bibliotheca Ephemeridum Theologicarum Lovaniensium 306, Leuven: Peeters, 2020, pp. 159–71.

———, 'Eschatology, suffering and the limits of theology' in *Game Over?: Reconsidering eschatology*, edited by Christophe Chalamet, Andreas Dettwiler, Mariel Mazzocco and Ghislain Waterlot, Berlin: De Gruyter, 2017, pp. 279–92.

Lange, Elizabeth A., 'Fragmented ethics of justice: Freire, liberation theology and pedagogies for the non-poor', *Convergence* 31, no. 1 & 2 (January 1998), pp. 81–94.

Lee, Jung Young, *Marginality: The key to multicultural theology*, Minneapolis, MN: Fortress Press, 1995.

Lewis, Thomas A., 'Actions as the ties that bind: love, praxis, and community in the thought of Gustavo Gutiérrez', *Journal of Religious Ethics* 33, no. 3 (September 2005), pp. 539–67.

Martinez, Gaspar, *Confronting the Mystery of God: Political liberation and public theologies*, New York: Continuum, 2002.

Martínez Gordo, Jesús, *La Fuerza de la Debilidad: La teología fundamental de Gustavo Gutiérrez*, Bilbao: Instituto Diocesano de Teología y Pastoral, 1994.

McCann, Dennis, *Christian Realism and Liberation Theology: Practical theologies in creative conflict*, Maryknoll, NY: Orbis Books, 2001.

Metz, Johann Baptist, Edward Schillebeeckx and Marcus Lefébure, eds, *Martyrdom Today*, Concilium 163, Edinburgh: T&T Clark, 1983.

Middleton, Paul, *Radical Martyrdom and Cosmic Conflict in Early Christianity*, Library of New Testament Studies 307, London: T&T Clark, 2006.

Milbank, John, *Theology and Social Theory: Beyond secular reason*, Signposts in Theology, Oxford: Blackwell, 1990.

Moser, J. David, 'Totus Christus: A proposal for Protestant Christology and Ecclesiology', *Pro Ecclesia* 29, no. 1 (2020), pp. 3–30.

Moylan, Tom, 'Bloch against Bloch: the theological reception of Das Prinzip Hoffnung and the liberation of the utopian function', *Utopian Studies* 1, no. 2 (1990), pp. 27–51.

———, 'Denunciation/Annunciation: The radical methodology of liberation theology', *Cultural Critique* 20 (Winter 1991–2), pp. 33–64.

Bibliography

Muñoz, Daniel, 'Anglican identity as Mestizaje ecclesiology', *Journal of Anglican Studies* 16, no. 2 (2018), pp. 83–102.
Nava, Alexander, *The Mystical and Prophetic Thought of Simone Weil and Gustavo Gutiérrez*, Albany, NY: State University of New York Press, 2001.
Nickoloff, James B., 'A future for Peru? Gustavo Gutiérrez and the reasons for his hope', *Horizons* 19, no. 1 (Spring 1992), pp. 31–43.
———, 'Church of the Poor: The ecclesiology of Gustavo Gutiérrez', *Theological Studies* 54, no. 3 (September 1993), pp. 512–35.
Noble, Tim, *The Poor in Liberation Theology: Pathway to God or ideological construct?*, Cross Cultural Theologies, Abingdon: Routledge, 2014.
Oliveros Maqueo, Roberto, *Liberacion y Teologia: Génesis y Crecimiento de Una Reflexion (1966–1976)*, Lima: Centro de Estudios y Publicaciones, 1977.
O'Regan, Cyril, 'Eccentric Existence and the Catholic tradition' in *The Theological Anthropology of David Kelsey: Responses to Eccentric Existence*, edited by G. Outka, Grand Rapids, MI: William B. Eerdmans, 2016, pp. 53–90.
Örsy, Ladislas, 'Authentic learning and receiving – a search for criteria' in *Receptive Ecumenism and the Call to Catholic Learning: Exploring a way for contemporary ecumenism*, edited by Paul D. Murray and Luca Badini Confalonieri, Oxford: Oxford University Press, 2008, pp. 39–51.
Outka, G., *The Theological Anthropology of David Kelsey: Responses to Eccentric Existence*, Grand Rapids, MI: William B. Eerdmans, 2016.
Pace, Thomas and Gina A. Merys, 'Paulo Freire and the Jesuit tradition: Jesuit rhetoric and Freirean pedagogy' in *Traditions of Eloquence: The Jesuits and modern rhetorical studies*, New York: Fordham University Press, 2016, pp. 234–47.
Parratt, John, 'Introduction' in *An Introduction to Third World Theologies*, edited by John Parratt, Cambridge: Cambridge University Press, 2004, pp. 1–15.
Petrella, Ivan, 'Liberation theology undercover', *Political Theology* 18, no. 4 (19 May 2017), pp. 325–39.
———, *The Future of Liberation Theology: An argument and manifesto*, Aldershot: Ashgate, 2004.
———, 'The futures of liberation theology' in *Radical Christian Voices and Practice: Essays in Honour of Christopher Rowland*, edited by Zoë Bennett and David B. Gowler, Oxford: Oxford University Press, 2012, pp. 201–10.
Pilario, Daniel Franklin E., *Back to the Rough Grounds of Praxis: Exploring theological method with Pierre Bourdieu*, Bibliotheca Ephemeridum Theologicarum Lovaniensium 183, Leuven: Leuven University Press, 2005.
Pollock, David C. and Ruth E. Van Reken, *Third Culture Kids: Growing up among worlds*, rev. edn, Boston, MA: Nicholas Brealey, 2009.
Ratzinger, Joseph Cardinal, 'The end of time' in *The End of Time?: The provocation of talking about God: Proceedings of a meeting of Joseph Cardinal Ratzinger, Johann Baptist Metz, Jürgen Moltmann, and Eveline Goodman-Thau in Ahaus*, edited by Tiemo Rainer Peters, Claus Urban and James Matthew Ashley, New York: Paulist Press, 2004, pp. 15–30.
Second General Conference of Latin American Bishops, 'Document on the Poverty of the Church' in *Liberation Theology: A documentary history*, edited by Alfred T. Hennelly, Maryknoll, NY: Orbis Books, 1990, pp. 114–19.
Shor, Ira and Paulo Freire, *A Pedagogy for Liberation: Dialogues on transforming education*, South Hadley, MA: Bergin & Garvey, 1987.

Siker, Jeffrey S., 'Uses of the bible in the theology of Gustavo Gutiérrez: liberating scriptures of the poor', *Biblical Interpretation* 4, no. 1 (1 January 1996), pp. 40–71.

Sindima, Harvey J., *The Gospel According to the Marginalized*, Martin Luther King, Jr. Memorial Studies in Religion, Culture, and Social Development, vol. 6, New York: Peter Lang, 2008.

Sobrino, Jon, *Christology at the Crossroads: A Latin American approach*, translated by John Drury, Maryknoll, NY: Orbis Books, 1978.

Sugirtharajah, Rasiah S., *The Bible and the Third World: Precolonial, colonial, and postcolonial encounters*, Cambridge: Cambridge University Press, 2001.

Thiel, John E., 'For what may we hope? Thoughts on the eschatological imagination', *Theological Studies* 67, no. 3 (September 2006), pp. 517–41.

——, *Icons of Hope: The 'Last Things' in Catholic imagination*, Notre Dame, IN: University of Notre Dame Press, 2013.

Toren, Benno van den, 'Intercultural theology as a three-way conversation: beyond the Western dominance of intercultural theology', *Exchange* 44, no. 2 (8 June 2015), pp. 123–43.

Useem, John and Ruth Useem, 'The interfaces of a binational third culture: a study of the American community in India', *Journal of Social Issues* 23, no. 1 (January 1967), pp. 130–43.

Ward, Graham, 'Intercultural theology and political discipleship' in *Intercultural Theology: Approaches and themes*, edited by Mark J. Cartledge and David Cheetham, London: SCM Press, 2011, pp. 29–42.

Zipes, Jack, 'Traces of hope: the non-synchronicity of Ernst Bloch' in *Not Yet: Reconsidering Ernst Bloch*, edited by Jamie Owen Daniel and Tom Moylan, London: Verso, 1997, pp. 1–14.

Index of Names and Subjects

action 9, 10, 28, 35, 47, 60, 72, 93, 98, 100, 109, 115, 123, 126, 127, 128, 130, 133n78, 138, 145, 146, 148, 150, 158, 184, 187
and contemplation/reflection 9, 86–8, 89, 94, 183
of God 27, 44, 51, 61, 103
human 29, 40n48, 89, 120
liberative 113
loving 110, 111–12, 114, 139
political 37, 85, 93, 141, 169
affirmation 54, 55, 131n28, 169
alienation 11, 32, 147, 148, 149
Althaus-Reid, Marcella (*Indecent Theology*) 153–7
Anglican Church in Chile 10, 11
annunciation 138, 150, 152–3, 157, 165, 169, 183 *see also* denunciation
anthropology 2, 8, 9, 13, 14, 21, 58, 120–2, 125, 137–8, 163, 178, 185–6 *see also* Kelsey, David
Christological 5, 7, 14, 182–4
liberative 3, 4, 118, 186
apostles 42
Arguedas, José María 148–9 *see also* Mariátegui, José Carlos
Ascension 73
attention 12, 14–15, 37, 66, 69, 72, 92, 93, 150, 167
Augustine 66, 168 *see also* Baker, Kimberly
authenticity 83, 148–9

Baker, Kimberly 75n2, 127
Beatitudes 72
Behemoth 27, 46, 47
being with 25, 83, 86

Bell, Daniel 86, 90, 92, 93–4, 98, 108–9, 112, 113
Benedict XVI (*Jesus of Nazareth*) 63–5, 144, 166, 168
Bible 13, 26, 40n63, 42, 51–2, 60, 61, 66, 142, 168
bishops (of Latin America) 42, 98, 152
blindness 154
Bloch, Ernst 141–2
blood 151, 172, 174, 175
body 74, 163, 171, 172, 174, 176, 178
of Christ (the Church) 62, 113, 114, 127
liberated 173, 175
of martyrs 177
Boersma, Hans 64, 66, 72
Boff, Clodovis 74, 111, 129–30
Bultmann, Rudolf 173

Cain and Abel 42
call 1, 14, 15, 21–4, 25, 30–1, 32–5, 42, 44, 49, 51, 60, 66, 71, 73, 82, 86, 89, 91, 93, 98, 99, 109, 110–11, 113, 115, 118, 120, 125, 128, 130, 137, 138, 144, 149, 157, 165, 168, 175
of God 45, 46, 52, 54, 103, 105, 107, 112, 123, 151, 156, 178
'*hasta que la dignidad se haga costumbre*' ('until dignity becomes the norm') 1
Caonao, massacre of 100, 101
Cardijn, Joseph 98
Catholic Action 98
Cavanaugh, William (*Torture and Eucharist*) 98, 113–14

challenge 3, 15, 16n4, 61, 94, 101–2, 103, 122, 142, 147, 168, 175
  of martyrdom 174, 179, 186
children
  of God 3, 34, 62, 84, 91, 93, 112, 126
  'of struggle' 93 see also Bell, Daniel
  third culture 12, 17n36
Christians 35, 48, 50, 51, 53–4, 59, 87, 91, 94, 99, 113, 126, 139, 145, 146, 150, 151, 153, 157–8, 160n76, 165, 169–70, 173
Christianity 71, 108, 145
Christology 4, 8, 9, 15, 58–9, 60–2, 63, 64–5, 67, 68–9, 71, 72, 74–5, 155–8, 163, 171, 178–9
  and anthropology 2, 8, 13, 183–4, 186 see also anthropology
  'from below' 63, 74
church 5, 13, 24, 37, 43, 53, 54, 59, 64, 66, 69, 73, 82, 92, 93–4, 98, 99, 100, 104, 111, 113, 114, 127, 143, 144, 147, 152, 154, 157, 170, 175–7, 187 see also children of God
  in history 42, 175
  in Latin America 152, 174
  life of the 103, 114, 143, 173, 175, 179, 186
  of the poor 42, 54, 174
  Roman Catholic 2, 6, 7, 144
  teaching of the 144, 156
communion 3, 21, 27–9, 30–1, 44, 55, 73, 86, 115, 129
  breach of, broken 31–3, 38
  with God 21, 22–3, 24–5, 26, 30, 31, 33–5, 37, 42, 55, 64, 103, 107, 110, 119
community 15, 21, 22, 24, 28, 32, 34, 35–8, 42, 51, 55, 61, 63, 69, 82, 83, 85, 88, 91, 94, 111, 113, 129, 140, 146, 148–50, 154, 157, 171–3, 175, 185
  Christian 52, 53, 54, 62, 71, 74, 86–7, 90, 92, 93, 94, 99, 114, 148, 174
  life in 23, 71, 112, 130
conferences of Latin American bishops
  Aparecida (2007) 6
  Medellín (1968) 6, 42, 95n15, 98

Puebla (1979) 6, 42, 155
Santo Domingo (1992) 6
confidence 145, 152, 155, 156, 175
conflict 26, 27, 32, 33, 43, 53–4, 100, 165, 166, 183
Congregation for the Doctrine of the Faith 3, 6–7, 49, 142, 156
  'Ten Observations on the Theology of Gustavo Gutiérrez' (1983) 142
  'Instruction on Certain Aspects of the "Theology of Liberation"' (1984) 142–3
conscientization 81–4, 85, 87, 88–90
contemplation 9, 88, 94, 106, 169 see also action
Cooper, David 84
Corinthians 172, 173
Council of Chalcedon 4, 8, 156
  'Chalcedonian principle' 22, 26, 31
creation 8, 21, 23–5, 26, 27–8, 30, 31, 32, 33, 34–5, 37–8, 45, 88, 92, 103, 107, 118–20, 121–5, 130, 163, 164, 167, 185
criticism 49–50, 98–9, 112–13, 142, 143, 145, 150, 153
cross 30, 46, 47, 48, 101, 168, 175, 176 see also John of the Cross
crucifixion 71
Cuba 100
Cullmann, Oscar 165–6
culture 11, 12–13 see also children, third culture

denunciation 103, 109, 138, 150, 152–3, 157, 165, 169, 183 see also annunciation
development 6, 14, 22, 139, 144, 151, 165, 176, 186
dialectics 63, 96n41, 125, 138, 148, 172
dialogue 13, 49, 70, 83, 89, 143
discipleship 54, 82–3
doctrine 64, 66, 106, 127, 143, 176

Easter 174
Ecclesiasticus 101
ecclesiology 93, 113
education 83, 85

Index of Names and Subjects

emergence 28
English 11, 53
Enlightenment 88, 102
Ephesians 26
eschatology 7, 10, 24, 25, 26, 31, 63, 139, 163–4, 167, 171, 174, 177–9, 183–4, 186
estallido social (social explosion, 18 October 2019) 1, 15
Eucharist 103, 112–14, 117n88, 129–30
Evangelii Gaudium (Pope Francis) 2
exchange 13, 121
exegesis 61, 66, 69, 173
existence 14, 28, 32, 45, 83, 129, 141, 168, 172–3
Exodus 32, 119
'Expanding the View' (Gustavo Gutiérrez) 6, 86, 143
Ezekiel 176

faith 9, 25, 27, 28, 30, 37, 44, 45, 47, 50–2, 63–5, 70, 86–8, 90, 91, 95n19, 98, 99, 100–3, 104–6, 107, 113, 115, 120, 128, 130, 139, 143, 151–5, 157–8, 163, 171, 172, 173, 183–4
'Faith as Freedom' (Gustavo Gutiérrez) 93
Farrow, Douglas 74–5, 176–8
Fierro, Alfredo 61
filiation 90, 112, 132–3n62, 151
flesh 44, 51, 65, 73, 110, 120, 127, 168, 171, 172, 177
forgiveness 30, 146, 149
Francis (Pope) 2, 6
freedom 25–9, 31, 35–7, 46, 47, 51, 81–2, 92, 99, 107, 122, 128, 146–50, 153, 154–5, 157, 183 *see also* faith; 'Faith as Freedom'
Frei, Hans 61, 69, 74
Freire, Paulo (*Pedagogy of Freedom*) 9, 81, 83–5, 87, 89, 90, 95n15, 97n58
Freud, Sigmund 84
Fromm, Erich 84

Galilee 74

God 4, 23, 25, 28–31, 32–3, 37, 40n63, 44, 47, 62, 64, 65, 72–3, 83, 86, 89, 98, 101, 104–6, 107, 110, 113, 118, 128, 138, 171–2 *see also* communion with; love
as Father 3, 7, 10, 14, 21, 58–9, 75, 82, 84, 90–3, 115, 137, 151, 164, 170, 171, 182, 185–7
in Jesus Christ 21, 31, 34, 44, 45, 51–2, 59, 60, 68, 74, 120–2, 124, 142, 168, 176, 184
Kingdom of 10, 24, 51, 99, 137, 142–3, 164–9, 173, 178–9
love of 9, 21, 24–5, 34, 46, 52–5, 88, 109, 111–12, 118, 125, 126, 128–30, 156, 182
machista 154 *see also* Althaus-Reid, Marcella
with the poor 47–8, 51–3, 55, 70, 105, 106, 152, 174 *see also* preferential option for the poor
work of 7, 8, 21, 26–8, 35, 45, 55, 106, 110, 119, 123–4, 131n26, 140, 151–2, 183–5 *see also* history, work of God in
God of Life (Gustavo Gutiérrez) 6, 60
gospel 4, 35, 42, 44, 45, 48, 51, 82, 83–4, 86, 89–90, 92–4, 103, 111–12, 137, 144, 152, 168, 175
Gospel narratives 60, 63–4, 65–7, 69–71, 72, 121, 157, 163, 171
grace 23, 26, 28, 34–5, 46, 52, 58, 92, 105, 106, 107, 109–10, 111, 123, 124–5, 126, 140, 152, 154, 174
freedom and 27, 31, 51, 183
nature and 21–3, 32, 102, 131n28, 183–4 *see also* nature
Guatemala 152

heart 44–5, 72, 91, 104, 109, 148
hermeneutic 8, 21, 25, 43–4, 48, 55, 61, 69, 95n19
history 22, 24–5, 26, 28, 35–6, 42, 43, 54, 67–70, 85, 87, 111, 119, 124, 127, 139–40, 145, 152, 156–8, 165–6, 170, 171, 173, 178–9
of the church 42, 175

human 21, 23, 26–7, 29–31, 38, 48, 49–50, 64–5, 72, 75, 85, 89, 107, 118, 120, 141–3, 151, 163, 168, 186
  read as preferential option for the poor 42–4, 45, 47, 48, 55, 169
  salvation 31–4, 62–3, 65, 126, 137–8, 164, 167, 183
  work of God in 29, 37, 45–7, 55, 110, 140, 153, 182, 184–5
honour 101
hope 24, 27, 29, 45, 47, 85–6, 105, 108, 111, 130, 141–2, 146, 157, 163–4, 169, 170, 172–3, 183–4
  Christian 139, 140, 145, 151, 158, 174
  eschatological 24–5, 143, 165–7, 174–5, 177, 179, 186
  Pedagogy of Hope (Paulo Freire) 84
  resurrection 171, 174–5, 178
horizon 119, 143, 175

'iconization' 67, 77n43
identity 21, 22, 28, 35, 61, 69, 70, 83, 120, 122–4, 126, 153
  'ambiguous "in-between"' 12 *see also* children, third culture
  Identity of Jesus Christ, The (Hans Frei et al)
  of Jesus 58, 59–61, 62–3, 65–7, 70–3, 74–5, 110, 119–21, 127–8, 179, 185–6
ideology 50–1, 60, 75, 85, 141–2
  Marxist 49, 143
  sexual 154, 157
imagination 125, 141, 156, 177
Imagining Redemption (David Kelsey) 125
Incarnation 11, 29, 30–1, 34, 44–5, 51, 53, 55, 58, 62, 64–5, 73, 122, 173, 178, 184
'Instruction on Certain Aspects of the "Theology of Liberation"' (Congregation for the Doctrine of the Faith) 49, 142–3
injustice 33, 36–8, 45, 46–7, 67, 82, 103, 105, 151, 152, 167, 170, 171
Israel 24, 165

Jesus Christ 30, 34, 38, 47, 48, 52, 54–5, 58–9, 61–3, 67, 69–71, 74, 82, 95n19, 100, 101, 109, 110, 119–21, 125, 126, 152, 173, 175, 185–6 *see also* God; identity
  coming of 46, 65
  disciple of 71, 82
  faith in 51
  God revealed, known in 44, 59, 60, 68, 91, 120–2, 127, 151, 176, 184
  gospel of 103
  Jesus of Nazareth (Benedict XVI) 63
  'point of convergence' 119
  resurrection of 64, 68, 73, 151, 171, 174, 178–9
  teaching of 42, 72, 102, 137, 165–6
Job 27–8, 30, 34, 45–8, 83, 86, 98, 104–9, 117n63, 171–3
On Job (Gustavo Gutiérrez) 6
John of the Cross 170
Jonah 146
journey 60, 107, 110
judgement 29, 61, 98, 107, 115, 138, 152, 178, 184
  faithful 100–1, 104–6, 108
  Final 71
justice 30, 46–7, 105, 106–7, 108–9, 143–4, 146, 151

Kelsey, David (*Eccentric Existence*; *Imagining Redemption*) 8, 9, 13–15, 59, 63–5, 67, 69, 71, 72, 74, 118–19, 120–7, 128–30, 167, 185
kingdom 2, 10, 24, 51, 73, 99, 137, 142–3, 151, 164–71, 173–4, 178–9
  see also God, kingdom of

Las Casas, Bartolomé de 2, 6, 98, 99–104, 114, 182, 186, 187
Lee, Jung Young (*Marginality*) 11–12
Leviathan 46
Lewis, Thomas 32, 123
liberation 22, 23–5, 28, 33, 35, 37, 63, 65, 68–70, 72, 82, 86, 90–1, 94, 100, 103, 109, 111, 113, 118, 124, 130, 139, 142–3, 146, 147, 150, 152–5, 157, 171, 175, 178, 182,

Index of Names and Subjects

184–5 *see also* theology, liberation; praxis of
  in Christ 22, 110, 156, 163
  historical 24, 26, 59, 63, 85, 119, 124, 151, 164, 173, 183
  of humanity 38, 81, 120, 143, 151, 184
  of Israel 165
  political and social 36, 84, 103, 156
  three levels of 31, 35, 92–3, 108, 138
  work of 28, 45, 100, 110, 123, 140, 141, 148, 149, 156
life 24, 32, 35, 47, 54, 71, 83, 87–90, 98, 99, 108, 127, 130, 139, 143, 145, 148, 152, 155, 170, 172, 174, 177, 179, 186
  Christian 23, 103, 110, 120, 151, 152–3, 168, 171, 173, 175
  human 23, 33, 37, 93, 124
  liberation and 32, 45, 146, 185
  of Jesus 44, 67, 110, 125, 137, 142, 151, 157, 173
  of the Spirit 109, 111–12, 114, 172, 176
limit 29, 63, 92, 107, 140, 142, 144, 154, 156, 164, 166, 168
love 1, 5, 27, 28, 35, 50, 85, 89, 91, 110, 124, 145–6, 149, 154, 157, 184
  Christian 43, 54, 102, 139, 150, 158
  of God 23, 24–6, 29, 30, 34, 45–8, 51–5, 67, 88, 98, 103, 106–7, 109, 111–12, 115, 118, 123, 125–9, 151, 156, 163, 182 *see also* God
  of neighbour 22, 31, 86, 99, 104, 118, 128–30, 185
  refusal and rejection of 31–2
Lumen Gentium 42

marginality 11 *see also* Lee, Jung Young
Mariátegui, José Carlos 148 *see also* Arguedas, José María
Maritain, Jacques 113–14
Martinez, Gaspar 5, 6, 139
martyrdom 111, 151–2, 174–7, 179, 186
Marxism 48–50, 141, 143, 148

Mass 101, 103
McCann, Dennis 64–5, 83
meaning 24–7, 31, 35, 43–4, 46, 52–3, 62, 65, 68, 71, 82–3, 89, 83, 103, 107–9, 114, 119, 121, 138, 165, 178–9
memory 168–9
metanarrative 50–1, 102–3, 114
methodology 59–61, 68–9, 71–2, 74, 98, 120, 130, 137, 185
Milbank, John 49, 98, 102–4, 112–13
mystery 48, 106–7, 109, 169

nature 21–3, 32, 102, 131n28, 183, 184 *see also* grace
  human 28
neighbour 21–2, 25, 30–2, 38, 43, 45, 50, 73, 82–4, 89, 90, 98–9, 105, 107, 110, 112, 115, 123–30, 145, 148, 168, 184
Nickoloff, James 138–9, 146

Onesimus 89
openness 25, 74, 88, 141–2, 146, 156
oppression 25, 27, 32, 36–8, 44, 48, 69, 86, 88–9, 99–101, 114, 140, 147–9, 152, 154–5, 163, 169
O'Regan, Cyril 122
orthodoxy 64, 156
  Radical Orthodoxy 98–9, 108, 112, 115n3, 147, 150
otherness 26, 61, 69, 72, 118, 125, 142, 174

paradox 29, 131n28, 140
Parousia 62, 73
Passover 103
Paul 21, 23, 35, 89, 107, 140, 172–3
Pentateuch 23
persecution 152
Peru 138, 146 *see also* Arguedas, José María; Mariátegui, José Carlos
Petrella, Ivan (*The Future of Liberation Theology*) 147, 149–50, 153, 155
Philemon 35, 89
politics 93, 139, 147, 178, 183–4
Populorum progression (Paul VI) 25, 34

poverty 36, 40n63, 44–5, 48, 51, 53–5, 70, 99, 105–6, 111, 114, 140, 170
power 27–8, 46, 85, 88, 90, 107, 110–12, 114, 139, 154, 175
Power of the Poor in History, The (Gustavo Gutiérrez) 6, 175
praxis 67, 81, 86–7, 93–4, 96n24, 99, 109, 126, 129–30, 145–50, 153, 155
  faithful 9, 98, 120, 123–4, 128, 185
  historical 85, 88, 123, 126, 138, 140, 157
  liberative 82, 85, 88–92, 94, 114, 118, 138, 148–9, 183–5
  of love 85, 90–4, 124, 137, 144–5, 147
preference 47, 52, 67
  preferential option for the poor 42–5, 48, 51–5, 126, 174, 183–4
proclamation 14, 30, 34, 37, 61, 82–3, 86, 90–1, 93, 137, 144, 151–2, 158, 165, 167–71, 174, 182, 186
promise 25, 30–1, 65, 111, 113, 139, 141, 157, 164–5, 170, 175, 184
prophecy 107, 164
Protestantism 14, 66, 122, 124, 131n28
Psalms 66

radicalism 154–5
Rahner, Karl 23, 113, 126, 132n52
  Rahnerian 'integralism' 102
Ratzinger, Joseph Cardinal 49, 141
realism 173, 175
reason, reasoning 48–9, 105
redemption 23, 65, 103, 121
reflection 42–3, 68, 74, 86–7, 89, 93–4, 101, 104, 109, 125, 147, 149, 171, 175, 177, 182, 183, 187
religion 93, 147
remembering 168
renewal 2, 87, 156
response 21, 82–3, 89, 102, 123–5, 140, 155–7, 174, 182–3
resurrection 46, 62–4, 68, 71, 73–4, 111, 112, 142, 151, 163, 169–79, 186

revelation 24, 27–8, 30, 42, 44–8, 51–2, 58, 60–1, 65, 71, 84, 87, 101, 105–7, 119, 157, 171
revolution 84, 88, 93
  Industrial Revolution 85, 88
Romero, Oscar 2, 140, 151

sacrament 53, 103–4, 114
salvation 21, 27, 33–7, 82, 102–3, 120–6, 174–5, 185
  history of 31, 34, 38, 62–3, 65, 119, 137–8, 164, 167, 183
scripture 27, 30, 42, 58–61, 66–72, 74, 103–4, 114, 156–7, 164, 177
  movement beyond 70, 73
Second Vatican Council 42
seeing, sight 38, 72, 98, 100–5, 112–15, 118, 123, 127–30, 154, 169, 170, 184–5
Siker, Jeffrey 32, 67, 70–1, 77n46
Sobrino, Jon 67–8, 75
solidarity 42, 47, 52–3, 61, 82–3, 88, 90, 91, 110, 111, 121, 126, 138, 148–50, 152, 170, 174
spirituality 30, 33, 35, 37, 43, 98, 111, 126, 152, 172, 174
story 23, 29–30, 32, 42, 45–6, 55, 71, 120–1, 123, 131n19, 146 *see also* history
  of humanity 21, 25–9, 31, 38
  of salvation 35, 119, 121–4
struggle 33, 47, 50, 54, 83, 90, 93, 111, 127, 141, 146, 149, 151, 169–70
suffering 45–8, 51, 83, 99, 100–1, 104–5, 106, 111–14, 127, 140, 146–7, 149, 152, 154, 163, 167–70, 174–5
Sugirtharajah, Rasiah 61

Tertullian 176
theme 32, 44, 64, 156, 157, 172, 174, 176, 184, 185
theologian 23, 50–1, 60, 67, 93, 98–9, 102, 104, 113, 147, 154, 177
theology 25, 42–3, 45, 48–50, 52, 58–60, 62–7, 71, 74, 83, 86, 90, 92–4, 104, 108–9, 112–14, 120–2,

125, 127, 129, 137, 139, 144–5, 148–50, 157–8, 164, 171, 174, 177–9, 182–6
  abstract 50, 104
  liberation 32, 55, 61, 68, 74, 84, 87, 90, 93, 96n41, 98–9, 102–3, 108, 126, 142–3, 147, 150, 153–6, 169–70
  mestizaje 12
  mystical 169
  Pauline 172–3
  of utopia 141–2, 145, 151, 153
Theology of Liberation, A (Gustavo Gutiérrez) 1, 4, 5–6, 8, 35, 38, 51, 75, 86, 93, 113, 139, 143
theory 69, 87, 96n41, 101, 104, 148
Thiel, John 177
Torture and Eucharist (William Cavanaugh) 114
totus Christus 59, 64, 66, 75n2, 120, 127
tradition 45, 66, 122–3, 138, 144, 147, 170, 175, 177
transformation 24, 34–5, 69, 81–3, 85, 88, 92, 99, 102, 109, 123–4, 129, 166, 173, 185
truth, truthfulness 21–2, 34, 46–7, 53, 58–9, 68–9, 83–4, 89–90, 98, 101–2, 104–7, 109–10, 115, 119, 128–9, 133n78, 137–8, 140, 141, 145, 149, 151, 152–3, 167, 169–70, 186
Truth Shall Make You Free, The (Gustavo Gutiérrez) 6, 144

union 30, 84, 103, 124, 127, 169
unity 21–2, 24, 26–9, 31, 35, 37–8, 44, 48, 50, 52–4, 63, 66, 68, 83, 87–8, 94, 111, 118, 120, 123, 126–30, 131n28, 132n52, 139, 156, 182–5
universality 52–5, 62, 73–4, 119, 126, 148, 165
Useem, John and Ruth 17n36 *see also* children, third culture
utopia 137–42, 145, 147, 151–3, 155, 157–8, 183–4

Vallejo, César 45
vision 21, 22, 28, 46, 49, 72, 93–4, 98, 99–102, 107–8, 115, 137, 140, 141, 145, 147–50, 151, 153, 156–8, 163, 166, 171, 183–4, 187
Vitoria, Francisco de 100 *see also* Las Casas, Bartolomé
voice, voices 22, 30, 47–8, 70–1, 107, 144, 149, 168, 187

We Drink From Our Own Wells (Gustavo Gutiérrez) 6, 98, 109, 111–12, 114, 172
women 92, 154, 155
word 29, 53, 86–7, 89
  of God, the Lord 24, 25, 60, 75, 166
Word, the (Jesus) 58, 65, 86–8, 93, 127
world 21, 24, 28, 35, 42, 44, 45–6, 51, 53–4, 58–9, 64, 75, 82–3, 87, 88–9, 92–3, 98, 100, 103, 105–7, 113–15, 127, 137, 146, 154, 170, 182–3, 186–7

Zealot movement 165

www.ingramcontent.com/pod-product-compliance
Lightning Source LLC
Chambersburg PA
CBHW022056290426
44109CB00014B/1122